ARE THE KIDS ALL RIGHT?

Other books by John G. Fuller

The Airmen Who Would Not Die

The Poison That Fell From the Sky

The Ghost of Flight 401

We Almost Lost Detroit

Fever: The Hunt for a New Killer Virus

Arigo: Surgeon of the Rusty Knife

200,000,000 Guinea Pigs

The Day of St. Anthony's Fire

The Great Soul Trial

The Interrupted Journey

Incident at Exeter

Games for Insomniacs

The Money Changers

The Gentlemen Conspirators

ARE THE KIDS ALL RIGHT?

THE ROCK GENERATION AND ITS HIDDEN DEATH WISH

JOHN G. FULLER

Times
BOOKS

Published by Times Books, a division of
Quadrangle/The New York Times Book Co., Inc.
Three Park Avenue, New York, N.Y. 10016

Published simultaneously in Canada by
Fitzhenry & Whiteside, Ltd., Toronto

Library of Congress Cataloging in Publication Data

Fuller, John Grant
  Are the kids all right?

  Bibliography p. 257
  1. Rock music — History and criticism.   2. Concerts.
3. Crowds.   4. Cincinnati (Ohio) — Riot, 1979.   I. Title.
ML3506.F84   784.5'4'009   80-5778
ISBN   0–8129–0970–4   AACR2

Manufactured in the United States of America

To Peter Bowes

ACKNOWLEDGMENTS

Without both the direct and indirect assistance of many people, no nonfiction book could be written. Those listed below include many who have been of inestimable help in putting this book together, along with the sources listed in the bibliography whose very informative works have been drawn on.

Special mention should be made of *Crowd Management: Report of the Task Force on Crowd Control and Safety*, compiled by Paul L. Wertheimer, Public Information Officer of the City of Cincinnati City Manager's Office. Its comprehensive analysis of crowd management, police services, architectural planning and design, emergency services and proposed ordinances and guidelines are being studied by communities both here and abroad to forestall a repetition of the Coliseum tragedy. Copies are available at moderate cost from the City Manager's Office of Cincinnati.

In addition: Jay Aronoff, John Bartimole, Walter Beckjord, George Bentley, Ronald Bingaman, Mayor J. Kenneth Blackwell, Mr. and Mrs. Richard Bowes, Forrest Buckley, James Chute, Cincinnati Fire Department, Cincinnati Police Department, Cincinnati City Council, Dr. Frank Cleveland, Charles Collini, John Cracchiolo, Roger Crauder, Richard Crisler, Brian and Mary Downey, Jane Eager, Bob Ferguson, Owen Findsen, Judd Fuller, Dr. William Gates, Rick Green, Ken Hammel, Bob Johnson, John Jordan, Dr. Milton V. Kline, Richard Klopp, Jim Knippenberg, Jim Krumrei, Father Krusling, Bill Lack, Jack Leach, Dr. Michael Lieberwitz, Walter Lingle, Bert A. Lugannani, John MacDonald, Al and Dave Maysles, Dale Menkhaus, Gary Miller, Roger Moore, Norman Murdoch, Tom Newcomb, Brother Tom Payne, Dr. Terry Pulse, Gary Pumplin, Cliff Radel, Rick Rauh, Brant and Becky Ross, Henry Sandman, Ed Schneuer, Sandy Sherman, Mike and Deborah Shumate, Terri Sigmon, Dr. Walter Smitson, Joseph Speaks, Jerry Springer, Tom and Peggy Stanken, Jeanette Stewart, Dr. Dan Storer, Dr. James Titchener, Andrew Tribe, George Turner, Jeff Waddle, Frank Wood.

CONTENTS

PART I 1

PART II 29

PART III 103

PART IV 153

PART V 233

PART I

DATE

DECEMBER 3, 1979

TIME

1:30 P.M. TO 7:00 P.M.

PLACE

THE PLAZA OF THE
RIVERFRONT COLISEUM

SHORTLY

after 1:30 on the afternoon of December 3, 1979, Lt. Dale Menkhaus picked up the phone in his office at District 1 Headquarters of the Cincinnati police. On the other end of the line was Richard Morgan, manager of the Riverfront Coliseum. The call was perfunctory. It seemed that the crowd for the rock concert that night was beginning to arrive a little earlier than expected. The British group that was to play, known as The Who, was unquestionably a big draw, known for the cannonading volume of its hard-rock beat. The off-duty police detail that was to patrol the chilled and windswept plaza that day was not due to arrive until four. There were to be twenty-five officers strong under the command of the lieutenant. It would help, Morgan suggested to Menkhaus, if at least some of the assigned detail could arrive perhaps an hour earlier.

Lieutenant Menkhaus, slim, scholarly, conventionally handsome and quietly firm, agreed with the idea. A young forty, he was a ripe veteran at this sort of thing, equating the action of the crowd with the decibels of the music. The Who ranked high in volume, up with Led Zeppelin and the Rolling Stones, if not a few decibels above them. For several years now, Menkhaus had studiously traced the correlation between whatever rock group was playing and the type of crowd.

In spite of their blustering, heavy-metal beat, The Who were some-

3

thing of an anomaly to Menkhaus. The group had remained mostly intact for a decade and a half, with a unified history longer than the Beatles. They had matured a bit since their early days. The psychographic profile of their spectators was probably a cut or two above the crowds who had run rampant on the Coliseum Plaza during two previous concerts, a group inappropriately named Kiss, and Led Zeppelin. The audience for The Who could be a bit more muffled, more intelligent, occasionally even cerebral. And slightly older, up to thirty, perhaps. This was a good sign.

Without moralizing, Menkhaus had always made it a point to assess the potential danger in pulverized beer bottles, smashed doorways, the OD drug cases, public urination, vomiting, public fornication and other attributes that accompanied many hard-rock gatherings. He was aware that most of the kids at a concert, the vast majority of them, were considerate, humane and affable. What was puzzling was the traceable shift from Dr. Jekyll to Mr. Hyde that occurred when the crowd was egged on by the small minority of bad apples, made more prominent by their behavior pattern than by their numbers.

On this winter day, Lieutenant Menkhaus was facing the usual problem of blending law enforcement with friendly persuasion. It was never easy. As a student of crowd control, he often faced uneasy choices. The line between healthy mischief and vandalism shifted between boiling enthusiasm and hysterical frenzy. "Once the kids get their tickets for a major rock superstar," he once noted in a report, "they think of nothing else for weeks before the concert. They arrive unbelievably hyped up in excitement and anticipation. They seem to change inside, and the harder the beat, the more strange they behave. These are the facts of life we have to face."

These facts had also been noted by his counterparts in most parts of the country. The hype went beyond the big sports events at Riverfront Stadium, just across the concrete footbridge. The syndrome was apparent there, when the Cincinnati Reds were in contention for the pennant, but Reds fans differed in nature from the hard-rock spectators. It was hard to define, and seemed to have little to do with drugs or booze. If anything, it was a tidal action of the crowd, an enormous, invisible pull that distinguished it not only from sports events, but from other concerts that lacked the high volume and crushing beat that accompanied hard- and heavy-metal rock. Menkhaus and other security men often wondered about this tidal pull, *why* it was different from so many other crowds they handled, and why it was so pronounced.

A John Denver concert, for instance, would be no problem at all, yet the crowd might include some of the same people. Even the peer security team, which patrolled the aisles during the concert and usually wore T-shirts, would don ties and jackets for a John Denver audience. In contrast, a previous Coliseum concert by the hard-rock group Alice Cooper brought a police harvest of 89 hits of acid, 7 pink pills, 3 brown pills, 40 red pills, 3.5 grams of cocaine, 8 Valium, innumerable Quaalude capsules, marijuana joints and miscellaneous Baggies full of other drugs.

Regardless of what might be in store on the cold and windy day of December 3, Lieutenant Menkhaus pulled together an early detail of fourteen officers and one sergeant to arrive at the plaza level of the Coliseum at three in the afternoon instead of the scheduled time of four.

Riverfront Coliseum sits like a large, chalky-white wedding cake, joined by the concrete footbridge to its sister edifice, the Riverfront Stadium. Sculptured in white concrete, the bridge widens into the broad upper-level plaza that lies as an apron to the main Coliseum entrance. The entrance to the building forms a V-shaped extrusion that juts out from the main arena like the prow of a ship. There is a bank of eight sturdy glass doors on each side, one bank facing the seven hills of Cincinnati to the northwest, the other facing southwest, toward Covington, Kentucky, just across the Ohio River.

Directly beneath the plaza is the street level. It is seldom used now. It lies buried for the most part under a maze of twisting superhighways that run across and along the river. The large green highway signs reach almost to the plaza's height reading: U.S. 71, U.S. 75, South to Louisville and Lexington, North to Dayton and Columbus.

Lieutenant Menkhaus lost little time in assigning his detail to five check points leading up to the plaza level. Some were fed by narrow concrete ramps that arch gracefully up and over the streets, and feed into the spacious open plaza. His instructions were simple: No one was to be allowed on the plaza without ticket in hand; no one was to be admitted carrying bottles or cans. Beside each police post were trash compactors ready to devour any contraband surrendered by the spectators.

ARE THE KIDS ALL RIGHT?

Shortly after 3:00 P.M., about the same time that Lieutenant Menkhaus assigned his first contingent to their locations, Deborah Shumate, her husband Mike and sister Carolyn parked by the stadium where the Cincinnati Reds and Bengals play in their respective seasons. The moment they approached the Coliseum, the wind coming off the Ohio River hit them, making the 34-degree temperature sting. Despite the four-hour wait ahead, Deborah felt ready to put up with it, especially since she would eventually be face-to-face with her favorite group, The Who, when the concert began.

Like her husband and sister, she was dressed for the occasion: long johns, two sweaters, a down parka, and a wool scarf wrapped snugly around her neck. Like her sister Carolyn, Deborah was tallish with the farm-fresh look of a Noxzema commercial, brunette in contrast to Carolyn's tumbling blonde hair. Both could have been likely candidates for the corps of Dallas Cowboy cheerleaders. But Deborah at twenty-three was already the mother of two, and Carolyn, at seventeen, was intent on finishing high school. Deborah's husband Mike was heavyset and powerful, a former defensive tackle on his high school team. She liked to describe him affectionately as the Incredible Hulk.

They were greeted at the footbridge leading from the stadium to the Coliseum by two police officers who were not uncordial, but asked them to show their tickets and open their jackets enough for a visual check and frisking for cans or bottles. This was routine and expected. The three had attended many rock concerts before, and took the inspection in stride. In fact, they were "clean," free of drugs or liquor. The lusty, sirenic magic of The Who was heady enough for them.

Although the concert was five chilly hours away, the plaza already held some 200 or 300 who stood about in scattered groups, some of them flapping their arms and running in place against the cold. Deborah was impressed. They were relaxed and casual, in high spirits but without frenzy. Even as the crowd grew over the next two hours, Lieutenant Menkhaus and his officers noted that it was orderly, not typical of some recent hard-rock audiences at the Coliseum.

By the time that the electric digital clock of Western-Southern Life across the throughway from the Coliseum showed five, the crowd had grown to well over a thousand. By now the group was clustering around the main entrance doors in a fan-shaped mass, a funnel shape pointing

6

toward the main banks of doors. There was plenty of room on the open plaza for thousands more to join behind them. Rumors were being noised about that the doors would open at 6:30 instead of 7:00 to let the crowd in out of the cold, and reward the stalwart faithfuls of The Who for their long and icy wait. Because the vast majority of the tickets were sold on the basis of "festival seating"—less euphemistically known as general admission—most of the early arrivals were there to get a choice seat or standing room on a first-come-first-serve basis. For many, this was a once-in-a-lifetime shot to see The Who. None of the growing crowd wanted to see Roger Daltrey, Peter Townshend, John Entwistle or the new drummer, Kenny Jones, from the vantage point of the rafters.

Deborah Shumate belonged to this group. From an early age she had absorbed The Who's albums like a thirsty blotter, knew every lyric before it was sung and passionately adored the resonant, field-holler voice of Roger Daltrey and the way he twirled his microphone like a cowboy's lasso at a live concert. This would make the galling wait worthwhile. Meanwhile, the crowd was getting somewhat tighter around her, almost imperceptibly.

For a brief moment, she felt a little panicky. But that passed quickly, as she shifted her weight from one foot to the other to relieve the tedium. The crowd was making her warmer than before. In fact, by 5:30 she was beginning to feel uncomfortably warm, despite the biting wind that had increased with the gradual falling of darkness.

One thing Deborah knew for certain: Her wool scarf had somehow been pulled tighter around her neck. It was actually beginning to choke her. She started to lift her arms to loosen it. She discovered that she simply could not move them an inch. They were pinned to her sides by the crowd's vise-like pressure. With difficulty, she twisted her neck to see about moving out of the crowd. She discovered she couldn't even see where the crowd ended. There was what looked to be an endless sea of faces, washed by the combined glow of three large bronze lamp posts, five globes on each; the lights along the Coliseum wall; and a full-bodied moon in the clear sky above. She could see no way to get out of the press even momentarily. Further, the crowd was beginning to sway, uncomfortably, dangerously. She tried to resist and to spread her feet a few inches apart, but discovered they were pinned together as tightly as her arms. She was, in fact, as straight and stiff as a pendulum.

"Please, Mike, please," she called above the background noise to her husband. "I think I'm going to die if I don't get this scarf from around my neck."

Mike was not one to sit back and let things happen. As an ex-Marine in the Vietnam War, inaction was not part of his makeup. But as he began to lift his arms to help, he found he could not move them from his sides. He could hardly believe he was pinned by such pressure. It was as if he were in the hands of a heavyweight wrestler and down for the count. He had prided himself on his strength and power, but had never encountered a crush like this—a quiet, growing crush that had sneaked up on him without warning.

With his palms stuck to his sides, he tried a different approach. Slowly, he cantilevered his elbows outward, using all the strength of his burly frame behind the motion. As he did so, he slipped his hands up his thighs and hips, and the cantilever opened a few precious inches of space. He pressed outward harder, and suddenly his elbows and arms popped out from their trap at shoulder height. Quickly, he framed his arms in an awkward fence so that Deborah could get her arms up high enough to untie her scarf. She struggled with it, now gulping for air. Finally, she got it loose, but her hands were now trapped halfway up her chest.

Deborah looked across at Carolyn. Her sister's sheepskin jacket was pressed tightly around her. Sweat was pouring down her face, in spite of the bitter wind and cold. Her hair was soaking wet. She was trying hopelessly to get the heavy jacket off, but like the others, her hands were useless, her feet jammed together, and all were swaying with the motion of the crowd, at least a foot in every direction. Conversation was almost impossible. With the wind, the constant noise of the crowd and its pressure, it was possible to talk only in grunts and cropped phrases. Worse, it used up precious breath.

Mike awkwardly forced his hands in Carolyn's direction, and managed to tug her jacket off, as she too gulped for more air. The jacket rested on several shoulders and eventually disappeared under the wave-like motion of the crowd, with gaps opening and closing as fast as they were formed. There was no way she could retrieve it.

By six o'clock, three long and unendurable hours after they had arrived on the plaza, the pain from the pressure became unbearable for

Deborah. She had been sure it could never have gotten worse over the past half hour, but it had. She thought back to an earlier moment in the afternoon, when she had phoned her mother in her apartment across the river in Covington. Deborah had been bubbling with enthusiasm over the anticipation of seeing The Who. Her mother, Betty Naumann, had not exactly shared Deborah's enthusiasm. She was a tolerant mother up to a point—but when the tone of rock music had shifted from the Beatles to a harsher, more rasping beat, Mrs. Naumann turned the other way. Now, here on the plaza, Deborah's enthusiasm was being tested. There was no question it was flagging.

"Mike," she half-screamed over the noise of the crowd, "Mike, I honestly think I'm going to die. I honestly do. I want to get out of here, Mike. I want to get *out!*" But she knew there was no way out.

Mike tried to comfort her, and to make more space for her with his arms, which now were frozen at shoulder height by the press of the crowd. The action helped only a little, enough to let Deborah catch a few breaths at a time. She gulped for air, and she thought of her children, Michael, three, and Mandy, one. She was now slipping into genuine panic. *Oh, God, suppose I never see them again*, she was thinking to herself. She reassured herself that her brother-in-law Bobby and his wife Roseanne who were sitters for the children that night, would take good take good care of them. *If they only would open the doors*, she was thinking. *We can hold out just a little bit longer*.

Words spilled out to Mike, hopeless words Deborah couldn't hold back: "Mike, I *know* there's no way out, but I want to get out of here, anyway. Please, Mike, *please*. I don't ever want to see The Who, I don't care, I don't care!" But the words were using up air, and Mike could hardly hear what she was saying. The pressure now was such that she could barely expand her chest enough to catch short breaths. She turned to see how Carolyn was holding up. But Carolyn was not to be found. She had simply disappeared in the waves of the crowd, and neither Deborah nor Mike were able to see any part of her.

The irony was that, from the back of the crowd where Sergeant Lamping was stationed, the mass of spectators appeared unusually calm and orderly. There was, however, some confusion about the time the doors were supposed to open. The prevalent rumor was 6:30, although

9

he knew from past experience the doors rarely opened until 7:00, about an hour before the concerts usually began. When Lamping checked his watch at 6:30, the doors remained closed. By this time, the crowd had swollen to some three thousand but the plaza could still handle more comfortably, especially in view of the well-mannered demeanor and appearance of the mass. There was some mild restlessness evident. The unusual swaying was not quite normal. Nor was the excessive urination against the Coliseum walls and on the walkways by those on the periphery of the crowd. But there were no facilities whatever outside the arena. There was no other choice.

The most important thing to Lieutenant Menkhaus was that the doors showed no signs of being opened by the private security police inside the building. Neither Menkhaus nor his Cincinnati police complement had any authority there. While the crowd pressure didn't seem particularly intense from his position at the rear, it was obvious that the sooner the doors were opened, the quicker the pressure would be relieved.

The wide network of walkie-talkies in the hands of both private and official police was chattering sporadically, linked to the downtown communications center by a dispatcher, who also monitored the patrol cars cruising near the scene. In addition, there was the central fire tower, several miles away in the city, ready to handle any citywide broadcasts to coordinate all the scattered elements.

At 6:30, Lieutenant Menkhaus was beginning to find his hands full as he patrolled the plaza. An anonymous young girl rushed up to tell him that a young man was down on the ground at the "Will Call" ticket window, and appeared to be in very bad shape. Menkhaus was able to work his way through the outer edge of the crowd to find the semiconscious victim sprawled against the wall of the building. He was on the periphery of the spectators, with three friends trying to help him. Menkhaus was informed by the friends that their companion had downed a pint of whiskey and taken two hits of speed.

With the help of the friends, Menkhaus carried the now-unconscious youth to a special door on the north side of the building, and on into the Coliseum first-aid room. Even with the drug arrests and the latest casualty, it was still a light evening for the police, in contrast to the Coliseum history over the past few years. ODs were so common that they had to be taken as a matter of course.

PART I

At 6:38, Lieutenant Menkhaus, outside on the plaza again, and out of the crowd, picked up his walkie-talkie and tried to contact Sgt. John Basham, in charge of the private police inside the Coliseum. By 6:41, Menkhaus was still trying to make contact to find out what was holding up the opening of the doors.

With the crowd packed tightly, there was still no overt evidence of inordinate pressure. The background noises swallowed most of the individual cries of discomfort. From almost any viewpoint, except for those in the center of the pressure pocket, the scene looked much like that of any rock concert: the expected jam, a bit of a crush, the long uncomfortable waiting, and the lack of movement in any direction. This lack, in fact, led many outside observers to believe that the crowd was exceptionally orderly.

While there was no crisis at hand, Menkhaus sensed instinctively the potential for problems. The cold and the wind, if nothing else, could generate a sharpened impatience. In spite of the orderliness there was a tighter than usual compaction, perhaps brought on by the cold.

On his radio, Menkhaus gave his call number — One-Sixty — and told the dispatcher: "Can you try Sergeant Basham again for Channel Four?"

With radio interference and occasional break-up of the signal, Menkhaus would wait nearly eight minutes before getting through to Basham. Meanwhile, Menkhaus checked the periphery of the crowd, hoping that it would remain as placid as it seemed. At 6:50, Basham finally contacted Menkhaus.

"I'll meet you at the side door. South side. Where we always come in."

Peter Townshend, Roger Daltrey, John Entwistle, Kenny (sometimes spelled Kenney) Jones, and the rest of The Who contingent had arrived in Cincinnati at about 2:00 P.M. on the day of the concert, almost the same time that the very first spectators had begun to gather on the windy plaza outside Riverfront Coliseum.

The previous night's concert in Pittsburgh had gone well, the first night of their eleven-city tour of the East Coast and the Midwest.

Townshend, sometimes sullen, sometimes exuberant, nearly always unpredictable, was now in his mid-thirties and torn between the rigors of

11

touring and the comfort of his country home in England. He seemed to be trying to decide if the piercing, screaming adoration of the crowd was worth being absent from his fireside. His hearing was now sharply reduced by a decade and a half of the pounding amplifiers that assaulted his ears with every concert. In fact, The Who had staged the loudest concert in rock history, in London on May 31, 1976. A decibel level of 120 was clocked at 50 yards' distance from the stage, equal to a nearby jet engine or a loud thunderclap—enough to cause partial deafness, and provoke what is called the pain level.

With Cincinnati as the second stop of the tour, The Who would be facing massive, sold-out crowds at Buffalo, Cleveland, Pontiac, Chicago, Philadelphia, New Haven and other stops along the big-coliseum route. Townshend had already grumbled about the burden of the re-formed group's first major U.S. tour when he told a reporter from *Rolling Stone*, "All because I said, 'Yeah, I don't mind doing a few dates.' I don't want to die, but I do want to drown in a way, go down with the ship."

Daltrey, sometimes called a half-pint Adonis because of his small stature and classical features, basked in the explosive approval of the crowds, and seemed unable to get enough feedback from them. Entwistle was stolid and noncommittal. Known as The Ox, he went along with the wants of the group, at the same time that he served as anchor for them. Drummer Kenny Jones and keyboardist Rabbit Bundrick were too new to the group to be surfeited by the one-night stands. They enjoyed the reflected glory of playing with a superstar group widely considered the greatest in the rock world, bar none—even the Rolling Stones.

In spite of the constant pressure and heavy schedule, there were compensations on the tour. The Who had five chauffeur-driven limousines at their disposal at each stop. Their contract with Electric Factory Concerts, the promoter for the Cincinnati engagement, called for lavish backstage meals, champagne, chilled beer, cognac and other niceties, as well as properly-lighted, air-conditioned private dressing rooms with hot and cold running water, private toilets, and comfortable furniture. They also requested and got three dozen large, clean, dry bath-size towels. A fully-qualified specialist in internal medicine on the staff of a first-rate hospital was required on 24-hour call in each area.

PART I

With the house tickets sold out over two months in advance, there would be a generously large pie to cut at each performance. For the Riverfront Coliseum concert, 18,348 tickets had been sold. Of these, 3,578 reserved seats went at $11.00 a ticket; 14,770 general admission tickets went at $10.00 each. All were sold within 90 minutes from the time tickets went on sale through Ticketron and the Coliseum on Friday, September 28, 1979, two months before the concert. The total take came to $187,058 with roughly 90 percent going to The Who after expenses such as hall rental, electricity, security were taken care of. The take-home pay for The Who would come to about $100,000 for the evening's work.

Under these conditions, a gross of nearly $2 million rested in the vaults of the ticket sellers before The Who had ever left England, a plump return for a seventeen-day, eleven-concert trip, and also a soothing poultice for whatever hardships were faced on the road, especially since the interest that accumulated on the presold ticket funds went to The Who's management. The Who's drawing power was incontestable. All of the eleven concerts had been sold out with the same alacrity as in Cincinnati.

As the crowd continued to gather and shiver on the plaza throughout the afternoon, the stars of The Who were checked into comfortable suites in the north tower of Stouffer's Cincinnati Towers, a pleasing, full-facility hostelry, considered by many to be the best in the city. The cheerful but cavernous lobby, four stories high, was peppered with special security police to protect the privacy of the superstars. Neither Cincinnati, nor any other city, is exempt from the groupie scene, where adoration and more profligate favors are lavishly offered to the rock crews, from superstars down to the "roadies" who handle the lights and rigging.

The group had been squirreled in through the back entrance of the old south tower, whisked into a sevice elevator and across a second-floor corridor, unobserved by the crowd framing the main entrance of the hotel to cheer them. Several of the contingent lost no time in going to the health club for a massage and a sauna.

Later in the afternoon, Daltrey and Townshend were able to drift down to the upper lobby and saunter unnoticed to the elevated skyway that connects Cincinnati's impressive shopping and business district with a labyrinth of second-level bridges, ramps, and shops.

Before they were recognized and had to retreat, they strolled into a modest skyway bookstore. It was just outside the second-floor lobby of the hotel. They browsed a few moments, quiet and unobtrusive. It was some moments before the proprietor, a motherly lady in her forties, recognized them. Their purchases were minimal: three magazines and one $12.95 hardcover book on how to mix drinks. The book's cover was die-stamped in the shape of a bottle. Although in the past The Who were known for their dynamic capacity to decimate and vandalize hotel rooms, their recent tours had been serene.

When they were spotted by a few devotees, the two stars retreated swiftly from the bookstore. They were of course used to this sort of attention. Townshend, tall, with a Fu Manchu beard, liked the adoration but continued to hate touring. Daltrey, who looked like an oarsman on the Yale crew with his new short haircut, liked both. Idolization is a high-potency nutrient that rock stars, among others, thrive on. The members of The Who were no exception. On this night, eighteen thousand fans would be on their feet for over two hours. They would roar with approval every time Townshend pin-wheeled his arms, jumped, or ran in place in between a series of power chords that would thunder through forty speakers, each as tall as a man. The crowd and the musical group would be fused, depending on the point of view, into one exalted or depraved mass.

The coffee shop of the Stouffer's Towers is on the mezzanine floor and resembles a sidewalk cafe in France, in spite of its indoor setting. The tables are clustered under colorful umbrellas; the atmosphere is distinctly informal. The Who gathered here for a light supper shortly before six that evening. To one waitress serving them, they seemed relaxed and casual, too casual in fact for her taste. She was worried they might not reach Riverfront Coliseum in time for the traditional warm-up before the concert. They were clear and away in a short time, however, and again retreated through the upstairs corridor to the little-used area where two of the five limousines assigned to the band were waiting to take them to Riverfront Coliseum.

As the limousines whisked The Who entourage along Fifth Street and down Race toward the Coliseum, the crowd on the plaza had swollen to thousands. Brant and Becky Ross had arrived there at five, a shivering hour and a half before the band's limousines pulled up to the lower level of the arena at Second and Broadway.

They had been married for three years. Both were quiet and studious-looking, Becky with a pert nose, rust hair, and a few freckles, Brant with the lean and wiry frame of the track man that he once had been. Both were passionate rock concert-goers, willing to put up with the push and pull of the crowds for many festival seating affairs, whether they were waiting to see Led Zeppelin, the Grateful Dead, the Stones, or especially The Who, whom they regarded with profound reverence. In fact, Becky Ross, an Ohio University graduate in business administration, had convinced herself she was just sick enough not to go to work at the IRS the day The Who tickets went on sale back in September. She was glad she did, in light of the rapid sell-out.

Brant Ross, a graduate of the University of Cincinnati who had now found a job that made use of his talent designing advertising displays, was glad that he knew of a semi-secret parking space near the ramp from the Stadium to the Coliseum plaza. They had only a short walk and the crowd was larger than he had expected when they arrived.

By the time the Rosses had shown their tickets and gone through the brief inspection by the police ramp, they had passed several scalpers, hissing out the going price of sixty-five dollars per ticket. Brant was happy he and Becky had theirs safely tucked in their pockets, but confessed to himself that he might have gone that high if forced to.

Because of the fan-shape of the crowd, which made the wedge wider than it was deep, they were not too far from the northwest bank doors, perhaps twenty feet, when they joined the rest of the ticket holders. It did not take long, though, for the late arrivals to surround them. Within fifteen minutes, Becky found that her face was almost pressed against the back of the man in front of her, at only slightly higher than waist level. He was quite tall, and Becky was just under five feet. Just as Debbie Shumate had found herself locked by the crowd, Becky was now totally enclosed, compressed, and helpless.

Becky suddenly realized she was afraid. Brant, aware of her discomfort, turned his back to the crowd in front of him and was able to open a small pocket of space for Becky's head and shoulders with his arms. But by five-thirty, Becky was convinced that she was going to get crushed. Although she tried to stop herself, she began to cry.

"Brant," she called above the noise of the crowd, "I hate to say this, but let's just go home. Let's get in the car and go home. This is just not worth it."

"Maybe it would be a good idea," Brant yelled to her, "if we got you out of the crowd. Then I'll go in and save the seats, and meet you back at the Beehive elevator. You can come in after the whole crowd is seated. There won't be any crush then." Brant was not tall, but he was tough and sinewy, and confident he could handle the crowd himself. The Beehive elevator was inside the Coliseum on the north end, providing access to the Beehive Club where dinner could be had by the special club members and the management.

Becky thought for a moment, then yelled back: "I don't want to do that, Brant. I don't want to get separated." Then she added after reflection, for a reason she wasn't sure of: "We just have ourselves, and nobody else, you know. . . ."

Brant reinforced the position of his arms, his back still to the doors, so that she could have more breathing space. Then the swaying began. It was strange and rhythmic. Brant had thought he'd seen it all in other concert crowds, but this was different. He felt like wobbly king pin, or Bozo the tipping clown. He was still able to keep Becky's head and shoulders reasonably clear, but wondered how long he could last. Becky was so tiny and fragile, he grew deeply concerned for her safety. Then suddenly, Becky slipped down beneath him, out of his sight.

With gargantuan effort, he was able to reach down and catch her arm. He squeezed her upward, holding on with a death-grip. She was on her feet again, but within moments, was unable to stand up. With Brant's help, she righted herself. They both agreed that she should work her way out of the crowd and to meet at the elevator later. The group around Becky was able to clear some space. She began to slip sideways and backward. By 6:15—after more than an hour of agonizing pressure— they had lost sight of each other, and Brant was forced to concentrate on keeping his own feet as the crowd pressure increased.

I was wrong, Brant was saying to himself. *I thought I had seen everything*. But a man next to him was calling to a friend, "This is nothing. You should have been here for the Led Zeppelin concert!"

PART I

Without any obvious pushing, the crowd seemed to have a molecular motion of its own. There was little anyone surrounding Brant could do about it. The group in his immediate vicinity teamed up to try to retard the motion, to help each other. The bodies continued to flow with an internal momentum. Then the terrible, damp heat floated up from the crowd. He was certain in his mind that Becky had got free. The people had made great efforts to clear a path for her. Now the swaying was constant. Ahead of him, he heard a girl cry out. Moments later, she was being passed back over the heads of people. For a flash, he thought it might be Becky, and he was terrified. Then he reassured himself that Becky had gone toward the back of the crowd. Another girl to Brant's right suddenly yelled that she couldn't breathe. Brant was able to turn and face her, as another man beside him was able to take half a step backward.

The girl was recovering from her hysteria, but she bent down to reach for a shoe that had come off her foot. Another swaying swept over the group. Brant fell down over her. Several others, like helpless dominoes, did the same. Brant reached out and tapped someone's leg. In the distance, he heard the sounds of chords coming from inside the building. They were fragmentary and disjointed. It was the band's sound check, he was sure. He tried to look at his watch, but his arm was trapped. He guessed it was 6:30. He felt he had been in the crush for an eternity. At the sound of the chords, the crowd squeezed harder, as if on cue for action. A tremendous pressure came down on Brant. He felt himself being pushed along the group, like "a pin rolling bread dough flat," he later recalled. He heard two shrill screams, and several muffled outcries. Some near him in the crowd were trying to reach down and pull him up. His hand slipped from them as they tried to grab him. *God, he was saying to himself, God, please get me out of this and keep Becky safe.*

Two hours before Brant Ross had slipped to the ground, Sgt. John Basham had arrived at the Riverfront Coliseum, at about 4:30 in the afternoon. As security officer and advisor on the Coliseum payroll, he acted as a link between the city police on the outside arena, and the private security force inside the building. He made a routine survey of the scene, noting that the city police were on full duty outside, and that the crowd was not too large. His experience, which was extensive, taught him that it paid to monitor not only the size of the crowd, but its mood.

In this case, he was pleased with what he saw. Even later, after 6:00, when the crowd had grown to several thousand, he was impressed with the orderliness of the spectators. As Sergeant Bashman walked around the crowd, surveying it from both the plaza and from inside the building, he noted that there were very few broken beer bottles, a good sign compared to the Kiss and Led Zeppelin fiascos. Further, he had watched the crowds passing by the various police-post checkpoints as they came up on the plaza. He was again surprised by how orderly they were.

Inside the Coliseum, at just about 6:30 Sergeant Bashman noticed that The Who had arrived, and were preparing the stage for their routine sound check. The stage was at the east end of the building, opposite where the crowd was waiting to enter. It was framed overhead with a bewildering battery of lighting gear strung from rows of pipes choking almost every square inch of the area above the stage. The clusters of six-foot-high speakers hung from a front truss were already hoisted high above the stage, twenty on each side.

The massive procedure of setting up the sixty-foot-wide stage had begun early in the morning when four enormous semi-trailer trucks had pulled into the bay for unloading. The operation required four riggers, three of whom were expert climbers, eight truck loaders, two fork lifts and their operators, and sixteen stagehands, along with an extra rigger to hang the safety cables.

The sleepy roadies had stumbled off the semis after the load-out and long drive from Pittsburgh for a backstage breakfast of doughnuts washed down by coffee, milk, and orange juice. For the hour-long lunch break at one, they would have hot and cold sandwiches, milk, Coke, 7-Up, and Dr Pepper, as specified by their contract. The first full hot meal for the crew would be at the dinner break at 5:00.

By the time Sergeant Basham went to meet Lieutenant Menkhaus at Section 616, the lights known as Super-Troupers were in place and ready with twelve spot operators manning additional follow-spots. At the sound and light mixing platform, a hundred feet back from the stage, fifteen hundred pounds of equipment rested ready to blend the lights and sound for the music that would thunder and shatter the hall to the ceilings when the concert began.

The final sound check was scheduled for 6:00. The Who would not arrive until 6:20. Meanwhile, the sound man was testing the "pink noise"—the roaring, neutral hiss that enabled him to check every frequency from 20 to 20,000 cycles, testing it to the highest load he was going to run that night—up to the pain level of 118 or 120 decibels.

Some time around 6:30, Mike Spoess of the private security guards was inside the Coliseum looking down on the stage. He was waiting to get his instructions to man one of the front doors at the main entrance. He had heard that The Who had arrived late, but could now see them testing their instruments from his vantage point in the arena ramp where he stood. Someone told him that the doors could not be opened until the band finished its warm-up, which he hoped would be soon. Over 6-feet 4 inches tall, and weighing in at 298 pounds, Spoess was assigned to the key doors of the entrance, because, though gentle, he could handle the toughest situations.

Having a daughter of his own, he was concerned about the spectators clustered outside on the plaza in the bitter December wind. He was hoping he would get his orders soon to let them in. Anticipating the acute discomfort during the long, cold wait, he had talked his daughter out of coming to the concert, and now he was glad that he had. The daughter of his next-door neighbor was there, however, and he wondered how she was holding up in the face of the growing crowd outside the doors. He was particularly sensitive about the possibility of any of the young people getting hurt. In two years of duty at the Coliseum, he was constantly aware of this possibility. His day job, as a materials inspector for the Palm Beach company, was a quiet one in sharp contrast to his moonlighting for the private security force at the Coliseum. The chain of command would come down to him from either Richard Morgan, the Coliseum's Manager of Operations, or Cal Levy, the local representative of the promoter. Their decision would be forwarded by his boss, Capt. Giles Galbraith, head of the private police. Spoess grew more anxious as the minutes crept by, but saw no sign of the order being given to open the doors.

For weeks before the approaching Who concert, the corridors of

ARE THE KIDS ALL RIGHT?

Cincinnati's high schools echoed with the buzz of excitement about the upcoming event. The Who were special because the group consisted of musicians, not merely three-chord wonders who thumped. Townshend was a thinker, a disciple of Meher Baba, the Indian mystic. When Roger Daltrey sang from the gut, he erupted with a Cyclopean, megawatt energy that made the auditorium tremble. Entwistle's throbbing bass did the same thing. Yes, the group used to smash their guitars and amplifiers at the end of a concert. But they had matured lately, confining the violence to some of the lyrics that lashed out without inhibition against the hypocrisy of the Establishment.

Their lyrics could be profound and incisive, evoking the contemporary scene and its tragedies. To the devout Who fan, wasn't *Tommy* a rock opera, as profound for its day as a Wagnerian tragedy? Wasn't it gutsier than any of the sophisticated show tunes of the American musical theater? The Who concert was an experience in which you could lose yourself in a sea of chords and percussion, a sensory overload that would be pounded out for over two hours, and that could make you forget everything including the piercing ringing of the ears.

It was all worth it, because the spinning 33-rpm Who albums, stored and treasured by all who could afford them, would be coming to life at the Coliseum. While parents looked on in either disapproval or wonderment, the rock enthusiasts would glue their stereophonic earphones on their heads and listen to the throbbing cadences of The Who, hour after hour, visualizing the concert stage as they did so. While their lips silently moved in synch with the lyrics, some could work out complicated math problems or absorb a history lesson without missing a beat. Others would sit between two hefty stereo speakers and raise the volume, trying to approximate the decibels The Who would achieve at concert pitch.

It was as if they were living on two psychological levels, two streams of consciousness. One level would be capable of absorbing homework. The other level would be soaking in the music and its beat for hours at a time. With the decibels high, the beat persistent, and the stereo music constant, something new was happening here, different from jazz, different from classical or the soft rock ushered in by the Beatles. There was a clue here that might contain part of the answer to what distinguished hard-rock spectators from others. Was it because the heavy beat

PART I

and high volume created a definite trance-like state, a hypnotic state? If so, the intense, obsessional loyalty created could put musicians in command of the way the fans would act when they entered the hall. It could explain a dissociation process that neither parent nor young adult could understand.

An approaching concert would intensify this anticipatory mood to extremes. In fact, on November 9, 1979, just about three weeks before the Who concert, Terri Sigmon, who wrote a column for the school paper of Western Hills High School, sat down at her typewriter to herald the coming event. After headlining the article *"Concerts, a real trip!"* she wrote:

> It's getting harder and harder to breathe. Caught up in the middle of a human ocean, wave after wave threatens to knock you off your feet. If they are still on the ground, for all the feeling beneath your waist has ceased entirely. Not even sardines are packed as tight as this mass of humanity of which you find yourself a part.

> You lost sight of the people you came with as soon as you entered the crowd, but that doesn't matter now. Nothing matters except for your fight to get to the front of the crowd. But that is also everyone else's goal and it's every man for himself as you shove, claw, and push your way forward. Covered with sweat, you feel as though you may faint at any moment, but you keep going. The roar of human voices is deafening and you're no longer sure if your voice is among the noise or not. All sense of reality has disappeared in the struggle to move forward. At last! You have finally made it as close to the front as you can. The crowd behind you tries to shove you out of the way and take your place, but you grab on to the closest thing in front of you, and refuse to move.

> Then it happens. What you have fought and waited for is about to begin. The lights dim. A voice comes over the loudspeaker, but his words are lost as a roar rises from the crowd in excited anticipation of what is about to happen. Suddenly all of the bruises, cuts, and crushed ribs seem worth it because of your "perfect" spot. The rock concert has begun.

The article was prophetic as well as perceptive, revealing the psyche of the rock concert spectator, as seen by a peer. It described a turbulent scene that was to be expected at practically every hard-rock, heavy-metal concert. From the moment the last ticket disappeared from the Ticketron windows, the date "December 3" was being circled in some

21

eighteen thousand homes not only in Cincinnati, but as far away as Louisville, Dayton, Columbus, Indianapolis and other midwest communities in a wide periphery.

North of Cincinnati is the affluent suburb of Wyoming. Peter Bowes and his friend Jim Krumrei, two students at the high school there that bears the same name as the town, shared a common enthusiasm for The Who. They planned their day carefully on December 3 to be sure of getting good seats.

Peter, a senior who liked to play the guitar, could thrash out complicated riffs from The Who albums. Peter was known with affection by everyone in the tree-lined neighborhood where he lived. Whether he was working part time at the local pharmacy, or as an assistant chef at In Cahoots, a popular restaurant near the university, his droll smile and infectious sense of humor sometimes hid his sense of purpose, which was marked.

At school, he was equally popular. He swam freestyle on the swimming team, loved to go skiing and played with a high school rock group that was always in demand.

Jim Krumrei had a craggy face and a shock of brown hair tumbled over one side of his forehead. Husky, tall and popular himself, he was proud of Peter's friendship. They would both be driving down to Riverfront Coliseum with two other friends, if Peter could arrange to leave early from his volunteer job at a nearby state school for the mentally retarded. Peter would spend three hours every weekday afternoon there, helping the troubled students to read and write.

Peter's self-imposed duty was part of a program that guidance counselor Ken Hammel had set up at Wyoming High School, called Wider Horizons for Youth. As part of an extracurricular enrichment program, it set up its volunteer students in professional work situations outside the school. It was a fresh idea, and it was working.

The professional staff at the state school liked Peter because he was always prompt and congenial. Peter was bearing down hard on a twenty-year-old student who was unable to write his name. For weeks, Peter had worked patiently with Byron, who seemed to respond to him remarkably well. At times, Byron would almost do it—with only a letter

22

or two out of order. At other times, he would regress. In spite of frustration, Peter kept at the job.

On the afternoon of the concert, Byron suddenly picked up a piece of chalk and completed his name successfully. Excited, Peter called Mark Carle, the teacher who guided Peter's work, over to the board. He asked Byron to repeat his triumph. Byron failed.

Peter was dismayed. "I've been working for three weeks, Byron — and now you do it wrong again!" Then he turned to Mark Carle again, and said: "That's all right. We'll get him do it tomorrow."

For the first time in weeks Peter asked Mark if he could leave a little early.

"Sure," said Mark, without hesitation. "What's the big event?"

Peter told him about the Who concert, and smiled. "You're only young once, you know."

"What time's the concert?" Mark asked.

"Not till eight o'clock," Peter answered. "But six weeks ago, I waited in line for four hours to get the tickets. I want to be the first through that door!"

Mark would miss Peter the rest of the afternoon, because he helped with three other students they worked with each day. Peter was already thinking about changing his major interest to psychology, and Mark was ready to help him.

At home about 5:00 that evening, Peter took out the Fender guitar that he had saved his money to buy. He practiced several Who arrangements while waiting for his ride to the concert. Not long after, he jumped into classmate Greg MacDonald's Chevy station wagon to pick up John Roosa, another classmate, and Jim Krumrei, who waited for them at his family's house, *Hilltop*.

In spite of the anticipated long wait in the cold, none of the four could think about eating. The thought that The Who were actually coming to Cincinnati dominated the conversation and overrode their appetites. Peter was able to talk good-naturedly about the frustration of his afternoon, and repeated his determination to get Byron to write his name correctly by the following day. Jim Krumrei had been listening to his favorite Who album that afternoon, called *Who Are You?* The conversation turned to the album cover. It showed a picture of The Who's late drummer, Keith Moon, who had died from a combination of acute alcoholism and a drug he was taking to overcome it. Moon was pictured in a director's chair clearly labeled NOT TO BE TAKEN AWAY. Moon would be missed. They wondered how the new drummer, Kenny Jones, would fill his shoes.

By luck, Peter's father, Dick Bowes, had a permanent parking space in the Procter & Gamble garage, not far from Riverfront Coliseum. They pulled up beside the exit, and waited for Peter's father to drive out of the garage and give them the card that would admit them to the special parking ramp. With spectators clogging the area, any space around the Coliseum was at a premium. Everywhere were the signs declaring SORRY — FULL.

The four classmates were up on the stadium bridge, crossing toward the Coliseum at about 6:00 — just about the time that Mike and Debbie Shumate had lost sight of Carolyn and Becky had slipped out of sight from Brant Ross. But to the foursome from Wyoming High, nothing looked unusual when they reached the plaza. They passed by the police checkpost and moved toward the crowd that fanned out from the main entrance. Within minutes, they were completely closed in. Jim Krumrei, tall and rugged as he was, was surprised at how quickly the pressure built up, both from behind and from the sides. Since the four classmates wanted to see the concert together, they locked arms which helped them to resist the swaying crowd. To Jim, the crowd's movement didn't seem to make any sense. People were shifting sideways, then back and forth. Nobody seemed to have any control of it.

By 6:45, the pressure began to get frightening. Jim was able to raise his arms high enough to help pass a girl overhead who had apparently fainted. Then Peter lost a shoe, and for ten minutes he and Jim tried to get it back on. They finally succeeded. But now Peter couldn't lower his arms down far enough to lock up again with the Wyoming High group. To stay together he put his arm around Jim's shoulders.

It was only possible to take the shortest of breaths. Jim found himself tipping his head back up to the sky to get some cool air. He was surprised to see an enormous cloud of steam rising from the other upraised faces, almost like a fog bank in a river valley. The moon was barely visible through it. Peter began saying that the pressure was so great, he didn't think he could hang onto Jim's neck much longer. Several moments later, Jim felt Peter's arm slip away from his shoulders. He looked

24

everywhere his confined neck would let him, but Peter was nowhere to be seen. Greg MacDonald and John Roosa looked too. Neither could find him, and no one could move in any direction to continue the search.

As the three Wyoming High School students looked in vain for Peter Bowes, Lieutenant Menkhaus reported his concern to Sergeant Basham about the swelling crowd outside on the plaza. They met behind a side door in Section 616.

For police and security guards, the view remained fragmented. None could squeeze into the middle of the crowd, even if they wanted to, without increasing the pressure that was steadily building. There was concern that a potential crisis was brewing, but because scenes like this were so common at rock concerts, neither the spectators nor the police anticipated anything beyond the usual crush, in this case an almost motionless one smothered by the noise of the crowd.

Sergeant Basham passed along the word that he thought that The Who had arrived late, and had not completed their sound checks and warm-up. The decision-making process of opening the doors was obscured by the maze of contracts between the Coliseum and the promoters, The Who managers, the ushers, private police, stage hands, electricians, and the unions involved. The key lay in the basic contract between the Coliseum and the promoters, that read: "DOORS OF THE AUDITORIUM will be open at the discretion of the Hall and/or Promoter." In this case, it would be either manager Richard Morgan or concert promoter Cal Levy, the local man representing Electric Factory Concerts, the Philadelphia concern that had booked The Who.

As Director of Operations for the Coliseum, Richard Morgan had his hands full the night of any concert, especially when hard-rock superstars performed. Inside the Coliseum, he had on hand that night twenty-six employees of the Cincinnati Private Police Association, and had to coordinate their activity with Menkhaus' city police. He also had to supervise the employees of what is called Volume Services—the hot dog, pizza, and soft drink concessions scattered along the ramps underneath the stands and sending out pungent, aromatic odors.

There were also forty-five ushers to keep track of, who were to guide the spectators after they swarmed through the eleven turnstiles that were assigned to thirteen ticket takers under Morgan's eye. He had a score of other responsibilities floating through his mind besides those directly related to today's event.

He had to buy and catalog every item purchased by the Coliseum with the exception of office supplies, advertising and some printing. He had to set up, clean up, check the box office, the heating and refrigeration, the electricals, the parking, the union negotiations and other contracts—the latter being a paper-trail maze to confound even a practiced eye. Among them were the Ushers and Clerical Union Local 375; the International Alliance of Theatrical Stage Employees and Moving Picture Operations Local B-38; the Treasurers and Ticket Sellers Local 754; the Service Employees International Union Local 158-A; the Cincinnati Private Police Association/Watchmen's Local 13130; the International Union of Operating Engineers Local 212—all in addition to handling the direct contract for the event of the evening, in this case with Electric Factory Concerts.

Electric Factory, in turn, was governed and controlled by the rigid demands of Tidal Wave Promotions. This organization represented The Who directly. In addition there was the Premier Talent Agency in New York to add to the confusion. Electric Factory was in a vise because of this multi-layered arrangement. The demands of the contract went right down through the essentials, requiring Immigration and Naturalization documents, approvals of the State and Justice Departments for The Who, a hospitality room, and a full payment of money in cash or certified checks, six hours before the music would begin. Underneath the festival atmosphere of the concert was enough grim legal language to make a Philadelphia lawyer blench.

As Electric Factory's representative in Cincinnati, Cal Levy had almost as much on his mind as Morgan. Levy was a husky man with a thick reddish beard, and a formidable demeanor. He was unpredictable, shifting from hostility to affability in alternating moods. He knew the rock business inside and out, and had the toughness to handle it. Larry Magid, the head of Philadelphia's Electric Factory was in Cincinnati for The Who concert, but was leaving the actual operations to Levy.

All of these machinations led down to the front-line manpower, Lieutenant Menkhaus of the city police, and Sergeant Basham of the security guards, who were face-to-face with the crowd. After their brief conference at 6:45 in Section 616, Basham went back to check the stage, while Menkhaus located Morgan inside the Coliseum. Both Menkhaus and Morgan tracked down Cal Levy. Morgan had arranged for some doors on the north side to be opened, and made the announcement over the public address system. Morgan also requested that the crowd around the main entrance, now estimated to be more than eight thousand, back up and give the people up front more room.

In spite of the announcement, the doors were not yet open on the north side of the arena. Here the plaza level narrowed to a balcony rather than the wide expanse in front of the main doors. As chunks of the crowd broke off to run there, they met others running back to the main plaza in frustration. The triangular shape of the prow that stuck out of the main building contained eight main glass doors on each of its sides. The doors would open outward into the crowd. The triangular prow had the tendency to divide the crowd into two sections, facing each other at roughly a 45-degree angle. But with the massive horde that had already gathered by 6:30 or 7:00 the plaza was solidly packed around both sides of the doors, with the prow sticking into the crowd's belly. And the ramp from the stadium was still pouring more bodies into the mass.

Officers Tom Lanter and Kerry Rowland watched the procedure apprehensively from their post at the rear of the crowd at the main entrance. There was no sign of the door opening anywhere, and their concern grew. At past rock concerts situations like this had often been a cue for the tossing of a barrage of bottles to smash into the crowd and against the building. With the extreme cold, conditions were likely to be exacerbated.

There could be no possible way that the small cordon of Cincinnati police could handle a riot situation on the plaza, expansive though it was. There was also evidence of drug and alcohol abuse among some of the spectators, including some heavy overdoses. Although they were in the minority they were conspicuous. Some slumped against the wall outside the crowd in stupor. Others reeled and staggered. They were few in number, and individually they were of small concern, but their possible effect on the rest of the crowd was significant.

"I don't know," Officer Rowland said to his partner. "I don't know what this crowd is going to do, or when they're going to do it. But if they don't get those doors open soon, something's gonna happen."

ARE THE KIDS ALL RIGHT?

Although the patrolmen were concerned, there was nothing evident to suggest that the biggest disaster in the history of rock music was about to take place, and that no one would be able to do anything to prevent it. Because the storm center of the crush was hidden from view and smothered by the noise of the crowd, none of the police officers or security guards yet had any real clue to the suffocating pressure that many of the spectators had been enduring for more than three hours now.

The answer to the big question of *why* the crowd was pulled so forcibly by the tidal action that followed would not be found easily. It lay in a phenomenon that is as little understood today as it was hundreds of years ago. But its current application can be traced back a decade and a half, to the time when Deborah and Mike Shumate and Brant and Becky Ross were just learning to listen to music, and Peter Bowes and Jim Krumrei were infants barely able to walk.

PART II

DATE

*THE MID-1960'S
TO THE MID-1970'S*

PLACE

USA, ENGLAND, THE WORLD

BACK

in the mid-1960's, fifteen years before they gathered on the plaza of Riverfront Coliseum, no one in the crowd could have predicted he or she would be drawn there by the charisma of The Who. For one reason, the Coliseum had not yet been built. For another, The Who as a group was unheard of in the United States, and barely known in England. But almost all who converged for the concert on December 3, 1979, had one thing in common: They represented the first generation who had grown up with hard-rock music. Rock was their music, completely. It was woven through their generation from the moment they were born. No other generation could make that claim.

Deborah Shumate (née Naumann) was just ten years old in 1966. She lived with her family in the suburb of Reading, to the north of the city, out along the busy Reading Road, in a section where a variety of brick and frame houses were blended like a patchwork quilt. There was a scattering of industry, a plethora of truck stops, and a pleasant oasis of residential, middle-income homes.

Fred Naumann, Deborah's father, was an operating engineer for the city of Reading's power plant. He was a patient man who liked country music. He was a little puzzled by the new rock music that was beginning to take over the radio, but he tolerated it as long as Deborah and her older brother Michael kept the volume within limits. Michael played

31

the guitar constantly, and well. Fred did not discourage this, and Debbie would sit for hours listening to her brother play and sing. She liked the way he played the song called "Bring It On Home," and thought his voice could match many of those on the stereo records that were piling up in the living room.

On the crest of the wave at that time were the Beatles, with Elvis remaining high on the charts. Both captured Deborah's rhythm and heart. She also loved the TV series *The Monkees*, which mimicked a group very much like the Beatles and their antics in the movie *A Hard Day's Night*. The fact that *The Monkees* was synthesized by a TV producer, and that invisible studio musicians prerecorded the instrumental track, failed to dim Deborah's enthusiasm for the show. Meanwhile, her sister Carolyn was a toddler of four, absorbing the music scene at least through her unconscious. But the music and the beat were there, and her interest would burgeon by the the time she was five.

Twelve-year-old Mike Shumate was deeply into the Beatles and Elvis, as was practically everyone his age and older at the time. Already the owner of a small tape deck, he glued his ear to it, listening to his favorites over and over, more interested in the beat than in the music and lyrics. At the age of five his foot had automatically started to tap to the beat of Elvis singing "Hound Dog," and from then on he was hooked.

Mike's first brush with the Beatles came a few years after that, under unusual circumstances. It was not uncommon for the Ohio River to show its muscles. In 1965, at the age of eleven, Mike woke up one morning to see his house surrounded by water, and a neighbor across the street fishing out his window.

He and his family had to be evacuated by canoe. The people he stayed with during the emergency kept their radio and record player going most of the day. Before long, he was addicted to the Beatles, especially when they chanted "She loves you, yeah, yeah, yeah" in their contagious spirit of affirmation. Interspersed with the Beatles, he absorbed the lilting cadences of "Puff the Magic Dragon," as sung by Peter, Paul and Mary. Mike did not yet recognize that the lyrics referred to smoking dope, rather than relating a nursery rhyme.

Mrs. Shumate was not averse to listening to the early rock music herself. But later, when heavy rhythm-and-blues began to come into the picture, she drew the line, leading to a sullen but not mutinous position on Mike's part.

In Wyoming, north of downtown Cincinnati, and out along Springfield Pike, Peter Bowes was a four-year-old in 1965, living in the pleasing environment of an affluent suburb that reflected the congeniality of a small town. Peter's father, Dick, was a Procter & Gamble executive who coordinated the college recruitment program—a program which had been scouring campuses for decades to find college trainees to meet the venerable company's expanding needs. From the company's beginnings as candlemakers, on through Ivory Soap, Camay, Mr. Clean, Joy, and Duz, and continuing on through Crisco, Duncan Hines, Crest, Gleem and other household words, P & G had been thirsty for well-scrubbed potential executive trainees, and the college recruiting program had been one of the mainstays of its growth.

Closeness was a basic characteristic of the Bowes family. Peter's older brothers and sister—Ben, Andy and Nancy—doted on him from the day he was brought home from the hospital. He could have easily been spoiled if it weren't for the quiet discipline of his parents. But Peter was bright and alert, and rarely had to be brought into line.

From his earliest years, Peter loved music. He was surrounded by music of all kinds, including classical. At four, he was taken to hear Peter, Paul and Mary, and was the youngest one at the concert. He was totally fascinated by it. Since everyone in the family liked a broad spectrum of music, his interest in it would continue to grow through the years.

At the age of nine, Brant Ross was a student at St. John's Catholic School. His love for music was now bundled in a cocoon. In the mid-sixties, Brant remained aware of little outside of homework, baseball and cowboys and Indians. Becky Bess, his future wife whom he would not meet until nearly a decade later, had not yet sensed her devotion to music.

Together, these Cincinnati youngsters represented a slice, a cross section. Their counterparts stretched across the country by the millions, and by the thousands across the city alone. As representatives of the first totally-immersed, rock-bred generation, they would find rock music a force, an energy, a philosophy, a politic, and even a religion of sorts.

Rock would bring them, almost fifteen years later, to Riverfront

33

Coliseum in December 1979, along with thousands of others. The pull that brought them there would be different in character from similar events of the past, unlike the force that compelled the crowds that thronged to hear Sinatra or even the Beatles. The difference in the nature of the attraction was subtle, especially for those who were most closely involved.

In 1965, these forces that were to meet on the plaza were only starting to form. The Who were not yet known by that name. The band was called the High Numbers, and was struggling for identity and recognition in the depressed London surburbs of Chiswick and Shepherd's Bush, in which the members were born and bred. They were out to make it, and make it in any way they could, with all the decibels their amplifiers could command.

At the Oldfield Hotel in Greenford, an ancient Middlesex village sprawled along A-40 outside London, a brash young drummer by the name of Keith Moon was sitting at the bar, belting down a series of drinks. The year was 1964, and the sound of music was getting louder all across England. The Beatles were high on their musical mountain, having already placed fifteen records on the American charts. But something was beginning to happen. A new, snarling, dissonant beat was starting to be heard among the British groups sprouting in the Beatles' footsteps. Up on the bandstand in front of him, Keith Moon could hear that new beat, and he liked it.

The group was playing some Beatle numbers, but they were playing them louder, thumpier and more aggressively. They were also playing some rhythm-and-blues, drained from America's black Southland and such blues singers as Howlin' Wolf, Bo Diddley, Muddy Waters and John Lee Hooker. This was Keith Moon's meat. It was the reason he was sitting at the bar with a single thought in mind: to get himself hired as the band's drummer, and replace the flaccid substitute session drummer, who seemed to Moon as ineffectual as a metronome.

Although the fledgling band on the bandstand of the Oldfield was called the High Numbers, it would soon be called The Who. It consisted of three testy nineteen-year-old Britishers named Peter Townshend, Roger Daltrey and John Entwistle. The reason they had a sit-in drummer was that they had just fired their regular, who had reached the ripe age of thirty-one, and was now obsolescent. When they hit the rhythm-and-blues numbers, their reedy British voices were pumped up and sandpapered into the growling guttural richness that characterized the blues of the levee.

It did not seem out of place. The beat was heavy and cacophonous, and the voices of the British singers from Shepherd's Bush and Chiswick seemed right enough imitating the gravelly Southern cadence. Peter Townshend, the tacit, informal leader of the High Numbers, relished a fierce attack on both treble and bass. As lead guitarist, he was fond of pounding out what he called power chords, swinging his arm down from a position pointing to the North Star, and slamming the strings with venom, then circling his arm to repeat the process. Daltrey appeared to rip his larynx apart to a heavy beat. John Entwistle, on the bass guitar, was becoming a master at thrashing the bass line with vengeance.

Keith Moon, sitting on the sidelines, liked all this. He sensed that the band needed him, even if they did not yet know it. Moon was a self-admitted looney. He had whisked through over twenty jobs in two years, beginning as a management trainee in an electronics company, and ending up as a drummer with another British group known as the Beachcombers, an imitation of the West Coast's Beach Boys. With a cherubic face and eyes as large as his name suggested, Moon had become frustrated with the dulcet sound of the group he had been playing with.

Moon's musical roots went back to the time when he played the bugle for the Barham Sea Scouts. He was a lousy bugler, but one day he picked up some drumsticks at the troop headquarters. He began beating the drums there with unbridled enthusiasm. From then on, his course was set. He didn't need lessons; he was a natural. Now, listening to the High Numbers, he could project himself in place of the indifferent drummer on the stand. All he needed was the courage to get up there and let the band know that he could save them. To get up his nerve, he bolted down a few more drinks. Not until he was sufficiently numb did he move to the the bandstand to stake his claim.

Facing Townshend and Daltrey, he said: "I can play better than any damn drummer in the business."

Townshend, unhappy with the drumming he was getting from the substitute, took Moon up on his challenge. He invited Moon to take a shot at the drums for a couple of numbers. Moon sat down at the borrowed drum set with a gleam in his eyes and a solid collection of drinks in his stomach.

ARE THE KIDS ALL RIGHT?

They began playing a song called "Road Runner." Keith Moon began with them and ended with them. His beat was maniacal. In the process, he smashed through two drum skins and decommissioned the pedal of the bass drum. He was startled at his own strength, he recalled at a later time, and scared to death. He mumbled apologies, and crossed to the bar to order another drink.

As he downed it, he saw Townshend approaching him. He called Moon over to the bandstand again, where Roger Daltrey asked Moon what he was doing the following Monday. Daltrey didn't complain about the pulverized drum set, and didn't ask him if he wanted the job. He simply told Moon they would pick him up in a van for a job on Monday, and that was it. Keith Moon had joined the band.

It was the beginning of a chaotic career. Not only for Moon, but for the rest of them. Townshend, alternately manic and dolorous, pushed the group relentlessly—playing every pub or club it could book. The Beatles were leading the way for the British invasion of the Western world of music. Townshend wanted not only to follow them, but to bring something else to the new music. He admired the Beatles, but felt they lacked those essential ingredients that he sensed in the crowds of his own generation that were beginning to pack close to the bandstand: frustration, alienation, aggression and violence. To Townshend, the Beatles didn't seem to recognize these elements. He repeated the themes constantly in interviews, especially when accused that the music was simple sadism. "It's not sadistic," he told a reporter from the British magazine *Melody Maker*. "It's aggression. I think aggression has a place in society today, whereas sadism and masochism haven't." To the London *Evening Standard*, he described his audiences in more detail: "They're in a crummy predicament, having to work to live. . . . They envy our music. They would love to get hold of a £200 guitar and wallop it. They would like to jump on stage and yell about why the kids can't have pills and how youngsters are being put down by people of forty who want to be twenty."

The smashing of a guitar was a symbol of aggression and violence that began with a single incident. With Keith Moon an integral part of the band, the group moved on to playing a regular gig every Tuesday night at the Railway Tavern, at the junction of Harrow and Wealdstone, not far from the great Harrow School where Byron, Trollope, Galsworthy and other luminaries once wore its colors.

36

PART II

The contrast between the ambiance of the school and the scene at the Railway Tavern was marked. The Mods parked their scooters outside, and clogged the dance floor in a din that savaged the central nervous system. The quarters were hardly luxurious, with a low ceiling and a dance floor the size of a postage stamp. The crowd and the band fed on each other. Playing "Summertime Blues" and "Shakin' All Over" with ultra-souped-up amplification changed these rhythm-and-blues numbers from a Southern drawl to a primal scream. The crowds, jammed close to the stage, became toys in the hands of the band. Townshend knew it, Daltrey knew it, they all knew it. And they relished it.

More important than the music was the physical action. Daltrey ran in place, bent over backward, twirled his microphone above his head. Moon pummeled the drums as if they were his enemy. Townshend leaped with every other chord. The more he did, the wilder the crowd became. At the height of an incendiary pitch one Tuesday at the Railway Tavern, Townshend jumped so high that he jammed the neck of his guitar through the low ceiling. The crowd roared. Then he yanked the instrument out of the ceiling and smashed it on the stage, breaking it into useless chunks. The crowd went berserk. Then Keith Moon jumped up from the drums, kicked his Premier bass drum over and crashed through the skin with his heel. Daltrey slammed his microphone to the floor. Now the crowd went insanely wild with applause. No ovation at the Railway Tavern had ever topped this one.

Standing in the back of the room, craning hard to see the band, were two would-be promoters and managers, Kit Lambert and Chris Stamp. By day, they were assistant motion picture directors; by night, they prowled the circuit of rock clubs from Watford to Harrow to Ealing to Shepherd's Bush, scouring the landscape for a promising new band to manage. They had never seen an audience reaction like this in all their tours. Whatever the music was—they could barely hear it over the din of the crowd—the bond between the audience and the group was incredibly intense.

Lambert and Stamp had found what they were looking for. And so had Pete Townshend and company. The group was not at all satisfied with their current manager, a door knob manufacturer. They were also frustrated because, though their local fame was growing, they had not yet produced a single record. They were more than willing to have Lambert and Stamp take over, although their former comanager, Pete

Meaden, had been steering them in the direction of a burgeoning market in England called the Mods.

The Mods were a unique and puzzling phenomenon. On the surface, they were held together by two flimsy bonds: music and fashion. Beneath the surface they were, what were called in England, working-class kids, who reflected Townshend's gut observations of frustration, alienation, aggression and violence. The interaction between the band and the Mod subculture was dynamic. It launched the group into a trajectory of rising power and influence over its own generation, and indirectly over others for years to come. That same interaction would also mark the beginning of the then barely-discernible influence that would follow in the wake of the new music, and would alter the pattern of the crowds and the way they reacted when brought together en masse under the impact of that music.

It is hard to tell which came first to the Mods, the music or the fashion. It may have been the fashion, because the Mods emerged in the early 1960's in the trail of England's notorious and destructive Teddy Boys, who combined their passion for style with frequent vandalism. The Mods followed suit, with their obsession for setting new fashion trends. But they drew the line at the mawkish pop music of the fifties embraced by the Teddy Boys. The Mods were much too cool for that. Instead, they extolled the esoteric modern jazz of America's Gerry Mulligan or Dave Brubeck. This was cool. This was where it was at. This, in fact, was where the name "Mods" came from, for they first called themselves the Modernists, after modern jazz.

In their constant search for the esoteric, the early Mods also latched onto the rhythm-and-blues of American black artists, to records that were hard to come by. The discs filtered in through American servicemen for the most part. Because the records were at a premium, their allure grew. They also marked a turning point in Pete Townshend's life. He and his roommate at art school, Richard Barnes, fell heir to a rich treasure of rhythm-and-blues records from two Americans who lived in a flat above them. The two Yankees had to leave the country swiftly because they had in their possession "certain substances," as Barnes puts it. As a result, Townshend found himself with all the musical raw material he needed to build a new British sound that would transfer the frustration of the black in America to the smoldering frustrations of the Mod.

38

PART II

In Townshend's windfall collection were many of the greats of America's blues, soul, and rhythm exponents: Chuck Berry, Bo Diddley, Muddy Waters, Booker T, Little Richard, Ray Charles, Fats Domino, James Brown, Howling Wolf and a dozen others—all in great favor with the Mods. Townshend liked James Brown especially, the Southern singer who was said to bring the Devil into gospel music, to turn it into a raucous explosion with a throbbing beat that would put a Nigerian ju-ju man to shame. Roger Daltrey, in turn, grabbed on to Brown's gravelly voice to sound as if he'd sprung from the Georgia cotton fields, where Brown had come from. Townshend pumped his guitar in imitation of Brown's monotonous, single-chord beat, using his instrument more as a drum than a guitar. Keith Moon would beat his drums as if he were deep in the Ivory Coast rain forest. All of this would lead to establishing Townshend and the band as the new British masters of rhythm-and blues.

When they became the new managers, Lambert and Stamp lost no time in renaming the group The Who. They were convinced the name would be much catchier than the High Numbers, or the Detours, which had been another name for the band in its search for identity. "The *what?* The *Who.*" It was a simple talk-making device, the new managers were convinced, bound to be circulated.

By 1964, the Mods had fully formed into their ill-defined but homogeneous subculture. They still had not settled on an anthem-maker for their music. The Beatles were too universal to be "in," too soft, too easygoing. The Rolling Stones, moving swiftly into the wide public floodlight, were thought to be commercializing the sacred rhythm-and-blues, and didn't have the knack for dressing precisely to Mod standards.

Following Pete Meaden's lead, Lambert and Stamp continued to pour The Who into the exact Mod mold, both in clothing and in music. Booking the group on Tuesday nights into the damp, black cavern of the Marquee Club on Wardour Street, Kit Lambert labeled their show "Maximum Rhythm-and-Blues," and turned the dead Tuesday nights into the high boiling point of each week. To make it at the Marquee was to make it big. About the only big-name British group that *wasn't* launched there was the Beatles. The Rolling Stones, with a two-year start on The Who, had played there when the club was just turning away from jazz to embrace the rhythm-and-blues tradition.

39

ARE THE KIDS ALL RIGHT?

The Mods lived for weekends, the great escape, the oasis separating them from the straight office-boy, sales-clerk, messenger-boy, typist girl, file-clerk, strait-jacket lifestyle that kept them in line during the week. Or they lived for lunchtime—the hour when they could cruise the clothing shops and tailors just off Carnaby Street—not on it, because that was too expensive.

If you didn't dress right, exactly right, you just weren't with it, man. The cut of the lapels, the jacket waist, the vents had to be exactly right if you wanted to be supercool. When you went to the Marquee or the Locarno Ballroom, you put yourself into a semitrance with the help of pills called Blues, Purple Hearts, or Depth Bombs, and danced all night and into Sunday morning, if not all day Sunday. The office or the store or the plant where you worked all week was simply wiped away by a giant eraser. Next to the clothes—and the pills—the music was everything.

Some Mods went all out for French clothes, spurred by the French teenagers who flocked across the English Channel to Brighton on summer days and at holiday time. Townshend himself went for a jacket made out of the Union Jack, to the discomfort of the old-boy school. Although there was no clear-cut society of Mods, they defined themselves by their trendy clothes, and no one knew how many there were roaming, and working, in London and in the Midlands, toeing the line just enough to keep the bread coming in from their straight employers.

To be completely with the "in" crowd, a Mod had to be constantly pilled-up. The drug of choice was Drinamyl, a Smith, Kline and French prescription form of amphetamines and barbiturates combined—both an upper and a downer. For the Mods, the street name was Blues or Purple Hearts, and they were swilled down in wholesale quantities. One Mod with a heavy overdose had his stomach pumped out, and in the process, over seventy Purple Hearts were discovered. They took the pills for a speed "rush" to stay awake all night dancing. They also helped for keeping awake on the job the next day. With a heavy reinforcement, some could avoid sleep for two or three days, and still appear to be functioning on the job that was all important to keep them in pills, clothes, records, and the price of admission to the rock clubs.

From the reactions of the Mods who swarmed to the Marquee, there was little question that The Who was the anthem-maker they were seeking. The energy and aggression that blasted off the dusty brick walls of the Marquee pumped the Mods to a fever pitch, especially when a battle was looming with the Rockers—another loosely-defined social group that paralleled America's Hell's Angels.

The Rockers wore leather jackets and long hair, and sported high-powered motorcycles. They continued to cling to the pop music of the fifties, and were considered by the Mods to be Huns from the north country, unkempt and unruly. On bank holidays and weekends, both Mods and Rockers would sweep down like motorized cavalry troops to Brighton or Margate or Hastings, the Rockers on their heavy bikes and the Mods on their elaborately-decorated Lambretta or Vespa motor scooters—an almost obligatory status symbol for the proper Mod. Some scooters would sport up to twenty meticulously shined headlamps.

The differences in vehicles, in musical taste, and in style were enough to set the stage for the furious conflict that arose when the two gangs met on the beaches and promenades of the hapless resort towns. There was no political focus, and barely a social issue involved in the fight. The differences in taste became a springboard for a knock-down, drag-out confrontation. It was hard to tell how the battles got started. Word would go around that "everyone" was going to Brighton, and everyone did, Mods and Rockers both. Fortified by pills, the usually gentle and fashionable Mods would find themselves with the courage of lions.

The battle scenes were hard to believe. On one chilly March day, over a thousand Mods and Rockers invaded the small seaside resort of Clacton during the Easter bank holiday. The gangs roared through the streets all night, shoved the townspeople out of the way, broke windows, turned over parked cars, broke into shops, fought and stabbed each other, and brought police reinforcements scurrying in from nearby towns.

The Whitsun bank holiday in May brought the mobs to Brighton and Margate, where Rockers were isolated from their gangs, then kicked, pummeled and stabbed as families looked on in horror and hid behind deck chairs they'd stacked like wagon-train stockades against the Indians. Next to the stones on the rocky beach, the deck chairs became the favorite weapon for smashing skulls and drawing blood of both Rockers and police. Two Rockers were beaten with deck chairs, then pushed off the roof of the Brighton Aquarium.

At August holiday time, the scene shifted to Hastings, and a Scotland Yard riot squad was flown in to quell the rioters. One of the squad was sacked the moment he reached the beach. He was kicked and mauled by a dozen Mods before his cohorts came to his rescue. A seafront cafe owner had both arms slashed with broken glass. All through the town, most of the night, hundreds of Mods roared a chant: "Mods! Mods! Mods!" Later, the body of a sixteen-year-old boy was found floating in the shallow water.

One London daily observed: "Shopkeepers looked on anxiously as the mob swept by. Hard-pressed police drove round in circles trying to keep up as the Mods changed direction every few minutes—always running. But why? No one knows—not even the runners."

Some of the kids did try to explain, but not too successfully. "You've got to be either a Mod or a Rocker," a seventeen-year-old girl said. A friend added: "Mods want to get rid of the Rockers—they can get out of the country. And the Rockers carry knives. Mods don't have weapons. Only deck chairs and milk bottles." A third friend offered this vague statement: "Mods like blues and blue-beat rhythm, and they go to clubs and dance. Rockers just listen to pop music."

After the battles came the band. Townshend and the rest of The Who would invariably be at the beach resorts, where their strength and power grew with the presence of the Mods. The interaction between the band and the crowd was explosive. Each fed on the other. The Who's music was gutsy, visceral, violent and all-enveloping. The overpowering noise and percussion of The Who wrapped up the entire package: the euphoria of violence in the battles of the day, the collective force of belonging to the crowd and its fashions, the packed closeness of the mass and the rush and exhilaration of the pills. As Mick Faver and Edward Baher put it in their book *Watch Out Kids*: "The Who provided total identification for this audience. On the stage, they were blatant pill-heads who generated an atmosphere of speed, frenzy and violence . . . an unreal spectacle of speeding Mods watching transfixed, packed shoulder to shoulder, as at deafening volume The Who go through their act to the culmination in an orgasmic ritual of frantic destruction, as Keith Moon climbs onto his drums and swings at them with an axe, as Townshend drives his guitar into the speakers until it splinters."

The Mods would throng to a Who concert at the Aquarium Ballroom in Brighton in such numbers that not a square inch of space was vacant. Pete Meaden, who had started it all for The Who, arrived there one summer night, and couldn't move into the doorway. The ballroom was

42

crowded that people were actually standing on each other's shoulders. The pull was growing stronger at every concert. The Who were about to become superstars.

Still, there was no rational explanation for the turbulence. One Mod said that his whole life was miserable, that he wanted to put an axe to his house and smash it the way The Who smashed their instruments. Another, after he shattered a shop window, said he pictured Townshend bashing his guitar into a speaker. Faber and Baher quote another Mod saying: "At times I'm frightened, but a handful of dubes [pills], and I feel really great. Like I own the world, and the peasants can get out of the way."

This was the scene when the Age of Hard Rock was starting, and later Heavy-Metal Rock. It would leave much of the character of rhythm-and-blues behind in favor of the throbbing fustigation that enveloped body tissues as well as ears at metasonic levels. None of the superstar groups that were about to emerge in the mid-sixties could be pigeonholed. Rock experts stumbled when they tried to define the trends that had developed from the relatively simple music that began with Elvis Presley and Bill Haley's Comets back in the fifties.

Every time a new superstar came into the limelight, a new category of rock seemed to spring up, either in Britain or the U.S. The simple term "rock and roll" became peppered with varied definitions: Ballad R &R, Vocal Group R & R, Uptown R & B, Jazz Rock, Surf, Pop Folk, Produced Soul, Tamla-Motown, Bubblegum Rock, Folk Rock, Soft Rock, Pop Soul, Progressive Soul—among others. The British invasion of the sixties started with a bang with the Beatles, who were basically soft rock. Then came the anvil beat of the Rolling Stones, followed by The Who—again, among many others. Acid rock moved in about the same time as hard rock, and both raced in tandem through the 1960's and the beginning of the 1970's.

At the time the hard-rock pattern was emerging on the beaches of Brighton and in the clubs in and around London, a full explanation of the Mod subculture was hard to come by. There were the obvious strands of violence and frustration of the era, not only reflected in the rock scene, but in the challenge of the Mods and the younger generation everywhere to the mainstream of society. They were searching for identity in a world where opportunity was mainly blocked, and freedom meant little without a goal to aspire to. Out of this milieu, the new hard and heavy-metal rock was beginning to grow—both as a reflection of the mood, and an instigator of it.

If a team of psychologists, sociologists and anthropologists were surveying the beaches of Brighton with ivory-tower detachment, they might have looked on with varied points of view in spite of their overlapping disciplines. Herbert Marcuse, of the New Left, might have been disappointed. He found the destruction, and the music that went with it, extraordinarily lifeless. To him, the music of the black, as the cry and song of the slaves and the ghetto, was real. For white bands to take it over, to jump and yell and turn it into a carnival, was inappropriate and simply imitative. To Marcuse, mobs like the Mods were insipid, rebels without a cause, vacuous. The monotonous beat, the aggression, the hammering, electronic volume of the music amounted to hapless frustration and little else. He found rock music "totalitarian" in the way it "overwhelms individual consciousness and mobilizes a collective unconscious which remains without social foundation."

Others, like psychiatrist Rollo May, might explain the actions of the Mods by the lack of any positive, constructive goals. They were living in a condition of emptiness, without anything to grope for or grow toward. The result was not merely stagnation. The collective emptiness turned to morbidity, despair, and eventually to the embrace of blind and undirected destruction. By losing themselves in the mirror-image crowd, the Mods avoided the fear of social isolation—and also of being ridiculed or rejected—in an attempt to fill their emptiness.

The Mods and their musical heroes, The Who, had an importance that transcended their time and space in the mid-sixties. They were a highly visible microcosm of the younger generation, and a harbinger of what was to follow in the coming years. They formed an exaggerated capsule of the mood and psyche of most of the youth of the Western world. Erik Erikson laid this type of restiveness partly on what he called identity confusion, a personality out of touch with its feelings. Such confusion, he thought, should grant youth a moratorium on certain restrictions to allow for "sprees" and other ways of "being different." But Erikson begged the question of what happened when the moratorium ran into borderline psychosis, criminality, or dangerous delinquency.

His theories, formulated in the fifties, had a direct application to the Mods. He found that growing and developing youths were deeply concerned with how they appeared in the eyes of others, and that in their search for identity, they had artificially to appoint well-meaning people to the role of adversaries. At the same time, they were eager to install lasting idols with whom they identified.

In Brighton or at the Marquee Club or elsewhere, this pattern was clear. Erikson discerned that the tendency was to over-identify, to lose themselves in their heroes. The Who, in reflecting the mood and aimless energy of the Mods, also tended to exacerbate the violence because of this over-identification. The musical idols would become what Erikson describes as "pseudo-identities."

But the roots of the antisocial behavior, he found, did not lie in the surface interaction between the heroes and the crowd. It lay instead in the industrial revolution, instant mass media communication and mechanization. With these, the identities that had been inherited from man's established cultures went down the drain. The resulting loss of identity created, in turn, deep anxiety, irrational motivation, and frustration. Finally, Erikson firmly points out, that frustration leads to aggression.

Erikson's observations were prophetic. More than a decade before the Mods emerged on the British scene, he wrote: "Young people can be remarkably clannish, and cruel in their exclusion of all those who are 'different' in skin color or cultural background, in tastes and gifts, and often in such petty aspects of dress and gesture as have been temporarily selected as *the* signs of an in-grouper or out-grouper. It is important to understand (which does not mean condone or participate in) such intolerance as a defense against a sense of identity confusion."

Whatever the theory, there was no question that the roots of the new music growing out of The Who's thundering volume were based on aggression. Townshend repeated the theme in a dozen interviews: "Ours is a group with built-in hate." The Mods agreed, and cheered him on. Taken individually, the Mods were probably as well-scrubbed, attractive, and appealing a group as any emerging young generation in history. They were as well-dressed as those on any Ivy League campus, and their ritualistic passion for the "right" clothes made them all the more appealing to the eye. The Who's comanager, Kit Lambert, claimed that the movement consisted of "clean living under difficult circumstances." Some took this as tongue in cheek; others didn't. He never elaborated on it.

The Mod obsession with style and posing—the way they leaned their

45

knees into the front panels of their motor scooters, even the way they put their hands in their pockets or slouched against a wall—reflected a basic narcissism. It was also a mild way of thumbing their noses at adult society. According to Dr. Gregory Rochlin, of Harvard Medical School and the Boston Psychoanalytic Institute, the wellspring of all aggression rises out of narcissism. Freud had noted it first—that powerful unconscious drive that pushed one into being entirely self-focused, and the need to be propped up and confirmed by his peers. From his study of the destructiveness and antisocial violence of the Roman Emperor Caligula, Rochlin concluded that when narcissism must be served, aggression follows. Rochlin goes along with Freud's observation: "Impeded aggressiveness seems to involve grave injury. It really seems as though it is necessary for us to destroy some thing or person in order not to destroy ourselves, in order to guard against the impulse to self-destruction. A sad disclosure for the moralist."

Tied to this was the theory that the neurotic expression of aggression was masochism, and the "need for punishment." The only way out was for the destructive impulses to be neutralized or "socialized." But to Rochlin or Freud, this was not easily achieved. A deeply-imbedded narcissism will hold on stubbornly. When young people try to form an identity, aggression rises swiftly. The death wish and the life wish clash. In the long run, aggression turns from others to the self.

When a group gets together en masse, the members imitate each other, act ferociusly and recklessly on the slightest stimulus and revert to Freud's "group mind," which belongs to neurotics and children—a herd. The narcissism grows in proportion to the crowd's size, and with it, the aggression. "It is not that conscience is dismissed," writes Rochlin,"or that it is somehow suspended or set aside. Rather, it does not come into question."

Rochlin concluded that regardless of the prevalence of Freudian narcissism, regardless of the dangers of repressing it in the unconscious, the essential needs of our social existence demand that we give up narcissism, since it is a greater menace to man than aggression. We must then redirect this neurotic form of self-esteem to work or causes or love for others, so that aggression can become "the benign energy of accomplishment."

The problem for the Mods and many others was that there were no open roads to creative work, no accessible causes to work for in the mechanized society they were growing up in. Although it was a period of relative prosperity, the jobs to be had were dead-end and menial. The horizons were fogged in.

Narcissism remained, and with the aggression that accompanied it came a sense of emptiness, of a vacuum to be filled. The new post-Beatles hard-rock music, entirely different in character from any that had ever been heard before, began to fill that vacuum with massive electronic amplification, never before available. It was a sound that could literally blot out the senses as much as the pills the Mod were taking to accomplish the same purpose. Whatever the results, a mold for music was being gelled that would dominate for years to come.

Slender, dark and often brooding, Peter Townshend shaped the music of The Who to fit the mood of the times and the pulse of his generation. The son of a jazz musician, he grew up in anger, at least in part because he had been endowed with a Pinocchio-like nose, and felt he had none of the charm of Cyrano. The middle-class doldrums of Chiswick left him with angst and frustration, which he often took out on his father.

"Whenever my dad got drunk," he told a reporter, "he'd come up to me and say, 'Look, son, you know looks aren't everything.' He's getting drunk and he's ashamed of me because I've got a huge nose and he's trying to make me feel good. It was the reason I did everything. It's the reason I played the guitar—because of my nose."

He attempted to escape by going to art school in London, where he was attracted to beautiful girls without being able to make headway with them. Again he blamed it on his nose, and gathered more anger.

When his grandmother gave him a guitar, he took his frustration out on that, determined to show the world that his talent for music was greater than the size of his nose. He dropped his classes at art school, and began his acrobatic guitar playing when he felt the girls on the dance floor were paying more attention to his nose than to his music.

Oddly enough, it worked. When Townshend leaped around the stage, the mood of the crowd fired up, the applause was thunderous, and no one had time to look at his nose. Further, smashing his guitar at the end of an evening's gig was beginning to become a habit—partly out of

47

his aggression and simmering inner resentment, and partly out of showmanship that brought the crowds back to see if he would do it again.

The instrument smashing drew crowds and screams of approval, but it was an expensive habit. The Who would be years in paying off the expenses. The band had managed to produce one single with the unlikely title of "I'm the Face," with "Zoot Suit" on the flip side. Its modest success was hardly enough to pay for a string of mangled $400 guitars and Vox, Marshall, and Hiwatt amplifiers. Townshend explained the destruction by saying that the violence catered to the suppressed aggression of the crowd, and that he liked smashing things up because it gave him a release. Moon explained it as frustration when someone in the band was too stoned to give out his best. Daltrey explained it, enigmatically, by saying that a guitar was just a plank of wood, and that The Who were doing what everybody wanted to do—up to buying a Rolls Royce and smacking it into a stone wall.

Even after Kit Lambert and Chris Stamp booked the group into the Marquee Club, expenses were outrunning income by several furlongs. The important thing to Lambert and Stamp, however, was that The Who continued to create an image that both reflected and provoked the innate violence of the Mods. It was a deliberate plan of action, and it brought in the money.

During 1965, Townshend was beginning to show his teeth as a song writer who knew how to hit Mod nerve ends. But in satisfying them, he was striking a universal chord of an entire generation across the world which felt the same unrest, frustration and insecurity. Townshend built on this when he wrote and recorded The Who's first hit single, "I Can't Explain." On the surface, it was a plaintive little love song about an inarticulate teen-age lover. But Townshend felt that the reason for its appeal, which brought it up into the BBC's Top Twenty with sales of over 100,000 copies, was that it reflected the insecurity and weakness of the young lover.

The next hit, written with Daltrey, was "Anyway, Anyhow, Anywhere." It flaunted arrogance and aggression, with lyrics that told the world that the kids could do anything right or wrong, that they didn't care, and never lost, regardless of what they did.

Pressing for controversy and challenge, Lambert told Townshend in

1965 to come up with a song that would "make a statement." If The Who were going to be leaders of what Townshend called "the teen-age wasteland," they needed a battle hymn that would rock the Mods and shake the rest of the world at the same time. Townshend sat down at a tape recorder with his guitar and thought about it. He pictured the chaotic scenes on the scores of dance floors where he played, with the Mods getting stoned out of their skulls as they pictured themselves as the coolest in-group ever invented. The result was "My Generation." It accomplished what it set out to do. The message simply stated that nothing else in the world was worth a damn except Townshend's and The Who's generation.

With the title phrase repeated after every line, the song complained that people tried to put them down, for the simple reason that they got around. The adult world looked awful cold, the lyrics added, and finally the protagonist of the song chanted that he hoped he died before he got old.

In further lyrics, Daltrey's commanding growl warned the outsider not to try to dig what they were saying—an emphatic instruction for the older generation to keep the hell out of their business. In addition, Daltrey embroidered his lines by delivering them with a deliberate stutter. His instructions sharply commanded the adult who might stumble onto the scene to just f-f-f-f-fade away.

Played at the auditory pain level, the song stirred the Mods, and nearly everyone else nineteen and under, to ecstasy. Its power far exceeded its awkward scansion, inept rhyme, and shoddy structure. It became the decade's "Yankee Doodle" rallying cry. Actually, the lyrics of "Yankee Doodle" made less sense, yet the song had stirred a nation to rebellion—as a protest against, of all things, the Townshend Act of 1767, nearly two hundred years before. Music critics could cringe all they wanted to at the banality of the "My Generation" lyrics, the two-chord harmony, the unsubtle volume, the blatant antagonism, the crudity. "My Generation" sprang from the streets of London, but was to be taken over by the kids of the world. It didn't need to be defended against stuffy critics; all it needed was rendition.

Hadn't Robert Burns brought fresh and tangy raciness into the fallow fields of British romantic poetry? Was there anything more vulgar than Burns addressing a hymn to a louse, especially in the crude vernacular of

ARE THE KIDS ALL RIGHT?

a Scottish farmer? Would Wordsworth, Byron or Keats ever write a poem entitled "Auld Lang Syne"? And what about Walt Whitman? Hadn't he shocked the ornamental precision of American poetry? Who else would have the guts to write of himself in the mid-1800's:

> Walt Whitman, an American, one of the
> roughs, a kosmos,
> Disorderly fleshy and sensual . . . eating and
> drinking and breeding. . .

Or:

> Through me forbidden voices,
> Voices of sex and lusts . . . voices veiled,
> and I remove the veil . . .
> I keep as delicate around the bowels as
> around the head and heart,
> Copulation is no more rank to me than
> death is.

Whitman summed it all up in his preface: "There is that indescribable freshness and unconsciousness about an illiterate person that humbles and mocks the power of the noblest expressive genius."

Even the staid Ralph Waldo Emerson backed him up by ascribing to Whitman "a freedom to use sound as discord to startle the ear." Emerson went further than that. In one of his own poems he wrote:

> The kingly bard
> Must smite the chords rudely and hard
> As with hammers or with mace.

If there were any band smiting the chords "as with hammers or with mace," it would be The Who, whose performances were as much physical as they were musical. They were also disorderly, fleshy and sensual, as Whitman was accused of being, and not at all averse to gorging and drinking and breeding. Daltrey was surly, contentious and angry, and by his own admission "knocking off as many birds as you could get in one night." With deep blue eyes, Greek-god features and abundant wavy hair that he tinted orange, he filled all the requisites as a

50

semi-official spokesman for the hard-rock revolution. For him, rock and roll was the highway to ride out of the gutter and away from sheet-metal working, at which he had been laboring for five years. Townshend called him a grass-head, he called Townshend a pill-head and both called Keith Moon a sot and a pill-head, which Moon readily admitted. Out of this came the inevitable: a long series of intramural fights that often brought fists into action. All three had testy and unpredictable tempers. They were anything but the boys next door, and they had no intention of being so.

John Entwistle was more or less the quietest of the aggregation, the only one willing to stand statue-like during a gig and pound out complex riffs on his bass guitar, as the others cavorted around the stage. He had studied piano and liked classical music. He had worked in a tax office for a couple of years, playing with bands at night on everything from a French horn to a trumpet to the bass guitar. He wrote songs too, rather witty and pseudowicked like "Boris the Spider," although The Who stuck mostly to Townshend's balladry. But without Entwistle, Kit Lambert once said, The Who would simply fly away.

Whatever the varied reactions to The Who and their music, the group was becoming increasingly popular. The idolatry tendered Frank Sinatra and Elvis Presley in America was far less riotous than the adoration beginning to be showered on The Who. The crowd response moved beyond the thrill of the music, into a lifestyle that swallowed that music whole, so that those who heard it carried the tribal beat before, during, and after the gig. The scene created an emotional release for the Mods, and other kids who joined them in increasing numbers. It also created monumental problems for the police, the street cleaners, the dance hall managers, and any innocent bystanders who got in the way.

With hard rock swelling in popularity, this kind of activity was not confined to the fans of The Who. Other new rock superstars were rising swiftly on the horizon with heavy volume, heavy beat, heavy lyrics and the direct provoking of the crowd to mayhem. The Rolling Stones, with Mick Jagger leading the way, started two years before The Who with the number "(I Can't Get No) Satisfaction," their own battle hymn of sexual and political liberation. Their course had been set in 1963, when young Andrew Loog Oldham took over as their manager and later announced with all the authority of a voice from a thunder cloud: "Pop music is sex, and you have to hit them in the face with it."

The Stones' image, like The Who's, was built on a single premise: parent shock. Sexuality and hostility were the keynote. "We're going to make you exactly opposite those nice, clean, tidy Beatles," Oldham told them. "And the more the parents hate you, the more the kids will love you. Just you wait and see."

The theory worked. But with it, the same phenomenon that The Who experienced with their followers took place. Jagger's power rose with the band's smashing success. He began to sense that he could stir the emotions of the crowd until they would do almost anything he wanted them to do. At a Berlin concert, he built up such a pressure of steam that the crowd ran wild, smashed the auditorium, the shops outside it, and anything else that lay in their path. Asked about it afterward, he said he had a strange feeling on the stage, that he felt tremendous energy coming from the audience, that he wanted to smash the microphone up. "I entice the audience, of course I do," he commented. "I do it in every way I can think of."

On practically every Rolling Stones tour after Berlin, there were riots—bottles smashed, smoke bombs thrown, chairs broken. Further, a new tendency began to show up: The riots began *before* the doors were open, riots created by people storming the gates trying to get *into* the hall. Audiences were beginning to go berserk wherever the new high-energy rock was being played.

The reaction continued to be radically different in nature from anything the Beatles created. Their crowds were hysterical and passionate—but they threw grapes, not chairs. The new type of frenzy didn't simply arise out of the aggression, arrogance and violence of the lyrics, or the deafening beat of the music. It wasn't even political. But it was incendiary. Again, something that had not yet been defined was creating scenes that were becoming common across the board, that were mostly confined to the new, specific genre of hard rock that The Who and The Rolling Stones generated.

In the spring of 1965, the attention of Lambert and Stamp, along with the members of The Who, was drawn toward the side effects that were springing up at nearly every hall where The Who were booked. In mid-April, the Who were scheduled to play at the Locarno Ballroom in

Swindon, next to the White Horse Hills, halfway between Oxford and Bristol. It was one of the many Mod gigs that were spreading the group's fame throughout England. But just a few weeks before the engagement, Kit Lambert received a letter from King's Agency, Ltd., that brought him up short. It read:

Dear Sir:

I regret to inform you that THE WHO'S engagement at the Locarno Ballroom, Swindon, on Tuesday, 15th April, has now to be cancelled. This is due to the fact that the promoter has had a lot of trouble there recently, and he feels that THE WHO are not the type of group that will go well in his ballroom.

The cancellation was a minor event. But the reason for it—potential and predictable destruction and damage—foreshadowed the trend that would go hand in hand with the new hard-rock music, as its almost exclusive trademark.

Still not discernible at the time was a clear, unambiguous reason why the crowd and the band interacted so violently with each other. The reason would emerge clearly only after the mood of the Mods and the music spread across the Atlantic, and saturated both Europe and America with its power over the coming years.

A sociologist, like a journalist, tries to avoid making value judgments. Both try to remain detached and clinical. This is not always easy. It might be impossible. Robert Nesbit, Professor of Sociology at the University of California, writes that the moral texture of the sociologist is never wholly lost, regardless of how he tries. Any community examined, whether Mods, Rotarians or Nigerian tribes, has its own moral values, and the observer adds his own to these to further alter an objective analysis of the group's lifestyle.

Anthropologists seem to have the same problem. Three schools of thought predominate. One would have it that no judgment of good or bad should be made in the study of a culture. Another would talk about his subjective appraisal, but as a moralist and not an anthropologist. A third would express personal value judgments, on the theory that the

53

scientist is fully a part of society, and should do his job as a citizen by saying what he thinks.

From any of these points of view, the German sociologist Max Weber might have observed that part of the new rock scene was based on the charisma of Townshend, Daltrey, or Mick Jagger as they led their followers into a state of what had to be called destructive frenzy. One fan of The Who stated that Roger Daltrey "had more power than Jesus Christ," and he meant it. The reactions of the fans packed next to the bandstand seemed to validate this. Weber felt that charisma could be found in every sphere of society.

Although Weber claimed that he was abstaining from value judgments, he would classify those with great charisma, who weren't great heroes, prophets, or saviors, as "berserkers." The essence of charisma, he wrote,"is simply the possession of—or belief in—supra-rational qualities." He goes on to say that the followers of a charismatic leader are drawn together by an emotional form of communal relationship. There are no officials or administrators—only disciples, believers and followers. Being outside the everyday mode of living, Weber contends, charismatic authority is at once opposed to any rational, bureaucratic or traditional authority. It repudiates the past and becomes a form of revolutionary force—even without any clear-cut revolutionary goals.

Weber puts the charismatic shaman of any group into the "berserker" class, whom he notes as being kind of a magician subject to epileptoid seizures as a means of falling into trances. He describes this as "the state of a 'berserker' whose spells of maniac passion have, apparently wrongly, sometimes been attributed to the use of drugs. . . ."

Although he shows his prejudice against a shaman, some of whose work is being creatively reassessed by modern scientists, he brings up an interesting point: Drugs have little to do in bringing the shaman into his trance state. Much of the destructive wave emerging from the hard-rock era was being blamed on drugs alone, but it was obvious that there were other factors at work.

The drug scenes at Mod rock clubs were, without doubt, heavy. In spite of the fact that the Marquee Club had foot-high letters painted on a wall: SPEED KILLS, and La Discotheque offered a £50 reward for anyone proving its management was responsible for the sale of Purple Hearts, a blizzard of pills was available night and day, all through Soho or anywhere the Mods gathered. One night after the Scene Club was raided, the floor was covered by a carpet of pills dumped from the pockets of the Mods in a desperate attempt to get "clean."

The desire to escape through the new music and the pills was an evident symptom of Erik Erikson's identity confusion, especially since the two forces teamed up with a double-barreled impact. But neither drugs nor music provided an answer to the apparently senseless destruction that followed in the wake of many of the hard-rock concerts.

The Who and the Rolling Stones symbolized the flow of the rock scene down through the years, from 1965 to 1980—the critical years of the rock revolution. There were other important tributaries, of course, other superstar groups who cut a channel wide and deep and swift.

Emerging also from England during this sesqui-decade were superstar groups like Led Zeppelin whose muscular beat was combined with some gentle harmonies; Elton John, the surrealist pop art exponent; Jethro Tull, offering uninhibited action and a rock-bound flute; Eric Clapton, considered by his fans as little short of a god; and the admittedly satanic Black Sabbath, among others.

On the American side of the Atlantic there would be bands like Alice Cooper, consisting of five male musicians pounding out shock rock; Kiss, a latecomer to the overcrowded scene, and lavishly embracing the grotesque; Aerosmith, another latecomer, whose decibels would demand the group be heard. All would be descending on Cincinnati later. They were in the second stratum, however, compared to their monumental predecessors: Jimi Hendrix, whose psychedelic music soared to the galaxies and beyond; Janis Joplin, who burned out her throat and lungs on every song; and Jim Morrison and his group The Doors, who played with psychedelic or psychotic force, depending on Morrison's emotional balance at the time. All had utterly passionate followers. But few were as enduring, persistent and pervasive as Pete Townshend's The Who and Mick Jagger's Rolling Stones.

Most of these superstar groups were linked by the very clear-cut nature and gust of the new rock milieu: the blistering volume, the libertarian lifestyle, the provocative lyrics, the merciless beat, the emancipation from sexual repression, the flaunting of law and tradition, the embracing of the drug culture, the advocacy of abandonment and rebellion and

55

the stimulation of violence through the sheer ravages of the acts in performance.

Underneath all this, and well hidden, were some other attributes that went unnoticed by many. There was a statement and a demand to be heard in the thundering volume. There was intelligence behind the provocative lyrics. There was an insistence on a new morality to be explored, a morality without pretense, false values, or double talk. It was embraced by the young; it alienated the old.

It would take at least a decade and a half—up through the end of the 1970's—to trace the effect of this juggernaut on the generation growing up heavily exposed to this sound, knowing little else in the way of music, drenched by its force, flooded by it on the radio, as hard rock singles and albums began to dominate the dealers' racks.

Traceable from the start, however, was the pattern symbolized by the rejection of The Who by the Locarno Ballroom in Swindon, and in hundreds of other halls like it across both Britain and America, to say nothing of Europe and other countries where the hard-rock tide was swelling. This pattern rested on the single and persistent fact: Almost everywhere a hard-rock or heavy-metal group played, from the mid-1960's on, there was trouble with the crowds. The mayhem was persistent, pervasive and predictable. It was different in nature from the occasional riots and disturbances at football games, hockey games, baseball games, soccer games or grandiose religious spectacles, where infrequent incidents would arise spontaneously and unpredictably. The causes for the new rock disturbances remained deep and hidden. But it would soon become evident that they were not *likely* to happen; they definitely *would* happen. They seemed to arise from the loins of the superstar hard-rock performers every time the crowd gathered—*and even before the music began.*

In a series of interviews with the British press in the mid-1960's, Pete Townshend revealed the image that The Who would like to project. "We don't allow our instruments to stop us doing what we want. We smash our instruments, we wreck everything. The expense doesn't worry us because that would get between us and our music," he told one reporter, and repeated the theme to others.

Managers Kit Lambert and Chris Stamp backed up the concept. To the *Observer Colour Magazine*, Lambert said: "Their rootlessness appeals to kids. They're a new form of crime, armed against the bourgeois." To which Chris Stamp added: "Their act creates emotions of anger and violence, and a thousand other things I don't understand myself."

In spite of many moments of introspective brooding, Townshend showed none on the performing stage. He reveled in audience acclaim, considering it the most exhilarating experience possible. He admitted frankly that each performance made him want more. "You want people to tear their hair out," he once commented. "You've really got to make them spew up."

He was doing it, too. Townshend related to these faceless crowds, felt deeply for them and their angst and frustrations. Whatever The Who played for them, whether it was a song called "Heat Wave" or another called "Shakin' All Over," or the constant repetition of "My Generation," the music invoked action, often riotous action, and Townshend was fascinated as he watched it turn them on. It was as if The Who and the Mods were holding full-length mirrors up to each other, each trying to outdo the other.

At the same time, the Rolling Stones continued to create chaos at every concert they played, whether it was up in the dingy midlands at Birmingham, Coventry or Leeds, or down around the London circuit. Jagger, with lips like a deflated inner tube, was fast becoming the sex symbol that had parents sealing their daughters inside for a sundown curfew. Brian Jones, vying with Jagger for first honors in the band, could stir inordinate pubescent yearnings with the roll of his soft, childlike eyes or a shake of his flowing blond hair. A brilliant musician, as well as a ranking sensual hedonist, he could handle at one sitting massive snorts of cocaine, plentiful drops of acid and a handful of uppers and downers washed down by Glenfiddich Scotch.

As The Who churned up the revolution in England, the Rolling Stones carried it to the Continent. At Halsingborg, Sweden, the crowd saluted the Stones by smashing bottles, splintering chairs, tossing fireworks and taking a swipe at the police. They rioted in Vienna, where over 150 were bruised and tossed into corrugated iron cells that had been especially built by the authorities in anticipation of what might—and did—happen. In Warsaw, several thousand angry fans tried to batter their way into the Palace of Culture, and got chased away by tear gas and high-pressure hoses. Mick Jagger explained his feelings by telling a reporter: "People talk about the riots that happen when we play. Of course there is a certain violent element, and to a certain extent, the kids are conforming to what is expected of them. But there is more to it than that. I've seen this wild behavior in so many countries, and the pattern is always the same . . . frustration. You can't solve the problem by locking them up."

But Jagger offered no solution for the problem, nor did he pin down any exact reason for why the riots happened at the hard-rock affairs. What was it that confined their volatile behavior almost exclusively to the sound of this sort of music? At what precise point was the spark, the ignition, the fuse set off—and what exactly set it off?

Keith Richard, lead guitarist for the Stones, saw the scenes less as rebellion than as a sexual reaction. He told writer David Dalton: "You can feel the energy building as you go around the country. You feel it winding tighter and tighter, until one day you get out there halfway through the first number, and the stage is full of chicks screaming 'Nyeeehhh.' There was a period of six months in England we couldn't play ballrooms anymore because we never got through more than three or four songs every night, man. Chaos. Police and too many people in the places, fainting. We'd walk into some of those places and it was like they had the Battle of the Crimea going on, people gasping, tits hanging out, chicks choking, nurses running around with ambulances."

Pete Townshend, writing himself in *Rolling Stone,* showed active acceptance of what was happening. "Damage, damage, damage," he wrote. "It's a great way to shake society's value system. It makes mothers disown their children. It makes school teachers puke. . . . They enjoy destruction because they despise phony values. . . . "

Even if the roots and causes were obscure, it was apparent that the superstars were egging the crowds on, and the crowds were egging the superstars on. The interaction was so Herculean that it went beyond the control of either.

But Townshend was a complex personality. Underneath all his aggression and brusqueness, he showed signs of idealism, sensitivity, creative genius and reverence for a universe beyond the cacophonous thumping of his songs. He was also an articulate, self-made intellectual, who spoke out about rock and himself at extravagant length. He viewed rock with a reverence usually reserved for saints. He believed it was the ultimate vehicle for destroying or building up anything, and especially for self-destruction, yet he never made clear whether he thought self-destruction—or any destruction—was desirable or not. Somehow, he seemed to feel that rock and roll would become the answer to all the problems of the day, yet he never went on to explain how.

"It is a single impetus and it's a single force," he told Jann Wenner of *Rolling Stone*, "which threatens a lot of the crap which is around at the moment in the middle class and in the middle-aged politics or philosophy." Then he went on to say cryptically: "It blasts out of sheer brashness, it's sheer realistic-ness. It's like suddenly everybody getting hung up on a bum trip: mother has just fallen down the stairs, dad's lost all his money at the dog track, the baby's got TB. In comes the kid with the transistor radio, grooving to Chuck Berry. He doesn't give a shit about mom falling down the stairs. He's with rock and roll."

The question was whether the problems of the age could be solved by the kid with the transistor radio. If the bulldozer was smashing everything in its path, shouldn't the architect and contractor be right behind? This was the imponderable, unanswered question.

In 1967, The Who and the Rolling Stones were moving swiftly ahead to their manifest destinies as two of the major supergroups of the new era. The Who dug the Stones, and the Stones dug The Who in a mutual, if mildly competitive admiration pact. Both floated in the drug miasma to greater or less degrees. Brian Jones of the Stones had an unbridled enthusiasm for getting catatonically stoned, and Keith Richard would keep himself in a euphoric haze for days at a time.

Jones, however, was increasingly slipping away from reality, and even those who shared the kicks with him were beginning to notice it. The drug menu he made his selections from was extensive. With cannabis as the first course, Brian was getting into everything: methedrine, acid, Valium, pharmaceutical cocaine, Indian hemp or reds—along with heroin to bring down the high rush from cocaine.

Jagger and Keith Richard covered a more narrow spectrum, but the inevitable happened when the famous drug bust of the Rolling Stones took place in February 1967 at Keith Richard's country estate in Sussex. The Rolling Stones contingent happened to be listening to a recording by The Who when the constabulary arrived. As headlined in the international press, both Jagger and Richard were given jail sentences, later successfully appealed. But Townshend and The Who swung into action by running a newspaper ad that announced they were supporting the Stones by releasing a new single featuring the Rolling Stones songs, "Under My Thumb" and "The Last Time." Backing up their friendly competitors, the newspaper advertisement pointed out:

> The Who consider Mick Jagger and Keith Richard have been treated as scapegoats for the drug problem and as a protest against the savage sentences imposed on them at Chichester yesterday, The Who are issuing today the first of a series of Jagger/Richard songs to keep their work before the public until they are again free to record themselves.

Brian Jones was also busted on dope charges, in another raid. Already on the skids, the bust only accelerated his slide downhill. Townshend, who admired Brian's music, worried about him. But Townshend was having troubles with Keith Moon's addiction, as well as his own. Moon was downing both booze and pills as fast as he could beat the tom-toms. Townshend was experimenting with LSD, and experiencing some scary memory blackouts, frequently joining Moon with a bottle. Still, Townshend continued to lock himself up with his tape recorder to create more songs that, while not earth-shaking, were enough to make the crowds scream for more. He would dub and over-dub the various musical parts in a room he called his "den of magnetic iniquity."

"The Kids Are Alright," complete with the alternative spelling of the last word of the title, was a wistful song about a restless adolescent who would go out of his mind unless he dropped everything and got out in the light. Contrary to the usual heavy beat, it was winsome and rather plaintive, but like so many Townshend songs it hit a responsive chord in the Mod heart.

Another was "Substitute," which examined good-humoredly the confession of a young man who knew he was a phony, and accepted it. Singing the piece with his usual authority, Daltrey stripped off the false-face of the song's protagonist, declaring that he looked tall but his heels were high, that his shoes weren't really made of leather, that he was born with a plastic spoon in his mouth. For some reason, this became the most quoted song of The Who's arsenal.

There was a strange song, too, coming from Townshend's guitar, on which he composed without being able to score music, or read it for that matter. Called "I'm A Boy," it tells of a boy who was made into a temporary transvestite by a mother who yearned for a daughter.

Still another of the early Townshend repertoire was "Pictures of Lily," which movingly describes a boy's first sexual experience when he falls in love with pictures of a girl. The subject is masturbation, and the song dramatizes an experience that practically every boy growing up goes through. Townshend's insights into the kids' frustrations put his songs up in the top five of the charts for the last three singles.

With his bluster and hostility, Townshend wanted to reach out on a more ambitious scale. He bristled under the accusations that rock music was considered a third-rate art. To him, it ranked at least as high as Andy Warhol's pop art, if not several niches above it. But he did not confine himself to listening to rock alone. He often listened to opera, especially Wagner, who opened up horizons for him.

An idea began to grow in Townshend's mind. His thought was that if he could string some songs together in a thematic series, The Who might pull away from the repetitive cycle it was going through. It would be an album first, a concept album in which the songs would tell a story. It might later become an opera. Townshend even had a title,"Deaf, Dumb and Blind Boy," about a kid whose only communication with the world would come through vibrations, which would be translated through the music of The Who. Speaking of the album, Townshend recalled in an interview: "When we were working on it, we started to call it a rock opera, knowing full well it wasn't a true opera at all. But the tag struck and we realized it was maybe a bit fanciful, but in spite of that we quite liked the idea." Then he added: "It was our first conscious departure out of the adolescent area. It was something that wasn't the same old pilled-up adolescent brand of music."

But this dream was far away from the riotous performances The Who were giving in 1967, with each performance ending up with what Townshend called "Pop Art Auto-destruction." It constantly stirred the crowd into following suit. The dance halls of Britain were getting too small for the growing power and popularity of The Who, and the time had arrived for them to expand geographically.

The logical target was America, where the young generation of the 1960's was caught up in a rock wave of its own. The Who was little known in the States, and rock fans there didn't know what to expect when the band arrived in the spring of 1967. The occasion was a special Easter concert put together by a brassy disc jockey called Murray the K.

The event was held in New York City at the old RKO Fifty-Eighth Street Theatre featuring a dozen or so different groups in an endless procession of musical thunder. Al Kooper, a young American rock musician, was curious about what would happen when The Who went on stage. He had read about this bizarre group from London in the English trades. Eric Clapton, who was performing there with his own group, Cream, told Kooper that Townshend was considered a god in England. These were powerful words coming from one who had been dubbed that same title by his own English contemporaries.

The Who was slated as the final act on the bill. Kooper and the other performers stood gathered offstage to see just what was going to happen. They weren't disappointed. When Keith Moon let loose on his riffs for "My Generation," the theater, front and backstage, exploded. Moon reached down into his bag of tricks to pull out a couple of containers that looked very much like Campbell's Soup cans. They were nothing so innocent. They were Brock's Crystal Palace Fireworks, Ltd. special smoke cannisters, Type Y2, that proudly announce on the label: "Producing a dense cloud of smoke lasting about two minutes." As Daltrey pounded his microphones to death on the floor, and Townshend flailed his guitar against an amplifier, Moon lit the smoke bombs and kicked over his eight tom-toms and two double-bass Premier drums.

By now, Townshend was using an old patched-up, break-away guitar and amplifier that their road manager, Bob Pridden, pieced together after the concerts. The crowd went insanely wild, and The Who's American debut was an overwhelming success. Meanwhile, The Who had their eyes on greater things in America. Coming up in June 1967 was the first of the great rock festivals. It was to announce to the world that rock was here to stay. The theme of the festival at the Monterey County Fairgrounds, near the California bay and city of 23,000 of the same name, was "Music, love and flowers." The alienation in the air was gentle. The profits would go to charity. The hippy movement was at its peak.

The festival was as much a pilgrimage as an historical rock event. Between forty and fifty thousand devotees of the thirty and more rock groups that were to perform for over a three-day period, swamped the town of Monterey. The pilgrims spread over the countryside in tents and sleeping bags. The police were jittery and the local citizens unhinged. But they really didn't need to be. Later, Police Chief Frank Marinello caught the spirit and dismissed half his contingent before the festival was over. "I'm beginning to like these hippies," he told a *Time* reporter. "When I go up to that Haight-Ashbury, I'm going to see a lot of friends." The main problem for the citizenry was reflected in the complaints about the sound of the music. It could be heard in heavy volume over six miles away.

For The Who, the Monterey International Pop Festival would launch their American careers more forcefully than any other performance. The rock fans had come to Monterey from all over the country. They would go back home to New York, Kansas, Georgia, Ohio, New England and other points of the compass, bearing the news that something new had swept in from England, a band that made strange sounds, did strange things and left strange feelings of elation.

There were other budding superstars there at Monterey who would suddenly leap into prominence from the springboard the festival provided. Jimi Hendrix was one of these, an acrobatic guitar virtuoso with an Afro-haircut and a mastery of the guitar that left other accomplished musicians gasping in admiration. Out of Seattle, he had migrated to England to make his mark there long before the Stateside audiences knew about him. Kit Lambert had booked him into London's Saville Theatre in a double act with The Who. Never had such a battle of decibels and rock brilliance been held. They would be meeting again now for the second time at Monterey.

In England, Hendrix had watched Brian Jones with the Rolling Stones as Brian taunted and whipped the crowds into emotional frenzy. Hendrix smelled success in the technique. He copied it. Brian copied Hendrix, and each outdid the other. By the time Monterey came about, Brian had drowned himself so much in every sensual drug he could get his hands on that he was being gently eased out of the Rolling Stones. He was considered by some to be almost a vegetable. But Brian liked Hendrix so much he trailed along from England to watch him perform at Monterey. Brian sported a flowing robe with an iron cross around his neck. The Stones could not appear; they were still hung up in London with the drug charges.

Another performer at Monterey was a young girl from Texas who was just beginning to stir up gale force winds. She was Janis Joplin. Her group was called Big Brother and the Holding Company. She was not exactly Girl Scout material. If she liked to shoot smack, swill Southern Comfort, mollify the sexual appetites of some Hell's Angels, then switch to double-gaited sex, she figured that was her business. She once tried to shake her liking for LSD by taking another powerful hallucinogen, dimethyltryptamine or DMT. When DMT began leaving her in worse condition, she increased her intake of grass and hash, reinforced by shooting cocaine. She shook the monkeys on her back temporarily, and was now stirring the loins of a growing fanhood on both coasts.

At one Manhattan club in early 1967 she let loose with her piercing screech and bodily undulations leading to her final number, "Down On Me." It took only a few verses before drinks were hurled through the air, chairs were smashed down on the tables and a riot was in process. Afterward in her dressing room, she told a friend, "Hey, I'm really making it."

Monterey would be her first big showcase, as it would be for The Who and Jimi Hendrix. Another rising star would miss the festival because of a New York booking, and he was furious about it. Jim Morrison and the Doors had been getting a lot of attention of the rock scene because of his uninhibited performances, his unquestionably brilliant mind, and his psychotic explosions onstage and off. The son of a prominent Navy admiral, he sealed his alienation from his parents by listing them as dead in his publicity bio, when they were not.

Morrison's intake of narcotics and alcohol exceeded even that of Joplin, Hendrix, Keith Moon, and Brian Jones. Although he was capable of writing sensitive metaphysical poetry, he was known as the master at stirring crowds to rioting, and he reveled in it. At one time, he deliberately planned to provoke a riot in Chicago, and succeeded. On that occasion, the band's beat and repetitive lyrics were deliberately hypnotic. By the time the audience was stirred to the peak of planned mayhem, a kid spread his arms and dove from an 18-foot-high balcony to the floor. Badly injured, he survived.

One reason Morrison was so furious about not being at the Monterey festival was that Joplin, Hendrix, and The Who would be presented in a jeweled showcase, and he would not. He felt he could outshine and outblast the inherent violence of their acts.

In a way, it was fortunate that Morrison wasn't present. Not long before, he had grappled Janis Joplin to the floor in a messy attempt at sexual calisthenics. She encountered him shortly after, and he sprang at her again. This time she cracked him over the head with a beer bottle she had in hand, and Morrison was taken home, bleeding from the scalp.

The rivalry between Morrison and Joplin at Monterey would not have been cordial. The contest for top honors among Joplin, Hendrix and The Who, was.

The music at Monterey got off to a festive, euphoric start. It seemed to live up to the theme of "love, flowers and music." Enthusiasm was rampant. The kids were gentle and discreet about the pot smoking and semipublic sex. The crowd consistently reflected the mood and atmosphere of whatever group was performing at the time.

When the brilliant Indian Ravi Shankar came to the stage for a full three-hour stint, the sudden contrast of the mood of the crowd was incredibly dramatic. Instead of the shrieking and the screaming and the whoops and the war cries, the audience fell into a reverent silence. They immediately conformed to his request to refrain from smoking, probably the only rock concert where such a restraint had even been observed.

A blanket of raptured silence floated over the scene throughout the entire performance. The music was calm and serene. When Shankar finished, he was given one of the heartiest ovations of the festival. His spell was magically absorbing, entirely different in nature from the response of the heavy beat of the hard rock bands.

When The Who took to the stage, few there knew what to expect. Their singles and albums had not yet penetrated the American market. Townshend, Daltrey and company built slowly. Then, as they crashed into "My Generation," the spectators turned a somersault from their silent worship of Ravi Shankar. The crowd leaped to its feet, reverting to war whoops and screams. Then Townshend brought his guitar down into an amplifier, reducing them both to splinters. The smoke bombs went off. Keith Moon slammed his drum set over, destroying them. Daltrey hit anything that didn't move with his microphone. One stagehand tried to save a microphone stand from Townshend's guitar, and barely missed getting his head lopped off. A mood far different from Ravi Shankar's now took over the audience. The cheering and screams ripped the air apart. In a matter of minutes, The Who had transformed the audience from a calm sea to a hurricane.

Backstage, Jimi Hendrix watched the proceedings with envy. The Who was a tough act to follow on any occasion. This one was downright formidable. He had one thing going for him. Brian Jones, still the idol of the Rolling Stones fans, was on hand to introduce him. To the rock fans, this was roughly equivalent to a special dispensation from the Pope.

There was no question about Hendrix's ability to handle the guitar. To this he added his sexual gymnastics that included making love to his guitar or using it as an enlarged musical phallus.

He dropped to his knees with the guitar stuck between his legs as an enormous erection, pumped it as if it had found a woman, flicked his tongue lasciviously, howled orgiastically, as the crowd screamed back in growing crescendo.

His charisma was fortified by his music, his leaping, acrobatic slumps to his knees, and backbends that he performed with the suppleness of a lemon-wood bow. Added to his raucous and sensual voice, Hendrix's performance smacked an already-dazed crowd into a frenzy that actually went beyond that which The Who had inspired. Hendrix finished with the song "Wild Thing," which brought a roar from the crowd, but he wasn't through yet. Not to be outdone by The Who, he pulled out a can of lighter fluid, splashed the entire contents over his guitar and lit it inches from his crotch. Arson in a performance had suddenly came into the rock scene, and with it, an augmented emotional explosion by the crowd.

The Grateful Dead was scheduled next on the slate, and they had to wait with leaden hearts for nearly half an hour before the applause for Hendrix died down. Somehow, the Grateful Dead felt they had to top all this, and the rhythm guitarist Bob Weir tried to get things going when he yelled to the audience: "Let's take those folding chairs and use 'em in the right way. Fold 'em up, slam 'em down, and dance on 'em."

The crowd not only did so, they swarmed on the stage and almost danced the band across the proscenium arch and into the pit. A potential riot was sparked, but unlike so many of the real riots across England and

America, it never ignited. It almost did, however, when Janis Joplin took over.

With a mating call more resonant than that of a bull moose, the frizzled, somewhat lumpy girl in a gold-knit pants suit smashed her foot on the floor, writhed her body orgasmically, shook her head like the top of a string mop, splayed her thighs in a semi-split and belted out her songs with all the force that she had used to crack Jim Morrison's skull. She also cracked the audience wide open, creating a din that equaled or exceeded her other competitors.

Grace Slick, both as the singing star of the Jefferson Airplane, and as an observer of the entire festival, found herself drawn to and swept away by the continuous violence on the stage. To her, the auto-destruction of The Who symbolized "the rush of energy of the art form." Jimi Hendrix drowning his guitar in a highly combustible fluid and incinerating it seemed to Slick "a theatrical act of destruction by flames . . . an excellent visual image to accompany the incredible friction and volume of rock and roll."

The interaction between the crowd and the stars was so tightly bonded that violence on the stage was breeding violence in the pack. At times, it was hard to tell where the performers left off and the crowd began. The two formed a seamless union. All the superstars who were blossoming at Monterey shared one thing in common: the absolute capacity to sway crowds in any direction they saw fit. They could, like Ravi Shankar, bring peace, composure, moderation, quiescence and quietude. Or they could, like The Who, Jimi Hendrix and Janis Joplin, create devastation and peril.

Luck held out at Monterey. There was peace and the threatened riot failed to mature. Meanwhile, four special performers there shared the joy of the spotlight, each of them ignorant of their impending downfall before the 1970's were over. They were Keith Moon, who almost stole the show away from the rest of The Who; Jimi Hendrix, who ignited the audience as well as his guitar; Janis Joplin, who was about to spring into incredible stardom; and Brian Jones, who was content to launch Hendrix into his stellar career.

Although he was unable to be at the festival, Janis Joplin's sparring mate, Jim Morrison, would be moving into superstardom with these four. As his fame grew, he faced with the others the same overhanging fate, a sword of Damocles that none would be able to avoid.

If anything was proved at Monterey, it was that the more physical or violent a performer was on the stage, the greater the audience reaction. Hendrix, Joplin and The Who were sensations. They upstaged nearly all the two dozen other acts. Each tried to outdo the others, and the contagion spread. Townshend had started it all. Hendrix, Joplin, Morrison and others began playing the reactions to the hilt. What counted was the capacity to get kids to rush the stage in an adoring mob, storm the doors and play follow the leader as one great human avalanche.

The Who set the pace offstage in other ways, too, as they began a series of tours through America. At the plush Hotel Navarro on Central Park South in Manhattan, Keith Moon discovered that the record player he had brought with him on the road was securely locked in the production manager's room next door. The door was double-locked, and the key, supplied by a bellhop, would not work. Using a knife, Moon slashed away at a closet wall to open a hole to crawl through. The mission was successful; the hotel bill was garnished with substantial extra charges.

At a Flint, Michigan, Holiday Inn, Moon got an early start on his bottle, and by the time he arrived at a birthday party thrown for him by the Premier Drum Company, he and the others in The Who contingent were reasonably smashed. Before long, the swimming pool was tempting enough to lure half a dozen party-goers into it with their clothes on. When Moon began to throw chunks of an enormous birthday cake at some of the others, they returned in kind. The place became a shambles. At the invitation of the hotel manager, the sheriff arrived to find Moon in his undershorts, the carpet saturated with gooey cake and The Who aggregation and their guests stoned out of their minds.

Moon jumped into the first car he found—a new Lincoln Continental parked near the edge of the swimming pool. When he released the brake, the car eased into the pool and quietly sunk under water. Moon extricated himself, climbed out, saw the sheriff waiting and ran to escape. In doing so, he slid on a piece of layer cake, slammed face forward on the floor and succeeded in knocking out a front tooth. He spent the rest of the evening in a dentist's office with the sheriff in attendance, and the rest of the night in jail.

Meanwhile, Moon's friends were spraying several cars in the lot with fire extinguishers, smashing a piano to splinters and augmenting the stains on the carpet. The bill for damages put a sizeable dent in The Who's budget. It came to nearly thirty thousand dollars.

But this sort of thing was routine for Moon. On the same tour, he took on another Holiday Inn at Saskatoon, Canada, by grabbing an axe and decimating the TV set, the door panels, the bedstead and the chests in his room. The same process continued throughout the tours, with Townshend sometimes joining in. In between the hotel-wrecking, sporadic intramural fist fights continued, especially between Daltrey and Townshend. Only Entwistle remained aloof. Some of the fights actually took place on stage.

Townshend explained the continued destruction in his notes to himself, published in *Rolling Stone*: "I see the faces beaming up at me as I destroy my £500 guitar. Why should they, poor bastards, dig that? They enjoy the destruction because they despise phony values. . . ."

From the point of view of the fans themselves, *Rolling Stone*'s Robert Weinstein explained it this way: "In spite of violent incidents at many Who concerts, thousands of loyal followers believe that the group is one of the important chroniclers of our times, expressing the lustful rebellion of youth and the nihilistic intermingling of love, God and country."

One passionate devotee of The Who told Weinstein: "Townshend is extraordinary. His lyrics speak to me. The need for self-assertion, the aggression, the anger and beauty are all there." Another told how The Who affected him at a concert: "Seeing Townshend smashing guitars and jumping about like a lunatic is quite moving. It also gets my adrenaline moving, and stirs similar feelings in me." Then he added: "The Who echoes and communicates countercultural trends. Their anger, prose and cynical stage machinations go far beyond clowning. They go into the very fabric of the culture of our day. And Townshend lives like a rock star should. He is outlandish, brilliant, and I can identify with him."

Townshend wasn't the only one the fans were identifying with, in spite of the fact that Townshend had been most responsible for pioneering the art of auto-destruction. Jimi Hendrix continued to light up and incinerate his guitar at a string of concerts, with stagehands standing by with fire extinguishers at curtain time. He also mimicked Townshend every time he could find a low ceiling at a club. "The Cafe Au Go-Go in New York was great," he told a friend, "because the ceiling was really low and dusty. I'd stick the guitar right up into the ceiling. It was like war. You didn't even need a smoke bomb. It's a freaky, funky scene."

In an elegant Swedish hotel where Swedish royalty was inclined to stay, Hendrix followed in the footsteps of Keith Moon. He began with the glassware, progressed to smashing the lamps and threw the gilt-and-brocade furniture out the window. The result was a night in the slammer and an astronomical hotel bill. Like Keith Moon, he was refused accommodations in over a dozen hotels. Hendrix's talent and his antics combined to have him, among dozens of other rock superstars, accorded an honor by a special team of three groupies who called themselves the Plaster Casters. While one girl made sure that his member was in top form, the others made a mold that would preserve it for posterity in plaster of Paris. Cynthia, the leader of the team, told a *Time* reporter: "Every girl should have the experience of plaster-casting at least once in her life. It's a beautiful experience."

Janis Joplin and her sworn enemy, Jim Morrison, continued to follow in the wake of the others, aware of the reaction that egging on the crowds would bring. In Louisville, Joplin stirred the crowd to such a pitch that they swarmed up on the stage in a relentless and unstoppable mass. A riot started. When the security guards tried to stop it, Joplin screamed at them that she demanded the crowd be allowed to do anything they wanted to. The houselights went on, but the pandemonium continued.

At a concert in Tampa, Janis overrode police instructions to keep the aisles and safety exits free, letting go a stream of obscenities at the police when they attempted to enforce the rules. Her commands to the audience won out, but she was booked on the use of vulgar and indecent language. At Madison Square Garden, she halted a song she was singing and screeched at the packed house to get up and dance. There wasn't any room for anyone to do anything except rush the stage like a horde of lemmings. The security guards were powerless.

Her managers begged her not to incite the kids, to keep them from jumping the barriers, but most of the time she refused. Promoters around the country began to be jittery about her appearances. Joplin wailed at the restrictions that were piling up on her. At one point she stamped her foot in her usual habitude, and yelled: "My music's not supposed to make you riot, it's supposed to make you want to fuck!"

Joplin was hardly a sex symbol on her own. In her private life, she displayed all the symptoms of a nymphomaniac, but with very few of the qualities that would make her attractive to a man. In all her arrogance, she was a rather pathetic figure, who once said that she often made love to twenty-five thousand people from the stage—and went home alone.

Jim Morrison, meanwhile, was turning the spotlight on himself as a chief exponent of whipping crowds to a frenzy. He drove fire, police and safety officials up the wall—along with those in the audiences who worried about their own lives and limbs when the mob began to get surly and out of hand under the singer's demonic and often psychotic manipulations.

His psychotic behavior was cruel. His mother came to try to see him before a concert in Washington, D.C. He refused to see her. When she went to the concert, he completed his song "The End" by howling at capacity volume, "Mother—I want to fuck you!" He repeated the screaming line, staring at her from the stage, and left for Philadelphia without letting her see him.

At the Anaheim Convention Center in California, Morrison belted out his new million-copy hit "Light My Fire," then began throwing lighted cigarettes out into the audience. The kids in the jammed auditorium responded by lighting matches and throwing them in the air, ignoring the consequences of what would happen if fire and panic broke out. No security force in the world could stop this. The control—or decontrol—lay completely with Morrison, once he had the crowd in a froth.

At the Singer Bowl in Flushing, New York, Morrison and The Doors joined up with The Who for a concert that, because of the high-voltage groups involved, received considerable hype. But the concert was almost aborted before take-off. Morrison opened his act with a primal scream. He grabbed his crotch and thrust it out at the audience. By this time, the surge forward had started. The mob climbed all over itself to crawl, wriggle, writhe, and twist up over the edge of the stage as a battalion of police threw up a screen. Then the wooden chairs started going, splintered and smashed against any surface available, including the police. Whether Morrison had planned it or not, he had set off another riot. The violence of The Who's act never had a chance that night, and they played as an anticlimax.

Viewing some film of the Singer Bowl riots, Morrison's chief comment was: "I was just a puppet of a lot of forces I only vaguely understood." In the tour that followed, injuries were frequent in explosive riots that broke out wherever Morrison and The Doors traveled. In Chicago, Phoenix, St. Louis, and Cleveland the scene was the same. Later, in Florida, the bloody events came to a head.

In an old hangar near Miami, a crowd of 12,000 was packed shoulder-to-shoulder in a torrid, airless hall. The band was over an hour late in arriving. Morrison was drunk. His act was rambling and disjointed. He howled at the audience that there was no laws here this night, no holds barred. They were to do any damn thing they wanted.

An hour into the show, the kettle boiled over. The crowd rushed the stage en masse. One promoter got on the PA and yelled, "Somebody's going to get hurt." Morrison continued to yell his head off, urging the spectators to come on up on the stage, and to hell with the security cops. Then, for a brief flash, Morrison exposed himself and simulated masturbation, as well as a bit of fellatio. Beer bottles flew through the air toward the stage and smashed. A flood of panties and brassieres followed. Three security guards and a karate expert pulled Morrison offstage. He faced trial and a heavy prison sentence. Concert halls throughout the country banned him. He was released on bail, pending trial.

The violence of The Who, now mechanically planned, seemed pale next to Morrison's. But it continued, with more wrecked hotel rooms, more violence in the performances especially on the part of Moon and Townshend, more wild and not particularly charming escapades. The crowds responded in kind. But at the same time, an opposite strain was taking hold on Townshend, a strain that reflected the dichotomy of his character, the polarity of his feelings.

His idea for "Deaf, Dumb and Blind Boy" had developed and matured quickly. By 1969, it had blossomed into a full-blown album, now called *Tommy,* that was to be the base for the rock opera that had simmered in his mind for a long time. He attributed this major shift in direction to the guru Meher Baba, to whom he had become devoted, from the mid-sixties on. To Townshend, Meher Baba was "a quiet explosion of divinity."

Baba, a Parsi, was hoping to swing the Western world to a more spiritual orientation. He believed in and taught the universality of God, and expounded on Sufi and Hindu doctrines that the intellect should be dropped in favor of pure love. The heart should remain open and fearless, in contrast to the analytical evaluation of the intellect. "God alone is real," he told his millions of followers, "and all else that you see and feel is nothing but a series of nothings."

Baba had a profound effect on Townshend. The guru steered him away from bouts with LSD, dope and other drugs. He was not quite so successful with Townshend's drinking. In fact, Townshend got adequately soused for the basic studio cut of the *Tommy* album, and credits his condition with part of its success. But most of the inspiration, he claims, came from his involvement with Baba.

The move from the dance halls of Chiswick and Harrow to the sublime power of the rock opera *Tommy* was a rather startling transition. Townshend was intrigued with the godhead figures of many religions, from Rama Krishna to Meher Baba and Jesus Christ. He felt they all had parallel stories to tell, but that the problem was to find a way to God through very clear and direct instructions from a guru like Baba. In *Tommy*, Townshend shifted his music from the expressions of teenage frustrations to the spiritual evolution of man. The character Tommy emerged as a boy who is saved by a pseudo-miracle and gathers enormous power to sway and influence his peers through it. He brings his followers to the point of demanding the way to ultimate Truth — and then they turn on him because he never tells them how to find it.

The lyrics and music of *Tommy* have power, poetry, insight, spirituality and revelation. The story is bizarre, but poignant and significant. In skeleton outline, it is no more or less awkward than the program notes and synopses for a Wagnerian opera at the Met.

At the age of three, Tommy sees his father and mother murder his mother's lover. The mother tries to beat the memory of the scene out of him. He becomes psychologically deaf, dumb and blind. Only his sense of touch remains. Through this, he becomes a champion pinball wizard. The parents try to cure him through a gypsy and a doctor who can find nothing palpably wrong with him. His cousin bullies him with cigarette burns and stick pins. His perverted uncle lifts his bedsheets and fiddles with him—one thing Tommy can respond to. He becomes preoccupied with his own image in the mirror, until his mother breaks it, out of rage and frustration.

When she does, Tommy suddenly is cured. Since he is National Pinball Champion, the miracle of his cure is spread across the country. He becomes a god, and tours the country as part of a religious rock concert. Thousands follow him to a spiritual holiday camp retreat. But they revolt when he insists on imposing religious discipline. Riots break out. The camp is utterly destroyed, and Tommy reverts to his original catatonic state.

There are shadows of Townshend all through this, and those of riotous fans and passionate groupies. Sally Simpson, the subject in one song, rushes the stage just to be able to touch Tommy. The lyrics describe the scene of the crowd going crazy as Tommy comes onstage, and of little Sally lost in the mob as the police try to beat the crowd back from the stage.

Sally ends up with a bloody beating by the police, and her face is permanently scarred, as the crowd goes crazy in true rock concert form. But the power and poignancy of *Tommy*'s final song are clear evidence of Townshend's sensitivity and perception when Tommy pleads for someone to see him, feel him, touch him and heal him.

But could such an abstract, poetic concept make any headway with kids who demanded a heavy beat and sensory overload? The question was answered soon after the album was released. By June 1969, it had soared to number two on the charts in England, and into the top ten in the United States. Townshend had shown himself as a composer and lyricist of stature. He was hoisted above the rock milieu, while at the same time he remained steeped in it.

But the other side of the coin was still turning up. In the spring of 1969, The Who were playing a concert at Manhattan's Fillmore East, then a leading rock hall that captured all the superstars. In the packed 2,700-seat auditorium was a young girl named Anna, who was attending her first rock concert with some trepidation. She knew little about The Who, although she had already heard of the album *Tommy*, which had just come out.

PART II

Shortly into the concert, Anna began to smell smoke. It was faint at first, and her date said not to worry about it, it was just the haze of marijuana. Anna said that was fine, but, the idea of smoking *anything* in such a packed theater was not exactly a comfortable one. She put the thought out of her mind, and tried to enjoy the concert. But the smoke got thicker. Her eyes began to sting and burn. She tried to rationalize these symptoms—they were caused by the strobe lights on stage that were flaring and flashing in time with the music.

She heard someone over the din, yelling from the back of the theater. Then a cluster of men, some in uniform, some in business suits, came down the aisle waving their arms and calling out to the band. The Who turned up the amps and played louder. As the smoke got thicker, the men tried to climb up on stage. The Who, in between chords, shoved them back again. The scuffle continued until one middle-aged man in a brown suit finally got up on the stage. He tried to speak into the microphones. Townshend stopped his guitar playing and let go with a Kung Fu kick to the groin. The man doubled over and Townshend shoved him off the stage.

Bill Graham, a leading rock promoter, finally got through to the microphone. Over the shouts of the audience, he told them that the men were from the fire and police departments, that there was a fire raging in the building next door, and that the theater had to be cleared at once.

The exit was fortunately orderly. Anna and her date went out through an exit door that led to a narrow alley. It was jammed with fire engines and firemen fighting the flame in the five-story building next to the theater. The members of The Who were standing just outside the door, next to the stage entrance. They were yelling obscenities at the audience for leaving in the middle of the concert. Anna was riled. Why should they yell and curse at the people for leaving a theater that was choked with smoke and stood in danger of a major panic or worse? But worse than the danger, the smoke, the fire or panic potential was what happened at the moment she passed by The Who in the alley. One of them spit at her.

Townshend and Daltrey were booked on third-degree assault charges for obstructing the duties of the law officer on the stage. Patrolman Daniel Mulhearn, a plainclothesman of the Tactical Patrol Force, went

75

on sick leave with a severe groin injury. Anna continued to wonder at the mentality of someone who would swear and spit at people for trying to escape from a fire hazard.

Townshend was not at all happy about himself in times like these, as he frequently told interviewers. There was a persistent battle going on inside him, and it was hard to tell which force was going to surface at what time. His fight with himself was constant; his bouts with the bottle were depressing. He was proud that *Tommy* had helped throw rock and roll off its monotonous three-chord structure. But he hated his own impulses and outbursts. At one time he wrote in *Rolling Stone*: "I now know that of all things on earth, nothing is so inherently evil, so contemptuous, so vile, so conniving, so worthless . . . as my own imagination."

After *Tommy* he went to work on a song called "The Seeker" that reflected his deep uncertainties. His reverence was profound in spite of his foibles. "God's endlessly present love isn't to be taken lightly," he wrote. "When you hold out an empty cup to God and demand that He fill it with wine, He fills it faster than you can ever drink. Then you know that the fault is your own incapacity to receive His infinite love, rather than His capacity to give it."

Townshend was grateful to Meher Baba. He had steered Townshend away from drugs, even smoking pot. But Brian Jones of the Rolling Stones had had no such luck. Townshend admired his talent, and had tried to help. Jones had now been eased out of the Rolling Stones, with a healthy payoff of nearly a quarter of a million dollars a year as long as the Stones stayed in business. On July 2, 1969, Brian was apparently enjoying a party at his house, but slugging vodka generously, along with a heavy dose of downers. No one is quite clear what happened, but Brian went into the pool around midnight and never surfaced again.

Jones was the first to experience the fate of four of the superstars who had been at Monterey, and the one other who wanted to be there, but wasn't. Townshend was moved to write a song, never released, about Brian's death. The lyrics suggest that this was all part of a normal day as far as Brian was concerned, and typical of the rock and roll world. Brian, the lyrics noted, was the sort who seemed to die on a daily basis.

The Rolling Stones, of course, were moving along the highest ridge of the mountains without Brian, grossing as much as $275,000 in two

concerts on a single night. Jagger was still demonstrating his unbelievable power to sway crowds. At a concert at the Inglewood Forum in Los
Angeles, Jagger whipped the audience into a frenzy with a medley of
"Gimme Shelter," "Midnight Rambler," and "Sympathy for the Devil." The drums and beat rose to such a climax that the audience rushed
the stage and clawed the security men just so they could touch Jagger. A
brawl broke out that could not be stopped even by turning up the
houselights. Trouble and danger to the audience at concerts of the
hard-rock superstars continued to remain monotonously predictable.

It was not until the late sixties that certain facts began to come together
in clear focus, facts that could lead to the best explanation and an
understanding of the consistent social violence and destructiveness of
the hard-rock phenomenon. The broad psychological and sociological
points of view were important, but they failed to delineate the precise
catalyst that triggered the actions of the crowds.

It had already been observed that the interaction between the
superstar and the crowds was electrifying in a way that surpassed anything in music history. There was also the evidence that the adolescent
generation had inherited anxiety and frustration from parents, leading to
narcissism and, from there, aggression. There was the loss of identity,
and the need to over-identify with new idols who reflected the generation's sense of anger and rebellion. There was the feeling that the new
hard rock, as writer Richard Meltzer put it, attempts "to free man by
rescuing him from meaning, rather than freeing man through meaning."

Herbert Hendin, of the faculty of Columbia University Department
of Psychiatry, was finding among his student patients the desire to escape
at all costs. He wrote of the prevailing syndrome: "You cannot be killed
if you are already dead (numbness). You cannot be hurt, if you withdraw
(detachment). You cannot be completely wiped out if you divide your
forces (fragmentation)."

Drugs, of course, were a way of achieving these mainly unconscious
goals, and at the same time fulfilled Freud's theory of the need for
self-punishment. Hendin observed: "Often students who are most in
trouble with the police over drugs are those from whom the need for
crime and punishment is more significant than the need for drugs."

But the freedom drugs were supposed to bring remained illusory. Janis Joplin sang about this in her song "Me and Bobby McGee," which indicates that freedom is only equivalent to having nothing more to lose.

There was the charisma of the superstar, too, that was becoming more visible every year—a charisma that had enormous power over the crowds that packed the concert halls. The crowds, in turn, reflected a furious energy of their own, psychologically amplified by the historically unique auditory amplification of the new electronic age. The battering of sound, the strobing of brilliant lights, and the blotting out by drugs of the central nervous system, had a macabre effect that also had never been experienced before.

With the density of the crowd came intensification, adding to the already tense situation. When the decibels approach the pain level, the tension grows higher. The crowd is fused, however, by the charisma of the superstar, and the hard-rock beat rivals that of a shaman in a tribal society. The superstar actually becomes a sort of a shaman, and whatever a shaman dictates, the crowd follows. Added to this is the catalytic effect the crowd has on every individual in it, an effect that destroys the sense of personal and separate responsibility for individual behavior. "Music is often used as the catalyst for increasing the emotional impact of situations," writes Perry London, a psychiatrist from the University of Southern California, pointing out further that under the charismatic spell of a shaman-like figure, it makes little difference what he says. The near-hysterical masses are already his adoring slaves.

As Gregory Rochlin also had noted, mass groups are highly susceptible to suggestion. "The fact that their members imitate one another, tolerating little delay, and that they carry some sense of omnipotence yet submit to orders and give up freedom to a fatherlike figure, encouraged Freud and many others since his time, to see in the psychology of groups parallels to the behavior of children and to the conduct of so-called primitives."

At many of the hard-rock concerts, then, there was this scenario: a tribal atmosphere with a loud and primitive beat; strobing lights; a charismatic superstar, to whom individual identities are transferred, and who believes in the need for aggression and violence; a crowd wide open to suggestion through idolization and the effects of drugs, intensified by a tightly packed space and lengthy exposure to megaloud, repetitive, and monotonic music.

The scenario could only point to one conclusion: *the creation of a mass trance state, or its synonym, mass hypnosis.*

Although hyponosis of any kind is still not fully understood, it is real, palpable, and documented. The National Science Foundation has studied it extensively, and both the British and American Medical associations recognize its danger and its value. Its scope and ramifications have still not been fully probed, but its power under varied conditions is undisputed.

Jimi Hendrix was one of the few rock superstars who first recognized what was happening at his concerts. He directly traced the source of his commanding power over audiences to the hypnosis phenomenon. In a *Life* magazine interview, he said, "I can explain everything better through music. You hypnotize people to where they go right back to their natural state, which is pure positive — like childhood when you got natural highs. And when you get people at their weakest point, you can preach into the unconscious what you want to say." Hendrix was as instinctively right as if he had been a trained psychiatrist. The music and beat created an hypnotic state. The unconscious became exposed and vulnerable. In this state, the id was available to whatever stimulus was at hand. With Ravi Shankar, it was serenity and adoration. With Hendrix, Joplin, Morrison and The Who, it was enthusiastic violence — and adoration. The crowd reflects with image of the superstar.

Because the trance state and hypnosis were so complex and elusive, their full impact could only become better understood as the hard-rock beat continued into the 1970's.

Looming on the horizon in the summer of 1969 was an event that became a major part of history. It was to be called Woodstock, after the name of the Catskill mountain art colony that once was the scene of musical and costume festivals in the 1920's and early thirties, a village that symbolized artistic freedom. There was to be an assemblage of over thirty of the greatest superstars in rock, not at Woodstock but at Bethel, some fifty miles south. Incredible crowds of nearly 50,000 kids a day were expected, an unimaginable total of 150,000 gathered on fields and pastures of an open-minded, congenial farmer named Max Yasgur. The crowds would be larger than the entire population of

Albany, the state capital; over three times the population of nearby Poughkeepsie.

The whole idea sounded crazy. But it was seized as a symbol, a rallying flag, a pilgrimage, and a holy mission of the rock religion. By the time the pilgrims began streaming along the narrow roads leading to Max Yasgur's farm, the estimates rose. When the concert was ready to start, the total crowd was between 400,000 and half a million. This was an open-air city now; it would rank as the fourth largest city in New York State and was larger than Tucson, Knoxville, Tacoma, Fort Wayne or Spokane, a swarming mass of unsheltered humanity converging from the farthest reaches of the continental United States.

A plethora of the magic names of both rock and folk would perform nonstop for three days, from Joan Baez and Arlo Guthrie to the Grateful Dead and the Jefferson Airplane, from Sly and the Family Stone to Ravi Shankar. And the three superstars who made such an impact on the Monterey festival all would be there—Joplin, Hendrix and The Who—all set to slingshot their fame to even greater heights.

Hendrix was riding so high that just before Woodstock forty thousand kids had mobbed the infield at Denver's Mile-High stadium, rushed the stage platform, flattened the security guards, and were repelled only by a cloud of tear gas that engulfed the stage and halted the concert. Hendrix barely escaped with his life in the equipment truck. He was now escalating his drug intake to match the rapacious appetite of Brian Jones. When he got the news of Jones's death, it socked him hard. His first reaction was to dedicate a new song to him called "Lover Man." Whether he pondered his own pattern of drug involvement was not clear.

Joplin was traveling the same path as both Jones and Hendrix. Her spectrum of drugs embraced all the colors of the rainbow. Her concerts were predictably set on a collision course between the crowds and the police. The emotions were stage-directed by Joplin, who continued to scream at every audience: "Get up and dance! Get off your butt!" By the time Woodstock arrived, promoters of her concerts were getting uneasy. Some halls and stadiums had begun turning her concerts down. Others were ready to.

Among the half million or so pilgrims who sludged along the jammed highways and country roads to Bethel was Frank Wood. He was just

PART II

beginning his career with radio station WEBN-FM in Cincinnati, after graduating from Harvard and the University of Chicago Law School. For several weeks, Wood and his wife, Cindy, had been hearing rumors bruited about that a giant rock festival was to be held in rural New York, with a magic lineup of the biggest superstars in rock. Visiting his family home with his wife in Cohasset, Massachusetts, Wood heard the rumors confirmed by some brief radio announcements that were, in light of the groups that were supposed to be in the talent line-up, oddly muted and restrained. Just to collar Joplin, Hendrix, and The Who, along with the others, in one giant cow pasture would be a logistical feat in itself. Wood determined that he and his wife were not going to miss it.

By the time August 16 rolled around, the Woods were in their old Volvo, moving along the New York Thruway in the direction of Yasgur's farm. Within thirty miles of the concert site, the magnitude of the festival became apparent. The traffic was impossible, and Wood's car radio kept pleading with concert-goers to stay away—there was danger of the New York Thruway being closed down entirely. Wood stubbornly kept crawling until he got within twelve miles of the site, at which point the Thruway became a frozen parking lot. Unable to decide what to do, the Woods pulled up at a coffee stop to talk things over.

As it stood at the moment, they were faced with a twelve-mile hike, with not a chance of hitching a ride. By luck, a local farmer, stranded near Yasgur's farm, overheard them. He volunteered to show them the way through some back roads if they'd give him a lift.

They agreed, and had trouble believing their luck. Squeezing along narrow country roads, they were navigated to within a mile of the site, a feat they considered to be something of a miracle. The closer they got to the concert grounds, the more they felt that this was something awesome, something bizarre, that it was more than just a rock festival. When they reached the natural bowl formed by Max Yasgur's pastures, they knew they were right. Nearly half a million people were spread across the fields, a tight package of wall-to-wall humanity. Far in the distance was a tiny rectangular stage, with what looked like toy electric lighting towers beside it.

What surprised Wood was that there were no fences, no ticket takers, no one collecting money. By the time he and his wife settled down on the meadow, the answer was delivered over the massive sound system that carried these words to them from half a mile away with perfect clarity: "This is a free concert from now on," came the voice of one of the promoters. "That doesn't mean anything goes. What that means is that we're going to put the music up for free."

This was a necessary concession. The fences simply couldn't hold back the pressing hordes. It was a question of the promoters taking them down before the crowd did. The voice on the speakers continued: "We've had thousands and thousands of people come here today. More than we ever knew or dreamed of or thought would be possible. We're going to need each other to help each other to work this out, because we're taxing the systems that we've set up. We're going to be bringing the food in. But the one major thing that you have to remember tonight is that the man next to you is your brother."

This was not merely sentimentality. With a crowd on hand equal to almost the entire enrollment of the U.S. Navy in the First World War, without discipline or command, things could get touchy. Frank Wood felt that what kept the crowd under control was that no one there had ever seen so many people in one place before. If anything spooked the crowd, Wood could see disaster spreading across the fields like a brush fire.

Practically everyone there was stoned, but Wood noticed that it was in a mellow and pleasant way, and the disturbances in the main crowd were remarkably few. When the food supplies dwindled, people began sharing apples, peaches, and sandwiches in a rare mood of mass generosity.

Backstage, in tents and trailers, the superstars waited, having arrived by helicopter, thrashing in from overhead in the night skies, almost drowning out the opening acts. Janis Joplin had checked into a local Holiday Inn a few days earlier bringing with her a $200-a-day heroin festival of her own that she was trying desperately to kick. She bided her time with loosely organized press conferences and a series of encounters with two lesbian friends and a male devotee. At her backstage tent preparing for what was to be a lackluster performance, she brandished a tequila bottle in one hand, and a fifth of Southern Comfort in the other. No one was happy with her performance, including Joplin herself. But the festival spirit of the spectators overcame even the worst, and euphoria was everywhere. Even the forty-mile backup on the Thruway, and its eventual closing, failed to dampen spirits.

Then came the rains. Frank and Cindy Wood found them refreshing at first. But by 4:00 A.M., the meadows were turning to mud pudding, and the all-night music failed to lift their spirits. Ravi Shankar, whose appearance was interrupted by the rain, huddled in a trailer, his fear of the enormous crowd growing. He turned to meditation. A kid in a sleeping bag on the outskirts of the crowd was run over by a tractor and killed.

With the rain came a new danger. Spectators were crawling up the giant lighting towers like caterpillars, soaked to the skin, brushing by exposed wires with thousands of volts rushing through them. Along the ground were exposed cables that could, according to one technician, turn the stage into a platter of french fried musicians. If the temporary towers should topple, there would be more of the same. The electricians worked desperately to switch over to safer circuits, as the loudspeakers blared instructions to get the spectators down from the towers. By a miracle nothing happened.

Frank and Cindy Wood finally found shelter in a Coca-Cola truck mired in the mud. They spent the rest of the night wedged between cases of Coke bottles. They decided they would not stay for the full three days. But sometime near dawn The Who came onstage, and Wood was determined to see their act. Sleepy-eyed, the Woods wriggled their way up near the front of the stage, a half a mile away from where they had been sitting. On the way up, Wood had the feeling that the entire population of the East Coast was there.

In spite of the mud bath, Wood was not disappointed by The Who. They made the whole thing worthwhile, as they segued into the music from *Tommy*, "My Generation," and other Who favorites. To Wood, they were dynamite, as they continued playing until dawn came and reminded him again of the enormity of the crowd that had faded into black during the night.

Townshend and the rest of The Who were not too happy about the whole thing. They had recently gone through a horrendously long tour in the United States, then returned to England for a short stay, only to come back for a concert in Tanglewood, a bucolic Massachusetts dell usually reserved for symphony concerts.

ARE THE KIDS ALL RIGHT?

After endless negotiations with Frank Barsalona, the concert magnate of Premier Talent, they had finally agreed to fly by helicopter to the Woodstock festival for a $12,500 fee — peanuts compared to what they would be earning in future U.S. tours. They were exhausted and edgy when they arrived, and the concert was now almost ten hours behind schedule. Someone slipped some acid in Townshend's coffee, which he learned about too late. He was in no mood to play, and when Abbie Hoffman forced his way up onstage and tried to take the microphone away to make an unsolicited political announcement, Townshend knocked him off the stage with his guitar.

After the Woods left, the concert went on, as the spectators huddled under parkas and ponchos, shivered in the recurrent rain, and enjoyed the plentiful marijuana that the police avoided noticing. Despite lack of food, water, and adequate toilet facilities, the euphoric mood kept up. Peace and tranquility reigned over most of the crowd. Even the severest critics had to grant that the affair was an exalted and benign event.

Two things occurred that were to spell trouble of sorts for future rock concerts. When Sly Stone showed up in the darkness to perform just before The Who began their act, production manager John Morris got up to say: "Sly Stone is about to come out and destroy your minds, but it's so dark out there we can't see you, and you can't see each other. So when I say 'three,' I want every one of you to light a match. Okay? Everybody got your matches ready? One . . . two . . . *three!*"

The natural amphitheater suddenly blazed with the brilliance of nearly half a million matches or butane lighters, illuminating the countryside with an awesome glow. Outdoors in a damp and muddy terrain, there was no safety problem. What was to follow, however, was a custom and ritual that would pervade clogged, sometimes tinder-box concert halls where the beauty of the spectacle would be matched only by the very real potential for fire and panic.

Another practice was much in evidence at the otherwise placid and benevolent gathering: the drug overdose. There were plenty of cuts, bruises and food poisoning cases to tax the emergency medical posts. But the most harrowing were the freak-outs, from both good and bad acid and the other drugs going around. They screamed in anguish and terror, swamping the medical trailer by the hundreds. The combination of overflowing portable toilets, food spoilage and ODs was causing some to press for declaring the site a medical disaster, and calling in the National Guard.

Wards were set up with mattresses in the employees' mess hall and in a local school. Helicopters carried the seriously ill to various local hospitals. Announcements were made declaring that the acid going around wasn't poison, but it was badly manufactured acid, as three hundred more cases swamped the medical posts. Volunteers tried to talk the freak-outs down from bad trips. An emergency alert was sent out for medical help, including additional Air Force helicopters. One overdose case remained near death, until a helicopter flew him out for intensive-care treatment.

The overdose, plus the bad trip and freak-out from acid, plus the synergistic effect of drugs and alcohol, plus just plain bad drugs, were all to become more and more part of the rock scene in the wake of Woodstock, a fact of life. The sight was never pretty, even to the most avid rock fan. The OD turned to blubber, ghostly white, and often fell wherever he stood to hit his head hard. Few realized that a toxic dose could be just a little more than a prescribed dose.

By the time Monday's daylight arrived, only 30,000 weary spectators were left to hear Jimi Hendrix. He arrived by helicopter with a guarantee — $18,000 down, $42,000 to be paid later — and a shaky state of health. He followed Sha Na Na onstage, but his performance was desultory. Nearly everyone, especially his friends, felt that something was radically wrong with him. A strange change in his personality was obvious. After his performance, he collapsed backstage and was flown to a nearby hotel, where he slept for three days.

One of the most miraculous pageants of history ended that morning, but its reverberations, good and bad, would continue perhaps forever.

The Woodstock festival had demonstrated that rock was able to produce a peaceful gathering, with four or five times as many spectators as the largest sporting event. A new label sprang up — the Woodstock Nation or the Woodstock Generation. Max Yasgur, the dairy farmer who braved it all on his farmland, made a public announcement that made him a hero of the Age of Aquarius: "If a half million young people at the Aquarian Festival could turn such adverse conditions — filled with the possibility of disaster, riot, looting, and catastrophe — into three days of music and peace, then perhaps there is hope, that if we join with them, we can turn those adversities that are the problems of America today into a hope for a brighter and more peaceful future."

After the long series of disturbances at dance halls and smaller concerts, Woodstock pointed the way for a possible new maturity for the rock scene. As people packed up and left, thoughts turned to the next decade. Would it herald an age in which music could be enjoyed without danger to life and limb?

Mick Jagger and the Rolling Stones had observed the Woodstock scene from a distance. The Stones were not exactly thrilled that they had missed the limelight. Woodstock had bent the beams of the Super-Trouper stage lights away from the roaring success of the Stones, who were on tour at the time of the festival. Jagger would have to administer an antidote, and the answer came before the end of 1969. With Mick Taylor replacing Brian Jones on the guitar, the Stones would give a massive free concert that would match the glitter of Woodstock and leave the rock fans reeling.

It was held on December 6, 1969, at a stock-car race track called Altamont, a jump away from San Francisco and Berkeley. By the time the crowds collected, a population nearly half as large as the city of San Francisco had gathered, and the scene was Woodstock all over again. The lines that gathered for toilets, food, and water seemed to stretch to the horizon. The security force was made up of over one hundred Hell's Angels, hired at the rate of $500 worth of beer to handle the crowd of 300,000. The Angels were roaring drunk before the first chord sounded and high on cocaine and hash.

Grace Slick, arriving to perform with the Jefferson Airplane, pushed through the crowd to get to the stage, and she felt bad vibes. They got worse when she saw their male vocalist, Cincinnati-born Marty Balin, get smashed unconscious when he tried to save an innocent victim from one Angel's five-foot-long billiard cue. The violence grew through the afternoon, as the Stones waited to make their dramatic entrance at nightfall. Meanwhile the Angels waded into the crowd and whiplashed spectators at random. A heavyset man pulled a knife, and threatened the people around him. There was a flood of bad acid, and screaming freak-outs were blossoming all through the crowd. The first-aid tent was splattered with blood, as long lines of stretchers waited outside.

Other ODs and freak-outs milled around the tent, waiting and screaming.

As darkness set in, Jagger slipped out on the stage in a flowing red cape. He danced and moved around the stage stepping away from the pools of blood on it. Disregarding the already frenzied pitch of the crowd, he built up the music with a raucous, threatening performance of "Sympathy for the Devil." The louder the band and the heavier the beat, the more the Hell's Angels continued to bash skulls. Suddenly, Jagger's arrogance changed to fear. He looked weak and vulnerable. He winced as a Hell's Angel gunned a motorcycle and roared into the crowd. He tried to get back into the song. Then he yelled at the crowd, "Hey—why are we fighting and what for? Let's cool out, let's relax." After that, he turned to the band and said, "Either these cats cool it, or we don't play."

But by now, nothing could stop the fire storm raging in and around the packed area by the stage. Suddenly, a young black man named Meredith was stabbed, stomped, pummeled and beaten just to the side of the stage.

Meredith died. Over a hundred were bloodied and battered. Nearly a thousand were treated for bad acid trips. A girl singer, well into pregnancy, was hit on the head by a beer bottle thrown from the audience. She ended up in the hospital with a fractured skull. Everyone began asking: What has happened to rock and roll? Was this the apocalypse? What happened to the spirit of Woodstock? Was it worth going to concerts anymore, if they were going to shift from festivals to blood baths? Were they worth taking your life in your hands? No sooner had the Woodstock Nation been established than it began to disintegrate.

For all practical purposes, the disaster spelled the end of the big rock festivals. The myth of the Woodstock Generation ended with fractured hopes, fractured peace and fractured love. Jagger had tried to stop the momentum, but only when it was too late. The era of the elephantine rock festival was over almost before it began. Still, individual groups continued to attract more attention than ever before.

As the seventies began, the hard-rock superstars turned to colleges and civic coliseums instead of the big festivals. But the same predictable pattern continued. The stars would egg the crowds on, and if they tried to tame them, it was usually too late. Washington, D.C. was the scene of a series of concerts that signaled the future of rock in the decade.

Grand Funk Railroad, a group out of Michigan, brought on riotous fighting at the Robert F. Kennedy Stadium. When the Allman Brothers Band, known for its capacity to stir the crowds to white hot excitement, played at American University, the crowd smashed its way into the gymnasium. That marked the end of rock concerts for that institution.

When The Who came to Washington, riding on the crest of their popularity from *Tommy* and from Woodstock, Pete Townshend had his own ideas about what happened at Altamont, even though he had not been there. He told Rolling Stone reporter Jonathan Cott, "There are reasons why kids do things and there are reasons why grown men do things, and they've got a lot more to do with rock and roll than they've got to do with anything else. But at the same time I felt that with a little bit of care, a little bit of thought in advance, you can avoid things like that."

But Townshend apparently didn't know how to avoid "things like that." At the Merriweather Post Pavilion in Columbia, Maryland, a full-scale riot interrupted The Who's concert. The Pavilion took the hint and shut out rock concerts forever. The ghost of the Locarno Ballroom in Swindon, one of The Who's first preconcert cancellations, refused to be laid to rest.

The demonic horrors of Altamont did little to persuade Mick Jagger that he should do something about smothering the violent persuasion of his act to prevent audience violence that continued to mirror his act. A new European Stones tour in 1970 stirred a riot in Helsinki, caused thousands of fans to break windows in Hamburg, and produced another stormy uprising in Berlin and the pelleting of police with bric-a-brac by the fans in Paris.

With the heavy obscenity charge hanging over Jim Morrison in Miami, he proceeded to get himself thrown in jail in Phoenix for drunk and disorderly conduct, and interfering with the flight of an aircraft en route to a Stones concert there. His drinking was far out of control. At a party given by Ahmet Ertegun, the head of Atlantic Records, he climbed up on the furniture, and started to maul several original paintings on the wall. At another party, he began urinating on the rug. A manager in Salt Lake City canceled one of his concerts after his stage behavior in Boston had left the audience in an hysterical frenzy.

PART II

He was now facing up to thirteen years of jail sentences. He was barred from Cobo Hall in Detroit after the audience erupted there on his urging. Between concerts he continued to defend himself in the courts of Phoenix and Miami. In September, 1970 Morrison flew to the Isle of Wight, a twenty-mile long island off the Solent and the Spithead in southern England, for a behemoth rock festival to be held there. The British had not yet given up the idea of giant festivals, and there was no doubt that Isle of Wight Festival would be big.

Not only would The Who, Jimi Hendrix, and Morrison be there, but also Bob Dylan and Joan Baez. Over a quarter million fans would be leaping across the water from England. It would be another Woodstock of peace and joy, or another Altamont—no one knew.

Hendrix was not faring much better than Morrison at the beginning of the seventies. He was often depressed and withdrawn. His music seemed to be deteriorating. His erotic physical antics increased. He was smarting from a drug bust in Canada where heroin and hashish had been discovered in his luggage.

Hendrix's theory was that violence of his act "drained the violence" out of the crowd. Yet there was not much evidence of this. If anything, the reverse seemed true. Hendrix had witnessed first hand what happens when a hyped-up crowd is unable to get into a concert it is desperate to see. At a Los Angeles concert date, his limousine was surrounded by a crazed mob that could not get tickets to the performance. It was a frightening experience. Police tried to save Hendrix and the limo from total destruction. Heads were bashed against the glass windows of the car. Bloodstains appeared on the windshield. At the concert, Hendrix was so affected that his playing was rough and shoddy.

At the Berkeley Community Theater, the pattern was the same. An announcement was made to the crowd outside the theater that the two performances to be given by Hendrix were sold out. The spectators broke through glass doors, scaled the sides of the theater to the roof, smashed through windows two stories high.

The pace continued when Hendrix played at the Isle of Wight Festival, where the crowd itself, lured by the music of the superstars, churned up its own momentum in an atmosphere charged with anticipation. The overflow crowd had one thought in mind: to get into the concert, whether there were any tickets left for sale or not.

89

ARE THE KIDS ALL RIGHT?

The promoters were prepared for trouble. An enormous security force was on hand—fortified this time by guard dogs. They were waiting for and expecting the worst. They got it. As the first thumping beats of the concert began, thousands of gate-crashers swarmed around the fences. Someone threw a hand grenade, opening an enormous hole in the barrier. Part of the crowd rushed through, while others dismantled more of the fence. Motorcycle mobs and frustrated, angry fans started smashing the lights and pillaging the temporary shops set up outside the festival site. As Hendrix mounted the stage, the screams and yells were so loud that even his ten-thousand-watt amplifiers failed to override them.

Bolstered by a heavy charge of methedrine, Hendrix tried to recapture his usual flamboyant energy. But something was wrong. He was out of synch with the band. He stumbled with the guitar and he stumbled on his feet. Then he stumbled into the dressing room and nearly collapsed.

But the crowd loved it, screeched for more, which they didn't get. Then Jim Morrison came on stage, just before The Who. There was something wrong with his act, too. He was sluggish, and The Doors could not make up for it. Morrison had lost his arrogance; he appeared to be a lifeless puppet. The festival site was already a shambles, and even The Who failed to stir the usual frenzy. This time, it had all exploded beforehand. The crowd was spent. All that was left of the 250-acre festival site were the results of the pillaging and looting. England had found its own Altamont—free of death and murder.

This repetitive and often predictable series of destructive disturbances was unique in history. They seemed to be increasing in frequency, and to grow in intensity in proportion to the increase in amplification of the new equipment coming on the market. Many of the rock fans themselves deplored the conditions of the rock concerts, including the overkill volume. But they couldn't resist flocking to the concert halls to hear their favorite groups. For the band, the art of pumping up decibels was becoming something of a contest. A 1970 article in *The New York Times Magazine* describes Grace Slick of the Jefferson Airplane in this way: " 'Our eternal goal in life,' Grace says, absolutely deadpan, 'is to get louder.' "

It is Marcuse, again, who wrote: "As this music loses its radical impact, it tends to massification: the listeners and coperformers in the audience are masses streaming to a spectacle, a performance. True, in this spectacle, the audience actively participates: the music moves their bodies, makes them 'natural.' But their (literally) electrical excitation often assumes the features of hysteria. The aggressive force of the endlessly repeated hammering rhythm (the variations of which do not open another dimension of music), the squeezing dissonance, the standardized 'frozen' distortions, the noise level in general—is it not the force of frustration?"

Since frustration axiomatically leads to aggression, destructiveness would naturally seem to follow. The scenes were reaching a point where the questions could be asked: Was destruction good? Was it an expression of a new kind of morality? There were a lot of things about old-fashioned morality that could be legitimately challenged. Adults had not brought the world to any ascending spiral of benignity. Their morality had not brought an end to war, poverty, discrimination or hatred. Still another question remained: Was the destruction syndrome at the rock concerts an answer to the problems of the day?

Nearly everyone involved in the rock business agreed that destruction was no answer—although there was a tendency to shrug it off. There are some social ethics that are hard to ignore. Perry London sums them up with simplicity in his book *Behavior Control*. "(1) People are entitled to do what they want, up to the limit that (2) they may not hurt other people." He goes on to describe a very practical morality, avoiding the type of moralizing that members of any younger generation hate to hear:

If aggression cannot be controlled, murder should still be avoided.
-If someone is to be killed, suicide is better than homicide.
-If another person is to be harmed, verbal aggression is better than battery.
-If society is intolerable, withdrawal is better than wanton destruction.
-If psychosis is needed, introversive ones like depression are better than projective ones like paranoia or extravagant madnesses, like mania. . . .

Negative in nature as this ethic is, it points up that aggression and destructiveness are not at all desirable. But this was what was happening across the board on the developing hard-rock scene. To the list could be added: If you have a crowd in the palm of your hand packed tightly into a concert hall, it's better to avoid asking for trouble.

There was no question that the leading superstars of the day were asking for trouble from the crowds, whether consciously or unconsciously. The incidents were part of a trend, not just a few isolated cases. Coupled with this trend was a strange apparent death wish on the part of several of the superstars, that went along with the violence of their routines.

Those that appeared to be in this category, like Hendrix, Joplin, Morrison and Moon, were setting the pace in the drug scene that was growing in proportion to the glamorization of drugs by many superstars. In his psychoanalytic case studies, Herbert Hendin was finding that heroin abusers pushed themselves into behavior so inimical to life that they were looking to kill themselves without wanting to acknowledge it. In other clinical cases, he found that amphetamine abusers tried to live in contradiction to their own most basic emotions. As amphetamines failed to contain or elevate emotions, the impulse for suicide grew and was often carried out.

How this was reflected in the rock milieu would soon become evident.

In spite of the success of the rock opera *Tommy*—the album sold over two million copies—the career of The Who continued to be chaotic, on- and offstage. The guitar and hotel room smashing continued, in direct contrast to the power and artistry of *Tommy*. Townshend's moods were as mercurial as ever, and he spilled out interesting, but confusing and contradictory interviews.

Keith Moon did not appear to be heading in a very propitious direction. Aside from his compulsion to chop things up and swill down whatever liquor and pills came his way, he encountered even more serious trouble. In a street fracas with a gang of four youths in London, Moon and a friend—his chauffeur—were accosted in Moon's omnipresent Rolls Royce. Moon, whose driving license had been lifted for violations, was drinking heavily and was in no condition to fight off the attack. In the brawl, the street gang dragged Moon's friend out from behind the wheel and kicked him under the car. Moon thought his friend had run down the street to escape the gang. Unaware of what had happened, Moon slid over to the driver's seat and gunned off to look for him. In the process he ran over his friend, who was killed.

The gang was arrested. But Moon was devastated by what had happened, and by the thought that he had killed his best friend, however inadvertently. Although Moon was held blameless in the death, he was charged with drunken driving. This and other incidents dimmed the success of *Tommy*, but in spite of the group's personal problems, there was an oasis of sorts in June 1970.

After The Who had performed the music from *Tommy*, in the spring of 1969 at New York's Fillmore East, Albert Goldman of *The New York Times* praised it lavishly as a blazing breakthrough that had "blasted out of the dreary, dying world of traditional rock into the exhilarating, intoxicating atmosphere of the future." He called the score "a powerful steel blade, blowing all the bull out of the current atmosphere with draughts of clean, cool, electric-spark-smelling ozone."

On top of using mixed metaphors, Goldman was wrong about traditional rock dying off. But he was right in another prediction. "No one has suggested yet," he wrote, "that the opera be mounted *as an opera* at the darkened Metropolitan Opera House, but the idea merits serious consideration. . . . Can you imagine the lords and ladies of the hip establishment turning out on opening night in their frumpy finery? . . . At intermission time, the distinguished audience could surf down the art-nouveau banisters or space-out by gazing at the Chagalls. . . ."

A year later, on June 7, 1970, his prediction came partly true. The event was not quite the way he envisaged it, but close enough to stand comparison. *Tommy* did open as a four-character opera at the hallowed hall of grand opera, the Met. No rock group had ever performed there before. They played two sell-out performances in one day, and the critics were kind, if not enthusiastic. One called it a "tribal scream of togetherness." No symphony of a hundred pieces ever had come up with the volume and percussion that thundered out of The Who's speakers.

Although the crowd was young and enthusiastic, something rare for a rock music crowd happened at the Met that night. No one smoked in the theater, neither pot nor cigarettes, this activity being confined to the rest rooms. Those who started were spotted in the beam of an usher's flashlight, and the attempt was quietly aborted. The kids in the audience were quiet, respectful, and well-mannered. One usher commented, "These kids are much more polite than their parents." An assistant manager of the Met said, "It's opera in a new language." Another opera employee muttered, "They're not making any more noise than a regular audience." Another assistant manager found himself blasted out of the audience by the volume, to retreat backstage. His comment was, "This is ritual. Galvanic ritual."

Whatever it was, The Who had had a concert with no mobbing, no crushing, no rush to the stage. Perhaps it was because The Who themselves were in awe of their surroundings. They refrained from egging the crowd on; they refrained from inviting them to storm the stage.

The reception of *Tommy* at the Met made Townshend happy, but the group wanted to move on in another direction. Townshend turned his attention to writing a song called "The Seeker," half inspired by Meher Baba, and half by getting himself drunk out of his skull, as he describes it. The song dealt with the premise that he was looking for his real self, while others were looking for theirs. Townshend claimed that the lyrics expressed Divine Desperation, but its lack of success in the market was less than divine.

Meanwhile, there were ominous signs on the rock horizon. Jimi Hendrix's behavior was growing more and more bizarre. On September 17, 1970, Hendrix spent an evening with friends, and took a heavy hit of acid, plus some downers. He went home with Monika Danneman, a striking German girl he had been seeing a lot of, who lived on elegant Lansdowne Circle in London along Nottinghill Gate Road. Hendrix did not feel at all well when they arrived there. He wanted to sleep undisturbed until he woke up, he told Monika. He took one sleeping pill, then several more when that failed to work.

Sometime during the night, he woke up and tried to get out of bed to vomit. By the time Monika discovered his condition, he was near death. In spite of the efforts of the doctors at St. Mary's Abbot Hospital, he died on the morning of September 18. The coroner's verdict: death from suffocation at the age of twenty-seven.

Janis Joplin, among millions of others, was stunned by the news. She told a friend: "This just decreases my chances. Two rock stars can't die the same year."

Two weeks after Hendrix's death, on October 5, 1970, Joplin ordered fifty dollars' worth of heroin to be sent to her room at the Landmark Hotel in Los Angeles. She shot up, then went down to the desk to change a five dollar bill to get cigarettes. She went back to her room, but never got to the bed. She was found dead on the floor beside an empty bottle of vodka, a bottle of Valium, and $4.50 worth of change in her hand. Her nose was broken in the fall to the floor.

The coroner's report read: accidental overdose of heroin, at the age of twenty-seven.

Jim Morrison, defending himself against court charges, read about Hendrix. He asked a friend, "Does anyone believe in omens?" Two weeks later, he read about Janis Joplin. This time he told his friend, "You're drinking with Number Three."

Ten months later, on July 3, 1971, he died in Paris under circumstances no one has quite explained. The cause was listed as a heart attack. He was twenty-eight. All three had followed the path Brian Jones took two years before.

Just a few days after that, The Who performed in Forest Hills Stadium. Local residents cowered inside their homes while the crowd reverted to the pattern that had marked the Altamont and Isle of Wight festivals. The Who did not perform all of *Tommy*, just a few songs from it. Instead, they were back in their old pattern, playing the anthems that had pleased the Mods in their early days. Outside the stadium, one young gate-crasher struggled with a security guard. In moments, he drew a knife and stabbed the guard to death.

A superficial observation of the crowds that responded to the continual chaos and violence of the hard-rock concerts could create a picture of uncontrollable zombies without intelligence or sensibilities. To rush the stage like lemmings, smash chairs and windows, throw bottles and even a hand grenade suggest that type of picture.

Yet it is obvious from even a casual analysis that the bulk of individuals in the crowds were not at all of that nature. Profiles of the rock audiences as individuals showed them to range from the most intelligent, through a wide spectrum of average, well-balanced personalities, down to a few incorrigibles. The one thing each had in common was a passionate devotion to the music and the superstar. A representative audience was no better or worse than any random slice of the rising generation.

The growing number of sociologists and psychologists studying the adolescent block were arriving at varied conclusions but marked by many similarities. One problem with their studies was that they talked as if the current adolescent crop was the first in history, and appeared to forget their own adolescent era, when they and their contemporaries were facing some of the same problems. The consensus on adolescent behavior included terms such as out-of-touch-with-own-feelings, alienation, frustration, loneliness, isolation, hostility, aggression, identity crisis, apathy, fragmentation, restlessness, subculture, purposelessness, resentment, socio-economic background, sensual experience, sex roles and scores of other elements playing a part in the development of the adolescent. But certainly these factors played just as important a part in adolescents growing up through the first half of the twentieth century, if not in all of history.

What was markedly different in the generation growing up concurrently with the hard-rock wave was the music itself, along with the first full impact of electronic technology, with amplification that could almost obliterate the music it was designed to enhance. This was not ignored by the social scientists, but it did not hold a center-stage position in most of the studies.

La Voie and Collins noted in the *Journal of Youth and Adolescence* in 1975 that rock music was an integral part of youth culture, and that it "contains informational value for the adolescent and provides a rich source of identification with peers. That is, rock music offers resources which are not available in the adult culture. Classical music does not provide these resources (i.e., it has little information about adolescence and life; it has no mechanisms for promoting identification with peers, etc.), and therefore classical music has little reward value. If one wants to be an enlightened adolescent, one can listen to rock music, the mode of communication of the youth culture."

The statement was true, but it still failed to explain why hard-rock music brought with it the frequent physical violence that it did, or the magnetic attraction of the superstar.

Prominent in many motivational studies of the adolescent is the importance of identification figures, figures which an adolescent admires and seizes on, identifies with, and imitates. Gail Sheehy, in *Passages*, notes that youth likes to identify with a charismatic figure, and the more extreme the model, the simpler it is to identify with. "Their exaggerated style is simple to mimic," Sheehy writes, and she adds that they "beckon the young seeker over a moat, in the imagination, at least, where the bridge leading back to the sanctuary of family would be burned." The thesis is that it is easier to identify with people than with ideas.

If this position can be accepted, the rock superstar becomes the "role model," and the violence of the musical act becomes a catalyst for conscious or unconscious imitation, even without the potential of the trance state generated by the music. This might explain part of the reason for the continued disturbances, but it wouldn't explain all of it. Nor would a closer look at the cross section of the all-rock generation growing up in Cincinnati who would converge at the plaza several years later. Their increased absorption of the new music was the same as that of millions like them across the Western world. Like 95 percent of their contemporaries, they were far from the riotous or destructive stereotype that some adults imagined.

Many of them had never seen Joplin or Hendrix or Morrison, but their singles and albums were there to solidify the myths that these parted superstars left behind. Barrel-chested Mike Shumate, coming into his own at Sycamore High School as 1970 began, had other favorites to soothe his regrets. He had already zeroed in on his personal choice, Grand Funk Railroad, scorned by the rock critics but adored by the kids.

As a teen-ager fully soaked in the hard-rock scene, Mike mourned the deaths of the three rock giants, and felt in a way as if all rock might be dying off. All he could say about Jim Morrison was, "It's the end of a rainbow that never ends. He may be dead, but his music lives on." He consoled himself with the thought of a pervasive rumor: Hendrix, Joplin and Morrison were not really dead. They had pulled a gigantic hoax to get away from the pressures and pace of the chaotic scene, and had spirited themselves away to some romantic, mystical island Valhalla where they could play together in peace.

For a while, he actually half believed it. But his passion for the Rolling Stones, The Who, the Jefferson Airplane and others helped ease the pain, and especially his first experience of a rock concert, when Grand Funk played in Cincinnati. It was a rousing introduction to the heavy concert scene.

Mike had gone to both the Reading Elementary and Junior High with his future wife Debbie, but she was two years younger, and a bit beneath his dignity at the time. She was already gathering together her own rock favorites, that matched his almost exactly by the time the new decade began. She still liked the Beatles, but her attachment to the Monkees had dimmed as she moved into her teens. The Who sounded different to her, more revolutionary. Her prize possession was a giant poster of Roger Daltrey on her wall. She surrounded herself with the music of *Tommy*, and envied the power of Grace Slick with the Jefferson Airplane, which was about to change its name to Jefferson Starship. Debbie would sit for hours with a friend listening to the *Tommy* album, and in spite of the heavy reality of the lyrics, they put her in an elevated mood every time she listened.

Debbie never liked Janis Joplin. She thought Joplin's voice was crude and whisky-tough, and her records reminded Debbie of the heavy drug scene that she despised. Debbie had inherited a pile of Hendrix albums from her brother when he joined the army and went to Vietnam. She finally put them aside because they reminded her of the war—and of how Hendrix had died as a victim of drugs. With Morrison, she felt much the same. To Debbie, drugs were synonymous with bad news.

When Mike Shumate quit school and squeezed himself into the Marines at seventeen in 1971, Debbie was in the ninth grade, and had no idea that he would be coming back to marry her. Nor did Mike. He was eventually shipped to Vietnam as a cook and baker, with assorted patrol duties thrown in. One night while patrolling checkpoints, a bullet whizzed through the window of his jeep, barely missing him. Another time, a drunken Marine took aim at him with a shotgun, just missing his chest.

Mike shrugged it all off. Close calls seemed to come his way often. He had fallen out of a tree when very young, and had sailed across the width of a street when a car hit him at a tender age. He never looked at things like this as tragedies; they were just part of life.

After the active war in Vietnam, Mike shifted over to Guam, where things were more relaxed. He and a friend from San Francisco monopolized the Pioneer turntable and four Sansui speakers and amplifiers in the barracks rec hall. Since both Mike and his freind were now steeped in the music of The Who, they played the album *Who's Next* for hours at a time to the wild boars and dogs that roamed the nearby jungle.

PART II

Their favorites were "Baba O'Reilly," and "Won't Get Fooled Again," which they almost wore off the record grooves.

In the barracks, Mike dreamed to the point of obsession about finally seeing The Who in concert. They were the greatest rock group in the world to him, and his one target when he got out of the Guam jungle would be to find them on tour somehow, and see in living color what he was constantly listening to in the barracks.

His friend felt the same way. They both wanted to announce and praise The Who to the world, starting perhaps with the Guam base where they were stationed. One night, basking in the romance of a full moon, they decided this was as good a time as any to begin. They amassed a total of twelve speakers, hooked them up and placed them strategically along the roof of the barracks. It was just before night duty began for both of them, and they would be well out of the way when the gratuitous concert began.

They put on "My Generation," cranked the volume up to maximum, turned the amplifier on, and scooted off to another part of the base. From the distance, they heard Daltrey's voice reverberating off the nearby cliffs, blasting loud enough to set off all the engines of war stored below ground on the site—enough to blow the island off the face of the earth.

Shipped back to the States later, Mike arrived in Jacksonville, Florida, just three days after The Who had completed one of their rare concerts in that area. He couldn't believe his bad luck. He swore that if The Who ever came within a few hundred miles of him again, he would be the first to buy a ticket and the first to be in line.

Brant Ross got his first battery transistor radio when he was twelve, back in December 1969. He spun the dial and hit Cincinnati's station WSAI, to be greeted by the sound of the Beatles, followed by a stream of others. His life changed from then on. WSAI was a top-forty station, catering to the moppet crowd. By the time the day was over, Brant had memorized "She Came in Through the Bathroom Window," "Downtown" and "These Boots Are Made for Walkin'." He also picked up a few news broadcasts that same day, and made a point of asking his father to show him where Cuba and Vietnam were. He broadened his geography as he plunged into the maelstrom of soft rock and bubble gum music.

By the time he reached high school, his taste had shifted along with that of many of his peers to the hard-rock sound, with The Who on the top of his list. The teeny-bopper sound was now rejected. He recognized the new rock as a powerful force, one that was not without its faults, but nevertheless irresistible. In spite of his admiration of The Who's music, he was not altogether happy with the expression of violence in their style of living. He sensed that it brought about an increase in vandalism, that there was danger of emulation or rock heroes that could lead young kids to very serious involvement with drugs.

The Rolling Stones seemed to be heavy on this scene, with songs like "Mother's Little Helper" about Valium, "Brown Sugar" about heroin, to say nothing about a song called "Sister Morphine," and one called "Moonlight Mile" about cocaine. Brant was scared off by the thought of heavy drugs, and the personality changes that could take place with them. He was scared off also by seeing what happened when the kids took downers and alcohol together. Like the majority of his generation, he tried smoking pot, but never became very attached to it.

Brant saw two sides to the coin. To him a group like The Who was displaying superior artistry, especially after *Tommy*, and they had something to say that should be said. But Brant had time just to listen to the beat, feel it, enjoy it and get on with a heavy schedule that included school, working in a local IGA store and keeping in shape for the track team. He ran both the 220 and the 440, with his best time for the latter being fifty-three seconds—not quite good enough in his league.

Brant worked hard at track, but he had a magical way of combining it with his love for music. With a fellow track man named Tony, Brant would often borrow the family car, and back it up to the oval. Then they would turn the volume up loud enough to hear it all around the quarter-mile circumference. The sound and beat seemed to lend wings to their running shoes, and broke up the monotony when they would run as many as forty or fifty laps at a shot.

Afterward, they would go back to Tony's small bedroom, featuring basically a mattress on the floor, a huge poster of the group Crosby, Stills and Nash and a battered record player. Tony was a gentleman. He would warn his mother that he was going to "turn on the stereo a bit" and close the door. Tony not only had a feast of albums; he had almost every rock magazine in print. They would relax on the mattress, leaf through the magazines, talk about their current favorite superstars and absorb the thudding music through ears and pores.

One day, Tony peeled the cellophane from a spanking new album by The Who called *Quadrophenia*. It had been bouncing around in Townshend's head for several years. It was the first concept album since *Tommy*, which by 1973 had soared to ten million in sales, and two years later would become a critically successful film directed by Ken Russell. Like its predecessor, the *Quadrophenia* album told a story, and it was slated to become a film in the near future. It was also operatic in tone and concept.

The story reverted to Townshend's preoccupation with the Mod culture. The protagonist, Jimmy, is split four ways, as the title suggests, a case of double schizophrenia. The songs in the album reflect the useless and dysteleological clashes of the Mods and Rockers at Brighton-by-the-Sea, the struggle to keep a job in the straight world while seeking escape with pills, the search for identity in a milieu that demanded the loss of it by joining the crowd.

Brant and Tony went for songs like "Drowned," "Cut My Hair," "Bell Boy" and "The Punk Meets the Godfather" almost as soon as they heard them. Even though the Mods were English kids, Brant felt a strong identity with them, especially for Jimmy and his confusion and his sense of alienation from the adult world. Most important, though, it was good music to run by on the oval track.

Brant and his friends had their own Brighton-by-the-Sea experiences, although they were peaceful and placid compared to the Mods'. The crowd from high school would drive out to an empty field, "fifteen miles from nowhere," where they would meet and party with a few six-packs of beer while they listened to rock on the car radios. They were on their own, no one was around to bother them and they had a sense of freedom they could rarely find elsewhere.

Whenever The Who came on, all the radios in the thirty or forty cars gathered in the field would switch to that station. It was a ritual, a testimonial of respect for their favorite group. If The Who ever came within earshot of Cincinnati for a live concert, there was one thing certain: Every person parked on that lonely field vowed to be first in line for tickets and first in line at the gates—including Brant Ross.

The varied forces that come together in the formation of a tragedy come into focus slowly, and are often obscured by crosscurrents before they meet to produce what eventually becomes inevitable. Visible in 1975, almost five years before the tragedy that struck at Cincinnati's Riverfront Coliseum, were the individual elements that would combine to create the theater where the event would take place. These elements would include the physical structure of the Coliseum itself, the managers and promoters, the music and musicians, the crowds, and the officials handling the crowds, all operating under the mood and atmosphere of the times.

The way these elements developed is important because a shift in any of them might have prevented what happened on December 3, 1979.

PART III

DATE

AUTUMN, 1975 TO
DECEMBER, 1979

PLACE

CROSSROADS, U.S.A.

CINCINNATI

lies at the crossroads of the South and the Midwest. It is known as the Queen City by virtue of its fulcrum position on the banks of the Ohio River. It has been both a musical and trade center since the opening of the West. On a direct fluvial artery from Pittsburgh to the Mississippi, Cincinnati has been pumping economic blood in four directions since the 1700's. The riverboat Delta Queen still chugs its colorful way, sailing down to New Orleans for the Mardi Gras, or over to Chattanooga, or even up to Pittsburgh or St. Paul.

Like all folk music, including the new rock songs, the fragmented Ohio River ballads of the black boatmen back in the 1800's were a reflection of the times, and sprang from the soul. There was little refinement; the songs were more powerful without it. Stephen Foster, working as a clerk for a Cincinnati steamboat agent near the Public Landing where Riverfront Coliseum would be built, heard the blacks as they sang their work songs and toted their bales on the levee. They inspired him to pass their message along to the world in his songs of the South and the levees.

Modern Cincinnati perches on seven hills overlooking the Ohio, busy with the manufacturing of automotive parts, aircraft engines and electrical equipment as well as other industry, including Procter & Gamble. Some of its restaurants can compete with more celebrated ones in Paris. Its symphony, civic opera, playhouse and art centers are burgeoning and lively. An integrated skywalk connecting a convention center and lavish department stores make strolling and shopping unusually pleasant.

For several years, the Cincinnati city fathers and prideful citizens looked forward to the autumn of 1975, when the spanking new Riverfront Coliseum was to open its doors.

As a sister edifice to the Stadium, the Coliseum was anticipating a World Hockey League expansion team, and perhaps a professional basketball club as well. What's more, the Queen City could now lure big-star touring attractions that required the heavy gross that eighteen thousand indoor seats could supply.

Riverfront Coliseum was the brainchild of two heirs apparent of prominent local families, both not long out of Harvard Business School. Brian Heekin, president of the multi-million-dollar project, and Bill DeWitt, Jr., vice president, made up in enthusiasm what they lacked in business experience. Thanks to the local Chamber of Commerce, they were able to finance the structure through commercial banks and savings and loan companies. Any facility that could take in more than $180,000 in a single night would be good for the state, county, and city.

There was no question that the facility would be under pressure to pull in healthy grosses. Young Heekin and DeWitt would be facing over a million a year in mortgage payments, plus over half-a-million due its public spirited bondholders annually, up through the year 2003. Architecturally, the building was soothing and impressive. Minnesota designer Frank Pattee knew about crowds and the importance of exit doors. He designed a ring of 134 doors around the perimeter of the building that would assure a smooth egress from inside the fireproof building. They led out to the broad upper level plaza, which the city itself financed for over $3 million.

Crowd flow is a specialty of its own in the design of public buidings. Experts from the National Bureau of Standards had long been studying "emergency egress" problems, which they approached with the same enthusiasm as an hydraulic engineer would a pipeline, or a hematologist studying the flow of platelets in the blood. Both hydraulic and blood flow were in some respects parallel to crowd flow. There was considerable controversy concerning the potential flow through the stairways and exit doors, to say nothing of the psychological factors involved in crowd behavior.

A researcher named I. Peschl had conducted a long series of laboratory experiments about the capacity of door openings in panic situations. He utilized student volunteers to simulate panic conditions by pressing against doorways until all the subjects were able to get through.

Peschl made some interesting observations. In large group experiments, people would often fall or stumble. A phenomenon called "arch formation," where a large crowd cluster builds up to impede the crowd flow would result from the self-dissolving of "arches."

Peschl's basic conclusion was that human beings in a panic situation behave identically as granular particles flowing from bins. Another researcher, L. F. Henderson, had slightly different ideas. He contended that people behaved according to the laws governing the propagation of gas particles in a low density crowd, while in a high density situation, the behavior was more along the line of hydraulics or molecular action in fluids.

Others contended that the speed of a group through an exit was determined by the pressures exerted among all its members. An interesting factor was that none of the studies involved the flow of people trying to *enter* a building, and with good reason. Panic situations were a traditional function of escape, and escape was not a function of getting into a building. The Coliseum's 134 doors were abundantly able to handle a panic exit from the new arena, whether the theory pivoted on the movement of fluids or of gas particles.

Young President Brian Heekin was as aware of the importance of crowd flow as he was of the importance of cash flow and profits. The city, state, and the bondholders were also aware that the cash flow had to be steady and adequate to keep the project in economic health. Long before the building was to open, Heekin was lining up the best possible draws in sports, special events and music. The number of dark days had to be kept to a minimum, and tempting lures had to be put out to fill the eighteen thousand seats on a regular basis.

Heekin and DeWitt both had stars in their eyes. They looked forward to the U.S. Olympic Boxing trials, the United States Figure Skating Championships, still a few years away, the Ice Capades, the Ringling

Brothers Circus, the Longhorn World Championship Rodeo, Frank Sinatra, John Denver and, of course, the constant circuit of popular rock superstars—the most consistent draws in the business.

But most of all, they were counting on the Stingers, Cincinnati's expansion hockey team, even though the new World Hockey Association was leaning heavily on aging National Hockey league stars and sprightly unknown youngsters who had not won their blades in professional hockey. Heekin had the backing of his socially prominent family, which had been in the city's social circles for generations, ever since Brian's grandfather had expanded his spice and coffee business into the Heekin Can Company at the turn of the century. The Heekin family was prolific—at a reunion in 1962, 300 Heekins showed up for the celebration.

Many in Cincinnati regarded the Coliseum as a rich man's plaything, and Brian, with his lean distant face and an air of indifference, seemed to fit the image. The executive officers and reception room were luxuriant, colorful and gaudy. Thirty-five booths where events could be watched in privacy were offered for takers at $16,000 each. Each booth included a living room, elegant mirrored lavatory, closed circuit television and sliding glass doors that led to a balcony jutting out over the highest tiers for a sweeping view of the events below. Each box or booth had easy access to the Beehive Club, bold and luxurious as the rest of the decor.

Since Cincinnati had long been by-passed by the top rock concert acts, there had to be a way for the new Riverfront Coliseum to be sure of a steady flow of the leading rock groups, who would almost certainly sell out the massive number of empty seats inside. Performers like Led Zeppelin, the Rolling Stones, The Who, Elvis Presley, Jethro Tull, Elton John, Kiss, Yes and other groups like Pink Floyd, Aerosmith, Wings and Black Sabbath—these made up a rock smorgasbord appetizing enough to pack the house.

To do this, the promotional operation of Larry Magid's Electric Factory Concerts in Philadelphia was a logical choice. Magid was a forceful rock promoter who had built his success through some tactics that were unpopular with his competitors. A forceful and outspoken man, peering out through thick glasses and wearing a heavy black mustache and sideburns, Magid had built up a booking business that grossed as high as $20 million a year. Using his control of groups booked

108

into the big-gross, 19,000-seat Philadelphia Spectrum as a lever, Magid could dominate other large markets like Memphis, Pittsburgh and, if he chose to, the new Riverfront Coliseum in Cincinnati. What's more, Magid would be able to guarantee the fledgling Coliseum up to thirty big concerts a year which in itself would suggest a cumulative gross of over $5 million.

Cincinnati tempted Magid as Philadelphia had done earlier. The Philadelphia rock scene had been sluggish before he took it over and turned it into a robust market. He smelled the same situation in Cincinnati. Here was a virgin market with a new coliseum and a fertile potential for multi-state audiences.

In Philadelphia, Magid *was* rock and roll. Outside of that city, he had booking power in as many as fifty others. Through his hold on the Philadelphia Spectrum, he dominated the market there. Through a pending arrangement with Riverfront Coliseum, he would set up a subsidiary promotion office called Riverfront Concerts. This in turn would extend a dominant hold over the new facility—a choice addition to his network. Without such access, other promoters would be all but cut off from booking profitable acts at Riverfront.

Magid's competitors smarted under his dominance and alleged that with his leverage he could hold a big stick over agents and talent. The superstar groups would have to play his game in a block-booking deal that was hard to combat. If a group wanted to play Philadelphia, they had to play Magid's game. Otherwise they could lose Cincinnati, Memphis, Pittsburgh, or wherever else Magid might be able to book.

On the other side of the coin, Magid was known in the business for paying his bills promptly, and his clout was respected, sometimes generously and other times grudgingly. His start in the industry came after dropping out of Temple University, when he began booking new rock talent for General Artists in New York in 1965. By 1969, he was helping a group of brothers in Philadelphia named Spivak to convert an old warehouse to a rock club that began outdrawing anything similar that Philadelphia had to offer. The overhead was low, the profits were good. These were the days when people danced to rock, and the Electric Factory provided tilted boxes along the wall, shaped like coffins, for dancers to rest against. Becoming the dominant owner of Electric Factory, Magid moved out of the old warehouse to the Philadelphia

Spectrum, home of the Flyers, an NHL hockey team, and more important to Magid, the home of his mass attraction, big rock concerts.

Just how the gamble of the Riverfront Coliseum owners would work out was anybody's guess. With nearly $10 million worth of bond obligations, manager Richard Morgan looked forward to the September 1975 opening of the giant hall with a combination of enthusiasm and jitters. There was no steady major tenant to carry the project along, and the hockey team was still barely a glint in Riverfront management's eye. Steady, guaranteed draws were hard to come by. It was already becoming apparent that Larry Magid and his rock concert billing were going to have to pull a heavy oar on behalf of Riverfront Coliseum.

The visceral gusto of rock fans for their stars was one thing that could be counted on. No other ticket would be so passionately sought after, nor was the price any obstacle, even for a teen-ager's limited budget. Fans had been known to drive from Alaska to the Midwest to see a concert by the Grateful Dead. Scalpers' tickets for The Who had been known to soar to $150 apiece at Madison Square Garden. How the Coliseum's emphasis and dependence on rock would sit with Cincinnati's devotees of opera, symphony, and art was a question mark. But the economic realities had to be faced.

Another reality was that tickets had to be sold, and in order to sell enough, the demand had to be energetic. Since ticket buyers often act on impulse, it was important to make it physically and mechanically easy to buy tickets in a wide interstate area surrounding the city. Fortunately, Ticketron was on hand in Cincinnati, Dayton, Kentucky and elsewhere, with a computerized setup at shopping center outlets. Telephone long lines carried the data to the computer center in Hackensack, New Jersey. Within seconds, the number of unsold seats were flashed on the screen, and the tickets automatically printed up. Already, Ticketron was figuring that three-quarters of its sales of Coliseum tickets would come from rock fans—and if the attraction was big enough, a sell-out could be accomplished in less than two hours.

Because it was already apparent that rock music was going to be the ultimate golden goose, it was not surprising when the opening event was announced. It was to be the rock group known as the Allman Brothers Band, which had a devout following in spite of an erratic and variable career. Duane Allman had been considered to be one of the towering

110

guitarists in rock. His brother Gregg was later considered an exalted superstar. Along with bass player Berry Oakley and the others in the band they played lusty, crusty Southern blues that left their fans en-raptured.

But they had encountered problems. Duane Allman, riding on both a crest of a new million-sale album and a motorcycle near his home in Macon, Georgia, drove to his death on the latter. Almost a year later, Berry Oakley duplicated the tragedy, as he too was killed on his mo-torbike only three blocks away from the scene of Duane's death. Gregg Allman, whose magnetism and allure had kept the group going, sank into a morass of drugs and alcohol, but still managed to remain op-erational. Before some large concerts, his colleagues would hire a doctor at $1500 a day—a benevolent jailer to keep Gregg Allman in shape to perform.

In spite of all their vicissitudes, the reconstructed Allman Brothers group was on hand to open Riverfront Coliseum on September 9, 1975, with considerable fanfare and a crowd of nearly seventeen thousand diminished slightly from total capacity by the fire department's watchful edict. Frosting on the cake was provided by a preamble performance of Muddy Waters, the great black Southern blues singer, whose songs and rhythm had reached over to England to inspire every headliner group from the Beatles to the Rolling Stones to The Who, all of whom converted their English accents to a pseudo-Southern growl.

Muddy Waters sang his guts out on opening night for a screaming, manic crowd. The Allman Brothers Band followed with everything from slow blues to race-horse galloping numbers. Big Time Rock had come to Cincinnati, and the future of Riverfront Coliseum was bathed in a roseate haze.

There were some gate-crashers, a problem which, if uncontrolled in the future, could lead to serious overcrowding. A thick cloud of ma-rijuana smoke baptized the new auditorium. Green fluorescent batons were tossed in the air and tumbled back down on unsuspecting pockets of the audience. A sharp crackling of fireworks punctuated nearly every set the Allman Brothers played.

It wasn't long before the fledgling operators of Riverfront Coliseum began to recognize the difference in the demographic and psycho-graphic profiles of their audiences. Richard Morgan made that clear when he said, "If you have a Lawrence Welk here, you won't need the security guards you would when Paul McCartney is here."

It also became apparent that you didn't need the same number of security guards for Paul McCartney that you did when Led Zeppelin or the group called Yes would appear. Throughout the trade, the consensus continued to be that the image of the group defined the behavior of the crowd. Some of the hard-rock groups literally played on the turbulent impulses of the audience as much as they played on their guitars.

This created another strange aspect that surfaced: an almost identical crowd, at two different concerts, would behave one way when listening to one rock group, and another when listening to another. Each group held their own special kind of power in their hands. That power was amplified in direct ratio to the devotion of the crowd, which in turn was subjected to an ionized reaction brought about by their own compaction. There was an exchange of neutrons as surely as there was in the fuel rods of a nuclear assembly. It all depended on how far the control rods were pulled out—and the performers sat at the control panel.

Larded in between the faltering hockey games of the Cincinnati Stingers and college basketball, the parade of rock groups continued to be slotted in throughout the months following the Coliseum's gala opening. It was obvious that here was the desperately needed bread and butter for the arena. The Stingers were playing to crowds as small as two hundred spectators. College basketball could barely cover the rent, although it helped with the overhead.

In contrast, the superstar concerts sold out within a few hours. Bootleg prices soared as high as ninety dollars a ticket. When Paul McCartney, the former Beatle, was booked at the end of December 1975, some fans drove in from as far away as Arizona and Minnesota for the concert. When The Who were booked by the Coliseum that same month, Ticketron offices were swamped. Four years later, in December 1979, The Who would sell out even faster.

Brant Ross, now eighteen and a freshman at the University of Cincinnati, learned early that the tickets for the 1975 Who concert were going on sale. He made sure he was in line at his nearest Ticketron office before the sun came up. He invested enough of his own capital to buy thirty tickets so he could make a modest profit by selling them to his school mates at the University. His enthusiasm for The Who was undiminished, heightened by his long workouts on the track as the music played on the car radio.

The previous summer, Brant had tagged along with the tour of the group Emerson, Lake and Palmer, selling souvenir T-shirts, making enough to help defray his college expenses. On the summer tour, he looked on the life of the rock star with a touch of envy. The adoration for the star was hard to believe. Backstage, the huge tubs of Heineken's and champagne floating on a sea of ice and ice water, the tables piled high with cold cuts, fruits and tidbits. The roar of the crowds as the group made its entrance, revealed a glamor he had never seen. Emerson, Lake and Palmer were loud and bombastic, twisting the classical music of Bach and Beethoven into eerie art rock that brought the audiences constantly to its feet.

He had now seen enough concerts to observe that the intensity of excitement reached its peak when the very hard-rock groups came to the area. It dwarfed the excitement of a home team playing in a championship game. The anticipation of the coming concert created a hyper-excitement that started weeks before the concert itself. The power that the superstar groups had was overwhelming. Sometimes, Brant wondered if the groups themselves realized how much power they held.

Another observation Brant made along with others who saw the same thing, was that the image of the group defined the action and behavior of the crowd. The loud hard-rock groups would work the audiences up to a state of empathy far past the boiling point. The superstars would also be stormed by many more groupies than the softer rock groups. The antics of the groupie to get anywhere near the stars or even the production crew were almost unbelievable, from setting up lookouts at airports and hotels, to bribing security guards, offering free dope and promising to bring the performers' fantasies into fruition.

With The Who coming to the Coliseum in 1975, the preconcert excitement around the University of Cincinnati campus was more apparent than ever before. Notebooks were decorated with "The Who" scrawled in elaborate lettering on covers and pages. Who albums blasted from dormitory windows. Brant would drive to the local Dairy-O and meet with friends as they played Who music on the car tape decks.

By the time Brant began selling off his thirty tickets to The Who concert, it was only a question of how fast they would go. He was almost mobbed before he started offering the tickets that bulged his pockets —at only two dollars more than the box office prices. Standing in the background was Becky, who at that time had not the faintest idea in the world that she would marry Brant. She waited until the group around him dissolved. Then she said to Brant that she would do *anything* to get one of those tickets. Brant, the businessman, told her bluntly that all she had to do was come up with ten dollars for the eight-dollar ticket. The problem was that Becky didn't have the ten dollars, and Brant was not about to find out what she meant by "anything." Becky never got to the 1975 concert, but she did get Brant for a husband not long afterward, brought together by the magic draw of The Who.

Also intent on trying to get to the 1975 Who concert was Mike Shumate. Steeped in the group's music all through his service in the Marines, Mike was still smarting from missing The Who concert in Jacksonville by three days. To his further frustration, he learned that The Who was giving their 1975 concert in Cincinnati just a few days before he would be released from the Marines. Debbie, who still had no idea that she would be marrying Mike, went to the concert with Norman, Mike's brother, and his date. The concert went off without incident, and reinforced Debbie's enthusiasm for The Who, especially for Roger Daltrey, whose voice and energy she considered the best in rock.

It wasn't long after Mike became a civilian and was back in Cincinnati, when he met Debbie at his mother's house. She was no longer the little girl he had known in junior high, and his interest in her took a giant leap. One evening when playing chess and gin rummy with her in his mother's living room, he said quite suddenly, "Debbie, why don't you let me take care of you?" She said, "You're a very kind man, Mike." Shortly afterward, Mike put his cooking skills to work in a local restaurant, and they got married. Their mutual devotion to The Who was a strong catalyst in bringing them together.

The devotion to a certain kind of rock or rock group was a common factor in uniting people in Cincinnati and everywhere else. Among the first questions on getting to know someone better in high school and after was, "What kind of music do you like?"—just as the Mods had been doing in England from the mid-sixties on. But there the

114

similarities stopped. There was no cult image similar to the Mods, with their impeccable dress and their carefully groomed hair. The hippy was almost the opposite—the blue jeans, the tennis shoes, the T-shirts, the long hair, the athletic socks, the picture of studied informality. But the music was there, always pervasive and almost always a great leveler. The Who, a symbol of the Mods in their early days, had reached out and become universal.

Meanwhile, The Who's popularity continued to swell. The previous year, New York's Madison Square Garden had sold out for three nights in a row as the result of a single late-night radio commercial. The 1975 tour was breaking house records. The film version of the rock opera *Tommy* had opened in early spring to critical accolades. It starred Roger Daltrey. In 1973, two years before, The Who had performed live the music from *Tommy*, backed by conductor David Measham and his London Symphony Orchestra. Measham stated flatly that *Tommy* was great music. While the performance had the support of the London Symphony Orchestra, The Royal Albert Hall lent none. It had banned rock concerts because of the threat of heavy damage. Even the prospect of Princess Margaret planning to be in the audience failed to alter the decision. Instead, the performance was shifted to London's Rainbow Theatre.

There were other events in 1973 that took the edge off the London success. On a quick U.S. tour that year, Keith Moon sat at his drum set playing in San Francisco's Cow Palace. In the middle of the concert, he began to falter. Then, during a frenetic set, he collapsed and fell face forward on his drums. Townshend asked the audience to bear with them, while Moon was rushed to a backstage shower in an attempt to revive him. It seemed to work. Moon came back onstage to turbulent cheering.

But he collapsed again, and was rushed to the hospital. Instead of suspected jet lag, it appeared that someone had spiked his drink with PCP. The same sort of collapse happened to two girls Moon had been drinking with before the show. In the wake of the incident, at a Los Angeles concert a few days later, Townshend smashed his guitar, after a long hiatus from the practice. On the same tour in Montreal, at a party after the show, Moon began smashing things up to the tune of six

ARE THE KIDS ALL RIGHT?

thousand dollars in damages to the luxurious Hotel Bonaventure. The entire Who contingent rested for several hours in jail, until compensatory damages were arranged.

But all this had been during 1973. The 1975 tour seemed to be promising and uneventful. By the time they reached Riverfront Coliseum in Cincinnati, they had tamed down and were playing serious music. It would stand them in good stead when they would return to Cincinnati in four years time at the end of 1979.

While both The Who and Paul McCartney concerts in 1975 were musical successes, there was one Cincinnatian who found neither of them at all pleasant. Richard Klopp was a young college student, a major in languages, and and articulate letter writer. Six months after the two December 1975 concerts, he was moved to boiling anger by the Coliseum's ticket-selling policy, which had announced the date tickets went on sale for a new concert three days after they had actually gone on sale. All the pent-up anger from his experiences at the December concerts rushed back as he sat down to write a letter to Electric Factory Concerts in very specific terms:

> Dear Sir:
> Since last December, I have enjoyed the dubious honor of attending two concerts produced by your firm at Riverfront Coliseum. In both cases, the personal safety of myself and my fiancée was jeopardized, while in addition, our esthetic enjoyment of the shows was diminished because of the deplorable conditions there. . . .
>
> The two concerts I have attended (The Who and Paul McCartney) were both sold out on a "festival seating" or "General Admission" basis. What this means for the promoter is money; for the concert goer who pays $7 or $8 a ticket, this means that he'll have to sit on the aisles or on the floor, blocking the exits, getting walked over or stepped on by others . . . and just jeopardizing his safety and the safety of others. If a fire or general panic were to break out, many, many people would be trampled to death. . . . This kind of deplorable—let alone dangerous—management cannot be tolerated. . . .
>
> At the Paul McCartney concert, for example . . . when the doors were finally opened (a half-an-hour late), the mass of people pressed forward, literally crushing those by the doors and forcing others into any and all available space. This is what happens when tickets are sold on a "festival seating" basis, and it is no festival. . . .
>
> Respectfully yours,
> Richard S. Klopp

116

PART III

To prevent the letter from being lost in the shuffle, Klopp sent out carbons to the fire department, the city council, Ticketron and Frank Wood's WEBN-FM in the hope that action might be taken to forestall such conditions in the future. While only councilman Jerry Springer acknowledged his letter, it would not be forgotten many months later, when it would surface again under the most chilling circumstance.

Around the time that Klopp was writing his letter that spring of 1976, the Cincinnati Fire Department was already taking a caustic look at Coliseum goings-on. At a concert by Yes, fresh out of Birmingham, England, certain members of the audience supplied contrapuntal explosions of fireworks throughout the entire concert. The private security force of forty stood by, but failed to apprehend anyone. Cal Levy, Magid's man in Cincinnati, indicated that a half a dozen spectators using flaming butane fuel cans were caught and turned over to the Cincinnati police, but he wasn't sure whether these were the pyrotechnical villains or not. He promised tighter security for the next concert, while the police and fire departments tried to figure how they could stop the firecrackers, cherry bombs and M-80's from getting into the building without heavy-handed techniques.

There were more than fireworks to complain about, however. Exits were constantly being clogged at the rock concerts, too many people were jamming the main arena floor and aisles were being choked. A meeting of two District One fire captains and Coliseum manger Richard Morgan was unproductive. But the action taken by the fire department's Captain Ed Schneurer was not. He filed criminal charges against Brian Heekin and two other Coliseum officials to be heard at the Hamilton County Criminal Court in mid-August, with the defendants facing misdemeanor charges for ten specific violations of the fire code. Later the defendants got off with a miniscule fine and a slap on the wrist.

Coming up in early August were two major concerts, scheduled back-to-back on the second and third, a fortnight before the Coliseum managers would be facing their hearing. They were both British bands and formidable superstars. The Jethro Tull group from Blackpool had taken their name from a British agrarian character of the 1700's. The band could draw a massive crowd of ticket buyers at a hushed whisper of its name.

117

ARE THE KIDS ALL RIGHT?

Elton John was one of the high-ranking superstars who combined a solid background in classical music with uninhibited antics on the stage. In addition to outrageous costumes and a reported $40,000 worth of wondrously strange eyeglasses, his music ranged from bluesy, emotional funk to rhythm and blues from the wellsprings of Muddy Waters, Chuck Berry and Elvis Presley.

In spite of his superstar prowess, the Elton John audiences were not considered a problem by the police who were charged with keeping order on the Coliseum plaza. John was not heavy-metal or acid rock to any extent, and much of his music was markedly sophisticated. He was known for cracking up his piano bench and tossing the seat out in the audience, but not for the traditions of The Who's past history when they smashed everything but the klieg lights.

Elton John's Tuesday night concert was scheduled to begin at 8:00 o'clock. The crowd began to gather before 6:00 o'clock. Many on the Plaza did not hold tickets, an obvious threat for overcrowding. With two to three thousand spectators already gathered, the crowd began getting unruly. The private Coliseum police could do nothing to calm things down, and were being bombarded with cans and bottles. Two squads of Cincinnati police came to the rescue, splitting the crowd in two sections.

The barrage continued for nearly an hour. In one case, the private security police overreacted and sent two spectators to the hospital. Since nine squad cars of the city police had to be sent to the Coliseum, downtown Cincinnati was stripped of normal police protection.

Inside, the concert went on smoothly, as Elton John brought the capacity audience to its feet, and tossed out his traditional broken piano stool into the crowd. The concert was a success, but the fire laws had remained unenforced.

On Wednesday, Jethro Tull swept into the Coliseum before the last chords had faded from the Elton John concert. The fire prevention squads also swept in to see for themselves that bars and chains were removed from the exit doors, and that the electronic announcement board carried a plea to keep the aisle and exits free and to refrain from setting off fireworks or any flammable material.

At the Coliseum that night, the aisle and stairs were clear for the first time in its rock history. Three people were arrested for safety violations, including one who lit a smoke bomb and tossed it into the audience. An attempt was made to stop the traditional use of butane lighters, sparklers and burning paper-cups in the ritual salute to the band, by turning up the houselights at the end of the show. The technique failed because the brief intermission with the houselights off allowed plenty of opportunity for the thermal acclamation.

With safety violations clearly on the increase, official resentment against the management of the Coliseum began to grow steadily. In the forefront of this critic's circle was Forrest Buckley, President of the Cincinnati Fire Fighters Union. Two days after the Elton John concert, Buckley, a husky, forceful outdoorsman, sat down and wrote the city manager: "It has been proven beyond a doubt that violations of the Fire Code exist during these concerts, and will continue to exist. To ignore these violations can only lead to a disastrous situation in which the risk of loss of life is very great. . . ."

As the year wore on and the concerts continued, there was no marked improvement evident in the Coliseum procedure. A Public Safety Study Team set up by the city received little cooperation from Heekin. The arena floor continued to be jammed. The fireworks were continuing. The blazing salutes opened and closed every show. Railroad flares had now been added to the arsenal. In spite of this, no arrests had been made by the private security.

At a special study team meeting, the Coliseum's Richard Morgan insisted that his staff was making every effort to control the situation, and promised that even tighter security would be imposed. Crowd control was looming at the *bête noire* that threatened the very existence of the Coliseum, not for the hockey or basketball games, not for the tennis matches, the circus rings, not for the Frank Sinatras, the Elvis Presleys or the John Denvers, but almost exclusively for the hard-rock concerts.

At the same time, there was a paradox here. The rock groups that threatened the viability of the Coliseum were also the source of its economic lifeblood. The giant superstructure had to depend on the giant superstars to exist. There simply wasn't enough steady business elsewhere, and it was the steady business that paid off the bonds and the mortgage loans.

A further axiom was developing: The heavier the beat, the greater the draw. A correlative to the theorem went beyond that: The greater the draw, the greater the problems of crowd control.

Another correlation was obvious. The heavy-rock groups, including the forerunner "maximum-rhythm-and-blues" groups like The Who, Rolling Stones and Led Zeppelin, brought in the most passionately devoted fans on the scene. They cut across all socioeconomic lines. As sane and sound as they were in the everyday world, they could be sent into an emotional tailspin at the twang of a guitar string.

Even some rock mavens deemed hard rock or heavy metal an assault to the ears. To anyone used to a different musical diet, it blasted discordant thunder. The electronic distortion, wah-wah pedals and feedback, all cranked through giant amplifiers and speakers pounded the body and eardrums until they throbbed and pulsated. No jungle drums could match the intensity.

Coming up on the Coliseum's schedule as 1976 drew to a close were two such groups. Aerosmith was one, in early December. Led Zeppelin was another, due the following April. With the renewed promise of Coliseum cooperation, the law enforcement arms hoped for the best. Theirs was not a posture of moralistic dictation. It was based on the question of crowd safety, with lives at stake. Somehow, their warnings were not getting through to the Coliseum management. Somehow, the renewed promises remained empty ones.

Aerosmith swept into town on December 9, played its concert, and departed for the next stop on its tour. Five days later, Assistant Fire Chief Charles Collini sat down and filed a brief report:

(1) Arena floor appeared to be overcrowded.

(2) Concourse walkway blocked by people standing.

(3) Large number of people smoking.

The growing pains for the Coliseum were continuing, but 1977 lay ahead with renewed hope on all sides. Meanwhile, the year-end figures were revealed, and they were promising. Magid had brought in fifty shows through his Riverfront Concerts subsidiary over the sixteen months the Coliseum had been in business. The average attendance was 12,695. The average gross at the box office was $89,958. For a new institution, a $4.5 million gross in its infant months was encouraging.

For 1977, there would be plenty of the big-gun, hard-rock groups, capable of pulling in up to $180,000 for a single night, if not more. Most of them were certain to sell out. And most of them would be booked on a festival seating basis.

The year 1977 was a relaxed one for the members of The Who. Daltrey, Townshend and Entwistle contented themselves working on a few solo albums, with Townshend plunging into the spiritual with an album called *Rough Mix*. It was another reflection of his continuing dichotomy between lusty materialism and metaphysical depths. In spite of the group's hiatus, there was no sign of their dissolving their partnership, as they had threatened in their earlier years.

Unlike the Who, Led Zeppelin was far from inactive. In the new 1977 tour, they continued to set attendance records as they had in the past. Their albums were selling in the millions. The group owed its name to Keith Moon, who used to describe his performance at a dud concert as "going over like a lead zeppelin." The intentional misspelling of the word "lead" has never been explained, but of course is a running custom among rock groups, from the Beatles to Aerosmith. Under the leadership of lead guitarist Jimmy Page, the band defined the meaning of hard rock in every stratum. The tempo was as explosive as the volume; the fans were as explosive as both. When they headed toward Cincinnati for two sold-out concerts on April 19 and 20, 1977, the anticipation of the fans was higher than it had been since the Coliseum had opened.

Among the Cincinnati fans who most looked forward to the Led Zeppelin concert was Jeff Waddle, a student of rock music as well as of journalism at the University of Cincinnati. Slim, soft-spoken, with an insatiable curiosity and analytical turn of mind, he could remain detached from the rock scene at the same time he immersed himself in it.

He found that the concerts could take him up to the highest heights and plunge him to the lowest depths in a burst of spontaneous energy that touched him deeply, for better or for worse. The crowd and the band fused together into an emotional incubator that generated an indescribable mood of elation and high energy for him.

His journalistic leanings prompted him often to step outside the scene and look at it with detachment. The potent lyrics and the earsplitting loudness could stir him to the point of drowning in the cacophony, and liking it. He secretly envied idolized groups like The Who, Rolling Stones, or Led Zeppelin. He wistfully admired a lifestyle that allowed freedom in any words that could be sung—along with lavish and extravagant living, palatial homes, gluttonous admiration, and the license to act on any unrestrained impulse.

In his positive thoughts about rock, he felt that it encouraged a loving brotherhood of sorts, and that it often made strong, intelligent social statements and criticisms. He also felt that people could understand rock as a powerful communication medium. But you had to be selective. If the messages were useful ones, they had a tremendous capacity to do good in society. If they were negative, that same capacity could do inordinate harm.

His appraisal of the Coliseum was that the officials there didn't realize the raw, naked *power* of rock and roll. The arena managers were simply not taking rock seriously enough. Did they realize *why* a teen-ager would mortgage his future allowance to pay ninety dollars or more for a scalper's ticket? Did they realize the restlessness, the anticipation, and the frustration that would arise if the doors were slow in opening? Did they know how a rock fan would react if he thought he might lose his ninety-dollar seat, or miss the concert he had been waiting for for weeks, if not months or years? Because of rock's power—which many outside it failed to recognize—the concert scene was dealing with incendiary passions that could be savage.

Many fans who got their tickets from Ticketron weeks or months in advance would often go through a ritual of staring at it several times a day. They would fixate on the impersonal electronic computer numbers, printed out on a flat piece of cardboard, as if it were endowed with magic. By the time the day of the concert arrived, they would be hyped up in a frenzy.

For Jeff Waddle—and for millions of others who grew up with it—rock had been the major cultural force in life. "Sometimes a particular rock song will stay in my mind all day," he once wrote, "and can sometimes control my mood (happy, carefree, melancholy, sad, mellow, etc.) as a result. I feel that many of the messages conveyed to me have moderately influenced many of my views of life."

Waddle's extensive experience at rock concerts had taught him the established axiom that if you don't get there early, you might as well forget the idea of getting a good seat—or any seat at all. On the day of the first Led Zeppelin concert, he arrived at about four in the afternoon on a muggy, steamy day. The concert was to begin at eight, but already the Riverfront Plaza was filled with several hundred concert-goers. They were spread about like picnickers, with all the paraphernalia of a day at the beach.

There were numerous ice coolers packed with beer and Cokes, and plenty of hard drinks to go around. The police benevolently looked the other way. The atmosphere was relaxed, and quite a few were already getting stoned or sloshed, depending on the drug of choice. By 5:30, some of the crowd was getting out of hand, while the open plaza was rapidly filling with hundreds of more spectators. The debris from the picnic coolers, including a growing number of broken bottles, was filling up whatever space was left open.

Except for the troublemakers, though, the crowd was enjoying itself. The plaza was open to anyone; tickets were not being checked. Some of the crowd were surly and rowdy. Others tried to tame them down, and several scuffles began. The drunks were now openly drunk, and the police moved in. Although the doors were not supposed to open until at least 6:30, an hour away, someone up by the doors yelled, "They're opening the doors now!"

The picnickers and the gate-crashers leaped to their feet in unison and drove toward the doorway in a herd. Waddle was caught in the unexpected rush, and found himself pinned in from all sides, his foot tightly jammed in somebody's metal ice cooler. He was buffeted by the crosscurrents of the crowd, with his foot pinned, and his body batted back and forth. His ankle felt as if it were breaking. He finally freed his foot, only to find that he was now squeezed in so tight that he had to gasp for breath. A small girl in front of him was turning blue, and her eyes were bugging out. There was nothing anyone could do, until someone was able to lift her up and hold her above the crowd.

For over an hour, Waddle was frozen in position, his hands caught above his head, sweat pouring, feet locked. He was jostled at one point, so that his hand was knocked down. It locked into a girl's hair, so wet from sweat that his hand was snagged in it. She tried to pull her head away, and Waddle tried to pull his hand back. The hand was so tightly snarled in the hair that clumps of it were ripped out. The girl screamed loudly, as Waddle tried to yell to her that he was sorry, but there was nothing he could do. All around Waddle was the same scene, with people moaning, crying and gasping for breath, and utterly no way to escape from the press of the crowd.

One man near the entrance doors was screaming that he had to urinate. He finally chinned himself up on a doorway, scrambled up to a low roof over the doors, and disappeared in the darkness above to relieve himself. When he reappeared above the crowd, someone far back out of the jam tossed a beer bottle at him. It fell short and landed into the tightly packed group near the doors. There were more screams, then a barrage of bottles followed from outside the pack, most of them falling into the crowd and shattering. Other bottles smashed against the wall above the doors. Several were hit on the head and began to panic— standing still, with no place to run. Intense pushing began in all directions. Waddle did everything he could to get out, but it was hopeless.

At 6:45, an hour and a quarter after the crush had begun, the private security men tried to open some of the doors. There was a horrifying push forward. Waddle was shot ahead like an arrow. He was smashed against a closed door until he was sure he would be pressed through the glass. His arms and legs felt as if they were going to break. He screamed for people to back up so the doors could be opened. Then he found himself crushed and twisted around a black metal stanchion. Somehow he untangled himself, then found that he was floating, feet off the ground, toward an open door. His glasses flew off, shot ahead, but he was able to snatch them from somebody's shoulder as he was swept through the doorway. His blue T-shirt was half-ripped off, his shoes heavily scuffed, and he was soaked in sweat. He eventually found a friend inside, and slumped down in a seat beside him.

Outside, there was more terror. The gate-crashers were now taunting the police, tossing rocks and bottles at them, rampaging through the parking garages, smashing windows and doors. Some were pushed down on the broken bottles, their hands and legs badly lacerated.

The police moved in, trying to stem the carnage. They became the target, and were battered with chunks of cement broken off from the Coliseum walls. As they tried to reach the attackers, a pitched battle sprung up, in the middle of angry screams and curses. An extra radio alert went out. Sirens responded almost instantly from cruising squad cars. Packs of frustrated gate-crashers scurried from one part of the plaza to another. Two youths spotted a police motor scooter near the guard rail on the plaza level. They ran toward it, lifted it up and tossed it down to the street level thirty feet below. Cheers went up. "Hey, man!" someone yelled. "They threw the pig's bike over the wall!" Everywhere a police officer showed himself, he became the target for a volley of bottles.

Outside the main entrance, the panic continued. A bottle was thrown over the crowd at the door, and smashed through it. In moments, a spectator plunged through the jagged glass. A girl was caught with a man's elbow in the throat. She gasped for air, and was beginning to lose consciousness. Gagging desperately, she did the only thing she could do—she pressed her chin down and bit him on the elbow. A girl in sandals was swept into the lobby with badly bleeding feet. Another girl was vomiting blood.

Some tried to crawl through jagged edges of the broken glass windows and door. Others tried to batter their way in with football tactics. Still others attempted to find a sewer pipe near the riverbank to crawl through. In the process, sixty were arrested and booked by the riot police, who cleared the plaza of the gate-crashers and continued a mop-up operation in the garages and parking lots for several hours after. In the meantime, the concert inside proceeded. It was described later by the critics as "an awesome ritualistic animal energy of rock . . . bathed in turbulence."

On his way home that night, Jeff Waddle began thinking about the article he wanted to write for the University of Cincinnati's student magazine, *Clifton*. There would be a lot to write about: The police-crowd antagonism, the utter foolhardiness of the fireworks freaks, the mob hysteria, the mutual responsibilities on all sides—and above all, the spectre of festival seating.

Why was festival seating so dominant on the scene? The crowds were supposed to like it because of the closeness and informality, the gregariousness. The superstars were supposed to like it because the packed front rows of standees on the arena floors fed their egos and displayed pure adoration in magnified terms. The concert halls and promoters were supposed to like it because it increased the gate measurably. But was it worth all that Jeff had gone through—where at several points, he felt he was looking death squarely in the face? Was it worth being showered by beer bottles, locked with his hands over his head for over an hour, smashed and crushed against a glass door, mangled against a steel stanchion, and totally gripped by panic? He was convinced of one thing. If situations like this kept up the way they were going, there could only be a disaster.

The second Led Zeppelin concert on the night following went without incident. Riot police kept the crowd divided up. No one was allowed on the plaza without a ticket. Crowd control was firm and disciplined. Lessons had been learned.

But six days after the first concert, on April 26, 1977, the Public Safety Study Team called an emergency meeting. The subject was the Led Zeppelin concert. The whole issue of festival seating was given a jaundiced look. There was no question that the gate-crashers had a better chance of slipping in during the confusion of the rush at the gates. While reserved seating would not be a panacea, it clearly appeared that many of the problems came out of the lack of reserved seats. The Coliseum's Heekin contended that none of the problems arose out of festival seating. To him, any superstar event created the same problems, whether there was reserved seating or not.

Heekin wasn't happy about the consensus of the team's members. He wrote a testy letter saying that the Coliseum was better able to assess crowd problems than the city police. He did not concede that the opinion of police officials should override his. About the opinion that gate-crashers could have a better shot at their goal through festival seating, Heekin wrote: "I think it should be spelled out that that is the feeling of the City, and not the feeling of the Coliseum, or of any of the coliseums we have talked to around the country."

The Public Safety Study Team had no real authority, and was not anxious to challenge the private property rights of the Coliseum. What's more, the big coliseums all over the country were continuing the practice of festival seating, and making money at it.

Meanwhile, Larry Magid held his strong grip over both the Spectrum in Philadelphia and the Riverfront in Cincinnati. Promoter Ross Todd, a Cincinnati independent, found it increasingly difficult to stay in business. Every time he tried to bid for a large-draw touring group, he found that he was frozen out of Riverfront Coliseum by Magid's tie-in with Riverfront Concerts. Since the big acts naturally wanted to perform

126

in the large arenas, the Coliseum was a unique and essential facility, and Ross Todd was shut off from it.

In Philadelphia, Magid's competitors were facing the same situation as far as the big arena, the Spectrum, was concerned. Rick Green, a young and energetic promoter operating the Midnight Sun Company, found that he couldn't book any groups at all in the Spectrum because of Magid. But he could at least rely on the 3000-seat Tower Theater in suburban Philadelphia, which he had been booking for several years. In 1975, the Tower Theater went up for sale, and Green put in a bid to buy it. He never got the chance. Larry Magid stepped in and bought it, thus excluding Midnight Sun from any measurable bookings in the Philadelphia area. Green had no other choice than to go out of business.

Steven Kramer, a determined anti-trust lawyer in Philadelphia, got wind of the situation. He began digging up the facts in the case. He found that Rick Green couldn't even bid for an act, because there was no place in Philadelphia to put it if he succeeded. Then Kramer began a long, painstaking preparation of multiple lawsuits against Magid that would engage him in 5000 hours of time, and over $100,000 in expenses. It would also lead to the charge of monopoly and restraint of trade.

Kramer was not fond of the way Magid did business. He found him abrasive, ruthless, and vituperative. In one year, Magid carried 92 percent of the local rock market, using his virtually exclusive contract with the Spectrum as a trump card. In another year, Magid booked fifty-six shows into the Spectrum while the other Philadelphia promoters struggled to exist on the leavings.

Beyond that, Magid's lack of attention to the safety and comfort of the ticket buyers was flagrant. Dating back to a Who concert at the Spectrum in 1971, up through a 1978 Rolling Stones concert at Philadelphia's John F. Kennedy stadium, riots and disturbances took place in the absence of adequate crowd control. In two consecutive years, Aerosmith was bombarded with missiles from the audience, resulting in serious injuries. Peter Wertimer, who worked for Larry Magid at one time, and later for Midnight Sun, found that crowd conditions both before and during the concerts Magid represented were out of control.

"Electric Factory would present what was referred to euphemistically as a dance concert, although the whole hall was generally packed so full that dancing was unthinkable," he said. "So what would happen on these occasions is that the most fanatic of followers of the attractions to be presented would arrive two and three hours beforehand, and there would be large crowds on both sides of the Spectrum."

He noticed that there was no attempt to form lines other than the ones that formed themselves. But as the doors opened, there would be a huge crush forward. Since the large glass doors were being opened into the crowd, people would either be squirted through them with the force of a fire hose, or be jammed into them. "I don't see how they could ever have collected tickets on the first several hundred people who went in," Wertimer added. "So very often you had an oversold situation on the inside. It's always a danger in security, no matter how loose the situation, if people get in free one time."

An oversold house is an invitation to danger. Or even if a house is not oversold, the gate-crashers flood the aisles and the floor space and create the same condition. The fact was that crowd control was a constant problem at Magid's concerts, and his critics claimed that Magid was at best indifferent to the comfort and safety of his patrons.

Magid's attitude toward the press was manifestly surly. He attempted to keep out critics from the Philadelphia *Daily News* and *Bulletin*, and even tried to get them fired. He pulled advertising out of papers whenever he felt annoyed at them. But his business continued to soar everywhere, especially in Philadelphia and in the new big market in Cincinnati.

Meanwhile, Attorney Kramer continued seeking depositions from promoters and others who would take a chance on standing up to Magid's power and strength by testifying. Encouraging to Kramer was an antitrust investigation of Magid brought by the Department of Justice in May 1977 before a grand jury. With so much time and money invested, Kramer was determined to win in the face of what he felt was outrageous dominance of the market.

The grand jury investigation against Magid was dropped, however, and his rock concerts continued while the money rolled in. Festival seating also continued, and by the end of 1977, over four hundred thousand tickets were sold at Riverfront Coliseum, most of them for rock concerts. *Billboard* magazine reported that Riverfront scored the second

PART III

largest total attendance in the country for equal-sized auditoriums. The only coliseum to exceed it was Larry Magid's Philadelphia outlet, The Spectrum. The beat was continuing for Magid, and along with it, the festival seating and the dangers that went with it.

The string of eruptions at Riverfront Coliseum continued to reflect the same trend across Europe and America, wherever hard-rock audiences gathered. The signs also continued to point in one direction: In addition to the violence and destruction, somebody was going to get hurt. The mélange of forces that blended to create the scenes made it difficult to analyze and to set up methods to counteract the inevitable trouble.

It was obvious that the majority of rock fans themselves didn't relish it. Richard Klopp's stinging letter of protest represented the attitude of most of the crowd who went for the music and not the mayhem. Jeff Waddle, who enjoyed rock as much as anyone in his generation, felt compelled to state clearly his protest in the article for the student magazine. The Coliseum management and concert promoters deplored the disturbances, although they continued to resist the pressures of public officials for better safety measures. The firemen and police were searching for ways to combat the trend, but were so outnumbered by the crowds that they found themselves ineffective if the situation grew out of control. Except for the borderline psychotic urgings of Morrison and Joplin, the superstars didn't want to encourage destruction or injury, yet their acts depended on high-wire energy and audience reaction that set the stage for the riotous reactions of the crowds.

Few in-depth studies were being made of the anatomy of the rock concert crowd. Most were generalized and peripheral, or confined themselves to the problems of drug abuse or the wide adolescent social scene. The direct effect of the hard-rock music itself, compared to other types of music, was being largely ignored.

There were studies on what the high decibels of rock could do to the ears. They were not encouraging. At an annual meeting of the Audio Engineering Society in New York, thirty scientific papers were reported. Of forty rock musicians studied, ten had chronic hearing problems. Another study showed that 75 percent of twenty-four rock musicians in their teens suffered hearing loss of high-frequency sounds. In Britain,

129

regular rock concert-goers suffered more hearing loss than a control group that seldom attended.

The Occupational Health and Safety Administration attempted to clarify where the danger level of noise began. The line began at 90 decibels, and anything over 115 decibels was considered unsafe. A decibel is a unit of sound pressure, with the count increasing by three as the volume of sound is doubled. Normal conversation rates a 60 level, a telephone ring rises to 75. From 5 feet away, a bulldozer can register 90. The most common sound in the range of the hard-rock concert volume is a loud thunder clap, which hits around 120. The rock bands at issue were consistently going above that, a level that most otologists agree can damage the hair cells of the inner ear. This leads to irreversible damage, and tinnitis, the constant ringing of the ears that is incurable.

A study by Columbia-Presbyterian Medical Center in New York concluded that decibels such as those The Who blasted at concerts could physically tear nerve endings apart, and that tinnitis could beome so permanent and intense that sufferers had killed themselves rather than put up with it. A *Rolling Stone* survey among musicians showed that the majority of those responding could no longer play music without feeling severe pain. Hearing loss was also reported by over half, and about 3 percent were faced with tinnitis. One of the respondents found that when he experienced high decibels, his ears would bleed. Townshend's doctor was warning him that he might be totally deaf by the time he was fifty.

One unusual study was being conducted by Dr. John Diamond, who had served as staff psychiatrist at New York's Beth Israel Medical Center, and as professor of Psychiatry at Mount Sinai Medical School. Born in Australia, he founded the Institute of Behavioral Kinesiology that fosters the fusion of psychiatry, psychosomatic medicine, preventive medicine, and a technique called Kinesiology. This technique is based on the theory that large muscles provided clues to what was wrong and what could be corrected in the body.

Dr. Diamond carried this into the behavioral field. He found that a large body muscle would test weak or strong, depending on whether a stimulus was bad or good for both the body and psyche. Some activities or thoughts enriched energy. Some depleted energy. A tested muscle could give a feedback that indicated in laboratory tests that the body knew instinctively what was right for the entire self, by-passing the conscious thinking process. In a sense, the tests were a direct route to the id. Several mental hospitals have found the techniques consistent and productive.

There were many tests made in the field of music, a favorite area for Dr. Diamond. He liked all types of music, and in his younger days had even promoted a rock concert in Australia on his own. The Beatles were a favorite of his, and he felt that the later rock music made an important social statement. He also found music to be a valuable therapeutic agent for his patients. The right type of music could help create a significant rise in the energy level. Beyond his own clinical observations, there was interesting statistical evidence, he found, in symphony orchestra leaders and musicians: Fifty percent of all males are dead by the age of 70. Among symphony conductors, 80 percent are not only alive, but are still actively working.

In working with musicians—rock, classical, and jazz—he found that muscle resistance tested strong in the playing of classical, early rock and roll, jazz, ethnic or country music, including Elvis Presley, the Beatles, Bob Dylan, Chuck Berry and Bill Haley and the Comets. All of this type of music registered a reinforced positive effect on the body, with the body muscle system acting as a gauge for the positive reaction of the mind.

One of the tests is simple. The subject holds an arm out straight from the shoulder, parallel to the ground. The subject listens to various types of music. Instructing the subject to tighten his muscles for resistance, Diamond exerts moderate downward pressure on the wrist. If the music's effect on the body is positive, the arm will not budge; the muscle tests strong. If the music has a negative effect, the arm drops to the side under the same amount of pressure, regardless of how hard the subject tries to resist. The loss of strength is instant when a muscle tests weak. Instead of needing forty-five pounds of pressure, only fifteen is required to lower the arm in most cases. Less than half a minute of exposure to the sound is needed for the test.

Diamond began testing thousands of recordings over a three-year period. Most of the music was invigorating; the muscle resistance tested strong. It was only when the most of the recordings of the post-Beatles groups were played for a subject that the muscles of the body went weak.

These groups included Led Zeppelin, Janis Joplin, the Rolling Stones, Jim Morrison's The Doors, Alice Cooper, Queen and others. These groups, defined as "Rock without the roll" consistently showed the same results: the loss of body energy, the weakening of muscle groups and the thymus, and an overall negative effect that Diamond calls body reversal. To him, the body is saying something that shouldn't be ignored.

The results of these tests were so persistent that Diamond went on to try to isolate the cause of the debilitating effect on the body. He analyzed over twenty thousand records. With the help of several rock musicians of his acquaintance, he eventually discovered one of the major causes was what he called "stopped anapestic beat." This was characteristic of rock that came in during the mid-1960's, and only rarely before that. The anapestic beat consisted of two short beats and one long beat, as if the music stopped and had to start again. Rock drummers knew this beat instinctively. Dr. Diamond found that this weakening rhythm was apparently counter to the body's normal physiological rhythm. What was notable was that this kind of rock—compared to the forerunner rock and roll—was that which was almost exclusively associated with the violence and destruction at rock concerts, the killing at Altamont, and the drug deaths associated with the superstars.

"Several jazz musicians have died as a result of drugs and alcohol," Diamond says, "but it's nothing like the similar deaths on the rock scene, one after another, some of them even dying in their own vomit. Can you imagine Toscanini or Casals dying that way?"

In all his clinical studies, Diamond found only two instances of classical music that produced the same indications of muscle weakness response. One is at the end of Stravinsky's *Rite of Spring*. The other is at the conclusion of Ravel's *La Valse*. In each case, the composer was attempting to convey chaos, and succeeded. Another non-rock case that produced a marked loss of body energy was a short recording of voodoo drum music from Haiti.

Mark Grant, a skeptical reporter writing for the *Los Angeles Times*, set out to contest Diamond's theory. As a musician himself, Grant found the ideas hard to believe. Diamond played a series of rock recordings for him, some with the anapestic beat, and some without. He did not tell Grant which type was coming up next. Grant made repeated attempts to resist and counteract the muscle test, but failed every time. Baffled,

PART III

Grant performed the same test on a volunteer patient in the doctor's waiting room, with the same results. "If Diamond is right," Grant observed, "a man who could normally bench-press 120 pounds would barely be able to press 40 when listening to a song like the Stones' 'Satisfaction.' "

Diamond has found other factors involved beyond the "stopped" anapestic beat, which can create the same negative effects even at low volume. At high decibel levels, the same deleterious effects take place regardless of the rhythm. In other words, the beat plus the noise level plus the newer electronic amplification, including widely-used digital recording, has the same clearly-documented weakening results.

As a member of the Royal College of Psychiatry of Great Britain and President of the International Academy of Preventive Medicine, Dr. Diamond was concerned about the broad implication of these results. In many of his patients, he found music had tremendous power to heal, to relieve pain and stress. Some experiments had even shown that the right music reduced bleeding. To find that hard-rock music caused the measurable loss of the body's life energy was discouraging. In his mind, there was little question that the new rock—not the old—reinforced negative energy, having a serious sociological impact in view of its intense popularity among millions of young people.

As Dr. Diamond continued his studies, other troubling evidence appeared. His clinical studies revealed that only the new rock music disturbed the symmetry of the right and left cerebral hemispheres. This in turn causes stress and subtle perceptual difficulties that result in restlessness, decreased work output, hyperactivity and the loss of energy for no apparent reason. Beyond that, extended listening to the new rock music began to show that there was a complete reversal in what Diamond calls "body morality": the normal beliefs of a subject or patient could be switched entirely by exposure to the music for as little as one or two minutes. With rock fans listening to recordings for hours at a time to the point of addiction, this was another disturbing signal.

Diamond tested for this reversal in beliefs by using the same shoulder (deltoid) muscle test he had used for brief exposure to the music. He designed a series of simple and obvious questions to ask the subject from both positive and negative points of view. Under normal conditions for practically everyone, the shoulder muscles would test *strong* when the patient was asked to say out loud: I want to love people and life. I want to be healthy. I want to live. I want to be good in my studies. I want to be strong. I want to be happy. I want to be well-liked, and so forth.

Also under normal conditions, practically everyone would test *weak* on the same muscle tests if asked to say out loud the opposing statements to the above: I want to hate life and people. I want to be sick. I want to die. I want to fail in my studies. I want to be weak. I want to be miserable. I want to be hated.

But the same subjects, exposed to a few minutes of the new rock music, showed a startling reversal. Their muscles tested uniformly weak for positive statements, and uniformly strong for the negative ones. The findings were so consistent that Dr. Diamond felt convinced that they were incontrovertible. If so, they would indicate without ambiguity why the new rock would lead to the violence and disturbances — and even a death wish — that were plaguing the hard-rock scene from the mid-sixties on.*

* The importance of Dr. Diamond's theory cannot be overestimated. The fact is that the simple deltoid muscle test, in which the arm is held straight out, parallel to the floor while the subject tries to resist downward pressure, can be done by anyone as long as there is test rock music available to be played. If done properly, the test response is repeatable and unfailing. There is nothing fanciful or ambiguous about the results.

To try the test, have an acquaintance stand in front of you, with left arm extended as above. It is important that the elbow be kept straight. Place your left hand on his right shoulder. Request him to resist every effort to press his left arm down, with your right hand on his wrist.

The first part of the test is done *before* the music is played. Have him repeat verbally and one at a time, a set of opposing statements of attitudes that are basic to living: "I want to live" versus "I want to die." " I want to be healthy" versus "I want to be sick." "I want to be happy" versus "I want to be miserable." Other opposing statements can be added.

After each statement, test the subject's muscle resistance by exerting sudden firm pressure downward on his wrist. The test actually reflects reaction time more than muscle strength. Unless the subject is psychotic, the arm will test strong and unmoved on the positive statements (I want to live, etc). But it will drop slowly down to the side and test weak on the negative statements (I want to die, etc.), in spite of his determined effort to resist, with the same or even less pressure.

This part of the test reflects the normal expression of a positive life force.

Now have the subject listen to a rock recording with a "stopped"

PART III

A consensus of other behavioral scientists showed that their more generalized observations pointed toward similar conclusions, many formulated on the basis of crowd behavior even before rock music evolved. As the hard-rock concerts continued, there would be plenty of opportunities to measure all the theories.

The new attitudes that swept in when the hard-rock floodgates were opened wide in the mid-sixties, brought with them a potential cleansing action, as well as a lot of flotsam, jetsam and crud. The conflict between the generations was not a one-way street.

The rock generation was, in its eyes, being scorned for popping pills, in the face of their elder's three-martini lunches and a nationwide wave of alcoholism that still represents the biggest drug abuse problem in the country. The young were maligned for smoking grass, when it was becoming a cultural norm for young American adults, and when scientific studies showed that in comparison to alcohol, cannabis was likely to decrease aggressive behavior.

The young felt they were being accused of riotous and boisterous behavior, when they could look in at any respectable country club on a Saturday night that would display enough depravity to last through the

anapestic beat, such as the Rolling Stones' "(I Can't Get No) Satisfaction" for about forty-five seconds. Then keep the music going and ask the subject to repeat the same opposing statements.

Test the arm pressure as above. Invariably, there will be a *complete* reversal in attitude as reflected by a strong or weak reaction of the deltoid muscle. For the positive statements, the arm will drop weakly to the side. For the negative statements (I want to die, I want to be miserable, etc.), the arm will resist the pressure and stay extended. In a matter of seconds, the signs of a positive life force are reversed.

The reversal is so dramatic and consistent that both the subject and the layman experimenter have difficulty in believing the results. Two college students, both avid hard-rock fans, tried the entire test four times on themselves before they came to believe the results. One of the country's leading ballet coaches was stunned by the test, feeling that her vast experience in rhythm and dance would keep her aloof from the effects of music of any kind. The palpable reality of Dr. Diamond's "body morality" needs only to be tried to be convincing. Since many of the songs of the Top Forty can create this body reversal, the sociological implications are broad.

week. The young people were angry at being accused of violence and destruction while they saw the elders were ordering the senseless slaughter of thousands of hapless Vietnamese, and creating the atmosphere that brought about the massacre of Mylai. The new generation was vilified for staging peaceful protests, while the National Guard mowed them down with gunfire at Kent State.

Youth was being blamed for anti-social behavior, while the inner cities rotted. They were accused of sexual promiscuity, while any visit to a corporation convention would reveal as many call girls and pick-ups at the bar as there were groupies at a rock concert. Regardless of social stratum, the younger generation held an almost uniform view of the state of the world it had inherited. This outlook was not confined to freaks or militants.

As this attitude was developing, the hard, "maximum-rhythm-and-blues," and heavy metal rock scene emerged as a protest and a cathartic release. There was no desire for niceties on the 1960's rock circuit. To many, niceties had brought the world to the state it was in. Through rock, "nice" kids developed a special morality of their own. It did not matter whether it was a backlash or not. The new morality was *there*, across the entire spectrum.

The new morality appeared to lead to two opposed philosophies: heavy hedonism or heavy spirituality. Or perhaps it could lead to a mixture of both, as Peter Townshend was demonstrating when he smashed instruments and hotel rooms, splashed down brandy, popped pills, smoked grass—and turned to his guru, Meher Baba, in order to try to accept the universe.

While many were slow to recognize it, rock was becoming the major force of the age. Like any other massive force, the rock culture brought problems.

One question was: Should the rock culture mimic the very qualities it was out to expose? There was plenty of violence, immorality, and greed extant in the rock scene. The leading superstars, record companies, promoters and managers were becoming millionaires several times over, while the songs were sung in praise of the kid in the street. Many superstars reveled in violence, and deliberately encouraged mayhem as their egos swelled.

Their power was boundless, once packed crowds were in their hands,

136

and they failed to assume any accountability for this power. They sang of sexual overkill and heavy drug scenes, and lauded destruction. They became idolized heroes and as a result, they were emulated, simulated, imitated and worshipped.

Where this would lead psychologically and socially was important, as was the direct danger of an explosive crowd to life and limb. The heart of the problem lay not fully in the rock culture, but as in any other scene, in its excesses. There was excessive power and influence, excessive use of drugs, excessive violence, and excessive noise level. This could and did lead impressionable and immature minds to drug poisoning, drunkenness (as opposed to drinking socially), vandalism (as opposed to creative mischief), hopeless crowding and crushing (as opposed to congenial closeness), senseless endangerment through fireworks, butane lighters, and bottle throwing (as opposed to cheerful exuberance)—and all of this controllable only by the superstar in whatever way he arbitrarily chose to use his power.

Charles Collini, assistant fire chief of the Fire Prevention Bureau of Cincinnati, had been observing firsthand the patterns of crowd behavior at all the major events in the city for several years. There was no question in his mind that the star performer had tremendous power and control over the crowd. This was difficult for him to get across to other officials who were rarely exposed to the front-line conditions at rock concerts. Few had the vantage point of close observation that he did. Collini agreed with the seasoned rock stage crews: the harder the rock, the harder to control the situation. If a superstar wanted mayhem, he got it.

The longstanding diagnosis for crowd disturbances at the rock concerts had been that there were "good kids and bad kids" in the crowd. Although the "good kids" were in the majority, it did not take much for "bad kids" to start things going and all hell to break loose.

It is in this area that the theory of a mass trance state, or mass hypnosis, comes in for close scrutiny. Combined with Dr. John Diamond's entirely separate ideas, the mass hypnosis phenomenon could explain a lot of things that remained unexplained. Freud had noted that *any* crowd is "extraordinarily credulous and open to influence." Jimi Hendrix had instinctively sensed this, and had elaborated further on his observation that he could hypnotize people "where they go right back to their natural state." In a publication called *Superstars*, he added:

> Once you have some type of rhythm, like it can get hypnotic if you keep repeating over and over again. Most people will fall off by about a minute of repeating. You do that, say, for three or four or even five minutes if you can stand it, and then it releases a certain thing inside a person's head . . . so you can put anything you want to say inside that, you know. Then you say what you want to say right inside that little gap. It's something to ride with, you know. I always like to take people on trips.

Hendrix wasn't the only superstar who noted this phenomenon. Ray Manzarek, the bass guitarist and keyboard player for Jim Morrison and The Doors told writer Jerry Hopkins:

> When the Siberian shaman gets ready to go into his trance, all the villagers get together and shake rattles and blow whistles and play whatever instruments they have to set him off. There is a constant pounding, pounding, pounding. And those sessions last for hours. It was the same way with The Doors when we played in concert. The sets didn't last that long, but I think that our drug experiences let us get into that much quicker.
>
> We knew the symptoms of the state, so that we could try to approximate it. It was like Jim was an electric shaman, and we were the electric shaman's band, pounding away behind him. The band would keep on pounding and pounding, and little by little take him over. God, I could send an electric shock through him from the keyboard. John could do it with his drum beats. You could see him every once in a while— twitch!—I could hit a chord and make him twitch. Just amazing. And the audience felt it too.

Evidence that the crowd did feel this power was shown when The Doors' Jim Morrison intentionally set out to produce the Chicago riot in the summer of 1968. He commanded, and the inevitable followed: a wrecked auditorium, a floor covered with pulverized glass, smashed windows and seats and mass contusions and abrasions.

As a charismatic figure, the superstar becomes in effect a shaman, as Manzarek observed from close quarters. Added to this is that rock rhythms closely approximate primitive tribal rhythms. In nearly every tribal culture it is axiomatic that dancing plus drumming equals trance.

PART III

The drum in nearly all such cultures is the shaman's primary appliance. Once the beat has taken over, the shaman is in total command, for good or bad. The power is his, and his alone. It cannot easily be countermanded by anyone but the shaman.

Except against any enemy, the primitive shaman does not command, suggest or ask for violence or destruction. His primitive rituals demand discipline. While the trance prevails for both the shaman and the tribe, the commands and suggestions are meant to work for the good of the tribal community, and not for the damage of it. If he asked the tribe to destroy, there is little doubt that the command or even the suggestion would be carried out. The forces behind hypnotism are powerful. The understanding of just how the forces operate shed some light on the consistent pattern of destruction that was so much a part of the rock scene.

Nearly every authority on hypnosis has noted the part hypnosis and suggestion can play in altering behavior paterns. G. H. Estabrooks, former president of Colgate University and American pioneer in the study of hypnotism, defines hypnotism as simply exaggerated suggestibility, arising from a trance state or from intense emotions. Under medical control, hypnotism and its parallel, if not synonymous ally, suggestion, can be extremely valuable and constructive, as evidenced by its extensive therapeutic use, now approved by the American Medical Association in trained hands. Over fifty percent of the patients of the pain clinic of the Walter Reed Army Medical Center are undergoing hypnotherapy. Medical records demonstrate successful hypnosis treatment for stomach and colon spasms, constipation, gastric irritation, rapid heartbeat, impotence, frigidity, psoriasis, insomnia and dozens of other health problems, even including the removal of warts. At the same time, the Association vigorously condemns the use of hypnotism for entertainment purposes.

In spite of continuous scientific study, confusion still exists about the nature and mechanics of hypnosis. One problem is that different people react in different ways to the phenomenon. It most often involves a trance state, although this condition is hard to define. The dictionary calls it a "dazed, abstracted, ecstatic or exalted state; a deep sleeplike state, profound and prolonged." Yet this far from encompasses the range of the condition. Some subjects won't admit they have been hypnotized, when their reactions have proved that they have. Although a deep trance is sometimes associated with a sleeplike state, many in the same depth of trance remain wide awake and alert, a "waking trance."

Nearly every expert agrees that the suggestibility level is far higher in the hypnotic state. But this alone doesn't account for the varied reactions among subjects. Most experts agree that the critical censor of the conscious mind is by-passed, allowing the unconscious to take over. The various stages of the depth of a trance have muddy borderlines, but basically consist of a light state (hypnoidal), medium state and the somnambulist state, that resembles sleep-walking.

Under the right conditions, hypnosis is remarkably easy to induce. The doctor and the stage hypnotist use the same technique. The object of the induction procedure is to suspend the function of the conscious mind so that the unconscious is fully opened to suggestion. For the most part, an eye-fixation technique is used, with a candle or bright object the target. A flashing or strobing light is particularly effective. By asking the subject to listen only to his voice, the hypnotist proceeds to suggest that the subject is relaxed, drowsy and unable to keep his eyelids open. With concentrated attention on both voice and object, attention to the current environment begins to disappear. The retina tires, creating distorted images and the strange physiological effects that ensue are credited to the prestige of the hypnotist. The image of the body begins to fade out, and the hypnotist himself begins to become an alter ego. An actual transference takes place, as in Freudian analysis, to create an intense feeling of rapport in which the subject becomes inordinately anxious to please the hypnotist in every way.

The transitional jump between hypnosis and waking is little understood. It does take place, however, with some widely known and startling results. If a responsive subject is told that every muscle in his body is stiff and unbending, his body actually becomes that way. His head can be placed on one chair, his heels on another, and someone can stand on his stomach while the body remains stretched between the chairs. Laboratory experiments have shown that positive and negative hallucinations can be produced, along with the speeding or slowing of the pulse. One doctor demonstrated to a medical colleague how a negative hallucination works. He told the subject, before the colleague arrived, that he would neither see nor hear the colleague. When he arrived, the colleague was placed by the window, and the subject told to look out the window to see if anyone was coming. The subject saw no one, outside or in the room. The doctor then handed a book to his friend by the window. All the subject saw was the book that appeared to be floating in air.

Dr. Lewis Wolberg, of New York University Medical School, defines hypnosis as "a spectrum of awareness that stretches from waking to sleeping—and some aspects are close to the waking states." He feels that the reason it is hard to nail down an adequate theory of hypnosis is that there are gaps in our understanding of brain mechanisms and psychodynamics.

Even more obscure in its workings is spontaneous autohypnosis. A windshield wiper or metronome can sometimes bring about a trance state. A cyclist pedaling through a long row of poplar trees with the sun behind them went into a trance because of the stroboscopic effect of the light hitting his eyes. Pilots have experienced a similar effect when looking through an idling propeller. But the trance is usually light, and the subject remains in control, perhaps just passing through a stage of daydreaming. If spontaneous deep hypnosis develops, it can be dangerous when not under responsible medical control. The radio and television networks recognize this, and no form of hypnosis technique is permitted on the air. The closest thing to trance induction is the singing commercial, where the music plants an indelible imprint on the unconscious. There is no question that this works.

A major danger in hypnosis lies in the spontaneous form that can arise out of a crowd and a leader who might not even be aware that he is creating an atmosphere of emotional contagion, as Estabrooks points out. With overcharged emotions, the crowd is highly sensitized, and whether the impetus comes from a trance state or from emotions, the results are the same: the removal of inhibitions and actions that are very hard to predict or control.

As both Estabrooks and Professor W. R. White of Harvard have noted, the more violent and less logical the appeal of the leader of a crowd, and the cruder the emotions in question, the greater the success of the crowd leader. A question often asked is why some kids go haywire at a concert and others exposed to the same trauma do not.

One answer to this is that some individuals are open to suggestion, and some are not. Expert estimates show that only 30 to 40 percent are likely to go into a deep trance state. About 20 percent are unable to even go into a light stage of hypnosis. This leaves a gray group area which might go into intermediate trance. Not all will respond in the same way when they do.

A stage hypnotist will go through his induction procedure, and carefully observe his audience. If there are a hundred people there, he can usually expect twenty or possibly thirty to be excellent subjects. From these, he chooses the most receptive to come up on stage, while the rest of the audience watches with full consciousness, mostly unaffected by the hypnosis procedure.

Since a hard, repetitive rock beat can often be as effective as a skillful hypnotist in creating a trance state, it has a power of its own. African tribal villagers can go into a deep trance soon after the beating of the drums begins. At high volume and with sensory overload, a trance can be quickly induced for some, or later for others, depending on the susceptibility of the subject. As the music continues, the trance (in many cases a "walking trance," as Estabrooks calls it) can become deeper and deeper, toward the somnambulist stage: halfway between sleeping and waking, with full capacity to move, speak and respond—but without the normal ego controls, as the id takes over.

Among the Bambara tribes of Niger, the shaman can create a trance in a matter of minutes with simply a heavy drum beat. The same is true with the tribes in Malaysia, the American Indian, the Veddas of Ceylon, the Sherpas of the Himalayas, the Voudon of Haiti—all of whom are neither more nor less suspectible to a hypnotic beat than the Western world.

Combined with the widespread use of the so-called hypnotic drugs such as Tuinal or Quaaludes, the somnambulism can become as deep as a medically-induced trance—but without the medical control. In an emotionally charged atmosphere, such as a rock concert, the sensitized brain can respond to even a miniscule suggestion coming from the superstars, combined with the Estabrooks's "social contagion" of the crowd.

Since the beat alone is enough, the hypnotic drug is thought by many authorities simply to increase the subject's suggestibility. Yet all the

142

while, he can remain awake and functional. Sleep will only be induced if it is suggested. It is often hard to detect even a deep trance state. The subject himself may not be aware of it, as Estabrooks points out.

The scenes that were constantly taking place at concerts were predictable: people fainting and being passed overhead, crowds rushing the stage, hysterical jumping and pumping of arms — reactions that could be closely associated with the hypnotic trance. Since the emotional atmosphere of a crowd is supercharged, it is not surprising that a groupie will rush the stage and slide on her stomach to grab a superstar's feet, as is often observed. Or to tear off her panties and throw them on the stage, an equally frequent event. The spontaneous trance can explain a lot of incomprehensible behavior, even on the part of normally sane, sensible and intelligent spectators. But recalling Ravi Shankar's performance at Monterey, his hypnotic spell created tranquility; Joplin, Hendrix and The Who created the opposite. The choice appeared to lie with the desire of whoever was in command of the crowd at the time.

Of course the phenomenon of mass hypnosis in an emotionally charged atmosphere can occur anywhere in any type of crowd. Billy Graham, Oral Roberts and dozens of other charismatic speakers display this constantly. What has to be concluded, however, is that for the most part, these affairs do not lead predictably to the type of disturbance that characterizes the hard-rock scene, where property is smashed and destroyed and vandalism takes over. It is probable that if this sort of charismatic speaker did urge the crowd to rush the stage, or knock down the seats and dance on them, these actions would follow. In fact, far worse than that did happen in the name of a grotesque religion in Jonestown, Guyana, under the aegis of the infamous Reverend Jim Jones. The actions of the crowd inexorably follow the attitudes of the charismatic leader, regardless of the subject matter. The actions have nothing to do with morality, religion, paganism or hedonism. They simply have to do with what the charismatic leader of any sort asks for, suggests, implies or demonstrates by his actions, the latter leading to emulation.

The long series of riots and disturbances since that advent of hard rock was clearly discernible and documented, once the pleasing euphoria of Woodstock had passed. Further, riots and disturbances had been admittedly incited in many cases, as Joplin, Hendrix and Morrison made clear. Many other superstars simply admitted to egging on the crowd, or indirectly inspiring violence by their actions on the stage. The smashing up of equipment and instruments onstage in front of excited spectators, many of whom might be in a waking trance state, went a long way in inducing them to follow suit.

Two forces were working simultaneously. The rhythm and beat created the trance state. This alone was not damaging. The attitude, behavior pattern and actions of the superstar laid on *top* of the trance state was what counted. What they suggested created the action that followed on the part of the crowd.

The same applies to a discotheque, where the beat, volume and flashing light parallel the rock concert. The difference is that the disco functions without a dynamic leader with real charisma. The trance state is there, but no one is exerting the power of suggestion, either by action or command.

Much of the problem appeared to lie in many of the hard-rock superstars not realizing their own power of suggestion. They were unconsciously, if not directly, breeding the type of atmosphere where the damage and physical danger took place, and even the young, peer, T-shirt security men were helpless to control the situation.

Although mass hypnosis could explain a lot of what happened inside the hall with the heavy beat, sensory overload, charismatic shamanlike leader, and strobing lights, there remained the question of the major disturbances *before* the concert began—outside the hall. As a test-tube reflecting the preconcert condition across the country, the crowds gathering at the Riverfront Plaza in Cincinnati had experienced turbulent eruptions at several concerts, as exemplified by the Led Zeppelin disturbance, before the doors had opened or the concert had begun. Predictions of future danger and injury at Riverfront were being reported from all sides, especially about the crush to get in the doors. The underlying reasons for this part of the puzzle could be traced more clearly as the hard-rock concert schedule at Riverfront moved on toward the end of the seventies.

By the time 1978 slid in, The Who were firmly set near the top of the rock and roll ladder. Financially, they towered above the most successful corporation executives. The smashed hotel rooms, and the smashed

144

guitars, amplifiers and cars were mainly a thing of the past. Even the lyrics of "My Generation" had lost much of their sting. The line of that durable anthem in which they wished they could die before they get old echoed with a hollow ring; The Who's average age was approaching mid-thirty. Three years of relative inactivity now had given them a chance for reflective reappraisal, although there was plenty to keep them busy.

Two of their films were in full production. One was *The Kids Are Alright,* a documentary of their stormy years put together from old clips and new inserts. The film began with a sequence from an early event in The Who's history, when they appeared on the network show *The Smothers Brothers Comedy Hour,* back in the mid-sixties. The Smothers Brothers were controversial enough on their own. The network brass was uneasy about their antics and their political posture, which was supposed to lean too far to the left for advertisers. The appearance of The Who as guest stars would not enhance the show in the sponsors' eyes.

The Who were not about to muffle their exuberance for the sake of pandering to network ethics. Townshend, Daltrey and Keith Moon came prepared with their arsenal of special effects, which included smoke bombs and the urge to wreck guitars, maim the amplifiers, mutilate the microphones, and add percussion to the drums with the aid of heavy-duty fireworks.

Keith Moon seemed determined to utilize these to the hilt, packing his bass drum with an overdose of explosives. The detonation came during a manic rendition of "My Generation." It succeeded in blasting Moon off his seat, pulverizing a cymbal and lacerating his arm. Not to be outdone, Townshend grabbed a guitar away from Tommy Smothers, and proceeded to decimate it against the studio floor. One *Rolling Stone* reporter rather enigmatically described the scene as "a glimpse of rock and roll as it was always meant to be: a force of elemental anarchy that dispels gloom without denying it exists." And the film's producer Jeff Stein fortified this observation by adding: "It proves that The Who were the greatest rock and roll band in the world." Allowance would have to be made for Stein's position since many outside critics would find the impact of the movie to be just short of total confusion.

Almost completed at this time was The Who's new film, *Quad-rophenia.* It was based on their album of the same name. Although the album appeared first in 1973, the film would not be released until 1979. It would be considered a British counterpart of *American Graffiti*, though without that film's success in America. It would spare none of the details of the lavish violence of the Mods and Rockers on the beaches of Margate and Brighton.

The music from the album on which the film is based ranges from roaring cacophony to poignant, sensitive operatic moments. Since the title reflects the chaotic condition of a personality split into four separate parts, some have speculated that the story represents the four members of The Who, and their emergence from the milieu of the Mods.

The Who acted only as executive producers for the film version of *Quadrophenia*, turning the direction over to a young director named Franc Roddam. Roddam was seizing on the scenes of violence on the Brighton beaches with all the enthusiasm of a herd master for a Merrill Lynch stampede commercial. Even Pete Townshend was slightly disturbed by this. He felt the film should mainly reflect the story of a Mod kid who was lost in the frustration of the times, and who sought some kind of spiritual insight to get him out of the morass.

Townshend was continuing his own search in 1978, fighting his battle against the constant dichotomy and ambivalence within himself. Although he was off drugs altogether, he was still belting down cognac to the point that he was getting drunk without wanting to be. He couldn't figure out for himself why he had espoused violence on the stage and in hotel rooms without feeling guilty afterward. He embraced rock as an almost religious experience, and said once that the only time he felt the joy of rock and roll was when he was on the stage. "When there's an audience," he wrote in a *Rolling Stone* article, "there's salvation. Mixed up in *Quadrophenia* was a study of divine desperation that is at the root of every punk's scream for blood and vengeance. . . . I stare into the future. Nothing that I have ever dreamed of had failed me. So I stare knowing that what I see will be . . . and yet I know that someday my luck will run out."

Though he loved the concerts and the gravitational closeness of the crowds, he hated touring more than ever. He loved and missed his family, and felt physical pain when he was away from them, yet he was fascinated by the extravagant admiration of the groupies. As the well-

146

spring of *Quadrophenia*, he reflected the scattered personality of the protagonist, moving from moods of arrogance, violence and egomania to states of both quiet and noisy desperation.

There was also another problem. Townshend was having increased difficulty with his hearing. The assault of 110 or 120 decibels for well over a decade was beginning to take its toll. He found that he was suffering physical pain in his ears at live concerts, in addition to hearing loss.

Townshend was also aware of the attrition that the stress of rock and roll was exacting from many in the business. The deaths of Brian Jones, Jimi Hendrix, Janis Joplin, Jim Morrison and others combined to make a statement on the stress of the rock scene, and it did not escape him. He often reflected on his own bouts of intemperance, and those of Keith Moon. At one point, Moon had been up to two bottles of brandy and a bottle of champagne a day, and was having a hard time sorting out the difference between creative mischief and aimless mayhem.

Moon had tried medical treatment several times, and had calmed down for a while. But now, in 1978, he seemed to be on the skids again. In spite of putting on some weight, Moon seemed in good spirits as early fall approached. He still would take some two dozen hits of speed, washed down by a fifth of cognac.

Although some of his friends disputed it, Moon claimed to be on the upgrade, denying rumors that he was becoming alcoholic beyond repair. He had been living in Los Angeles for some time in recent months, living a surf life of sorts, and trying his hand at acting in a few rock films. He returned to London, and he claimed that he felt a new sense of maturity and purpose.

As if to substantiate that, he had recently taken over the job of public relations manager for The Who's Shepperton film studio, an ancillary business they hoped to develop. He seemed to take the job seriously, though not without slipping back into a few of his romping gags.

On September 6, 1978, he was the guest of Paul McCartney at a party at a posh restaurant called Peppermint Park. With Moon was Annette Walter-Lax, a model from Sweden and his inseparable mate since his recent divorce. The occasion was a prelude to preview screening of a new film called *The Buddy Holly Story*.

Holly had been a pop star of the 1950's who was credited by many

English groups of the Mersey tradition for supplying them with root material for their own burgeoning growth. The young Texan had been killed in a tragic plane crash in early 1959, but his echoes remained for everyone from the Beatles to Bob Dylan to Eric Clapton. According to David Frost, who sat near him at the party, Moon was affable, complacent and contented.

After the film preview, Moon and Annette went to a night club. Moon seemed lively as ever, not neglecting the generous assortment of drinks available at the bar. The festivities went on until first light. Not long after, Moon and Annette left for the Mayfair flat he was renting. There was talk that he and Annette might soon get married, a hopeful sign to those close to Moon, as his apparent new sense of maturity grew.

Moon was habitually taking a drug called Haminevrin at the time, both as treatment for his problem drinking, and as a tranquilizer. As with everything else, Moon tended to take the drug in excess. Just what he did on going to bed that morning is not known. However, it appeared that Moon not only took a heavy dosage before he got in bed, but also another when he woke up in the morning, and then went back to bed again.

Haminevrin is a drug not fully understood even by the medical profession. It is clearly not meant for long-time use, which Moon had been doing. It is dangerous to take, unless the patient remains in bed. It also has a critically dangerous synergistic effect when combined with alcohol.

At about two in the afternoon, Annette came to wake him. He did not respond. Later, the autopsy confirmed that he had died as a result of an overdose of Haminevrin.

The shock to the remaining members of The Who was immeasurable. To Roger Daltrey, it meant the end of the group. They would never find another drummer to replace him. Entwistle felt it would take more than one drummer to do so. When Pete Townshend went to the studio the following day, he broke down and cried. But he pulled himself together and wrote out a statement that said: "We are more determined than ever to carry on, and we want the spirit of the group, to which Keith contributed so much, to go on—although no human being can take his place."

It took about four months of soul-searching for The Who to find an answer for their drumless aggregation. Townshend was still torn about going back on the road, in spite of the urgings of Daltrey and Entwistle. A drummer named Kenny Jones had worked with them on several recent recordings, and seemed to have a lot of fire, but none of the problems, of the late Keith Moon. He was a veteran, having made his reputation as a drummer with the group the Small Faces. In January of 1979, he was drafted into the band, along with keyboardist Rabbit Bundrick.

There had been a long hiatus in live shows. The Who had not toured in the U.S. since 1976. In spite of Townshend's ambivalence about touring, it looked as if The Who would once more assemble their five tons of electronic equipment and hit the road before 1979 ended. They would, as a matter of course, hit Larry Magid's Spectrum in Philadelphia. From there, Magid would see that they moved on to Cincinnati's Riverfront, where houses were selling out on a regular basis—if the draw was good enough.

In Cincinnati, the duel between safety officials and the Coliseum's Brian Heckin was still continuing, with on and off intermissions over the months. At one point, Fire Chief Bert Lugannani had written to Safety Director Richard Castellini: "It may be appropriate to have another meeting with Mr Heekin, but past experience has been that very little happened until we made a citation. Conditions improved for a while, then regressed to business as usual."

It was obvious that all the steps taken by the city officials to control the violations were getting nowhere. They were especially concerned about the upcoming concert at Riverfront Coliseum on September 14 by the group called Kiss.

Kiss consisted of American rock superstars with literally a million dollars' worth of stage paraphernalia, an arsenal of blow torches and smoke bombs timed to let go throughout the concert. They were the ultimate commercialization of the rock violence movement. They used heavy makeup and grotesque costumes that, with their high-decibel music, projected the image of four vampires loose in a boiler factory. Their message was shock—especially to parents of the younger teenybop crowd they appealed to the most. At one point, a Gallup poll ranked them quantitatively as the number one rock group in the world. They had none of the poetry of The Who, and their attitude toward any kind of cultural classic was expressed by a quotation of Gene Simmons, cofounder of the group, to *Rolling Stone* in 1977, "Shakespeare is shit."

Included in the group's repertoire was Simmons' ability to shoot fire out of his mouth, along with the occasional vomiting of what looked like blood. Their image was carefully designed to reflect scenes of sex, violence, destruction and death, although with a certain innocence that softened it for the younger set. They had sold a total of twenty million albums. When cofounder Paul Stanley started to make up songs for the group, he knew three chords: A, D and E.

In a letter to the acting city manager about the forthcoming Kiss concert, Forrest Buckley, president of the Cincinnati Fire Fighter Union, continued his warnings:

> In that the Kiss group performed here about a year ago, and considering the numerous violations of the Fire Code that occurred during that performance, the Cincinnati Fire Fighters Union hereby requests that you order the use of off-duty Fire Division personnel to ensure the life safety of the patrons attending the concert.

Buckley had begun his protests back in 1976, three years earlier. He felt strongly that the management of the Coliseum and the promoters were not carrying out their responsibilities, and that if they didn't, something was going to happen. To Buckley, the crux of the matter lay in festival seating, and apparently nothing was being done to eliminate it.

The Kiss concert came and went on schedule, the week after Buckley wrote his letter. The extra off-duty fire inspectors were not hired. But the pyrotechnical displays of both the superstars and the audience were there. A plethora of angel dust was circulated, and Lt. Dale Menkhaus had his hands full.

After the crowd had entered, and the Kiss concert had begun, the plaza was strewn with so many broken bottles, there was no place to step. Many never made it into the concert. They sat or lay outside the doors on the plaza, heavily stoned. Whatever open space there was between the broken bottles, there seemed to be vomit. Two of the spectators jumped from the plaza level to the street below. One lay there laughing, with both legs telescoped in compound fractures. The other was dead.

There were two and a half months for the Coliseum to recover from the Kiss concert before The Who came into Cincinnati on its 1979 tour. Not having seen the group since 1975, the fans of The Who had sealed their allegiance by the 90-minute sellout of Who tickets, six weeks in advance.

When the first clusters of the crowd gathered on the frigid plaza that December afternoon in 1979, The Who tickets were a scalper's delight and gate-crasher's envy. The Who were back in town after a four-year absence, and that was what counted. By the time the crowd had built up and the tidal action had separated Deborah Shumate from her sister, Brant and Becky Ross from each other, and Jim Krumrei from Peter Bowes, the suffocating pressure of the crowd had replaced the joy of holding a ticket.

PART IV

DATE

DECEMBER 3, 1979

TIME

7:00 P.M. TO 10:00 P.M.

PLACE

THE PLAZA AGAIN

THE

disaster that was about to take place swept in like a sudden squall at sea, with no time to reef the sails, or even to think. The preconditions had been set in a continuous pattern over the last fifteen years. There had been predictions, conjectures and astute observations as to why such a disaster could take place, but they were academic. They would be easier to understand in retrospect.

Jeff Waddle, the journalism student at the University of Cincinnati, arrived on the plaza with his date Marilyn, at about 6:00 in the evening. He came there with certain misgivings. They arose from his experience at the Led Zeppelin concert in April 1977, more than two years before.

Jeff had also been to The Who concert at the Riverfront Coliseum back in 1975. He had watched them as they drew the crowd into their hands, blasting their songs in mounting crescendo. When they wanted the crowd to stand, they never had to ask for it. The blinding stage lights would flash in brilliance and color, and the crowd would rise to its feet, hands pumping overhead, screaming: "Awright! Awright! Awright!" —and ending with a gasping, satisfied "Yeaaaaah!" The atmosphere was contagious, the frenzy would grow and thousands would be fused into an amorphous rock and roll brotherhood that transcended the crush, the sweat and the bruised ribs.

Yes, the grass, the Quaaludes, the Angel Dust, the LSD, the speed,

155

the smack were there—although in reasonable moderation. The question that nagged Waddle was: Was the higher energy response a great release and safety valve, or was it a reaction to the decline and fall of a civilization?

No one knew the answer. It was the attraction—in this case The Who—that brought the people into the Riverfront Plaza in this sort of mood. On the night of the December 3 concert, Jeff Waddle and Marilyn found themselves thirty or forty feet away from the bank of doors, and like everyone else, shivering in the cold. Whatever was to happen, Jeff determined not to let himself get in the panic situation he had faced at the Led Zeppelin concert. He was worried, too, that Marilyn might think the less of him if he betrayed his fears, which were considerable.

He was relieved to find that the crowd on the plaza appeared to be calm. Since he and Marilyn were at the back of the crowd, he got none of the trapped feeling he had experienced before. The people near him were hanging loose, cheerful enough. They seemed reluctant to get packed in tightly, and even those up front showed little of the intense restlessness of the Zeppelin experience. Jeff's anxieties were reflected in his constantly looking up at the Western-Southern Life digital clock across the throughway. When the clock showed 6:30, Jeff noticed a half-dozen high school kids near them, jostling and pushing each other. But they were in good spirits, and singing The Who favorite "Can You See the Real Me?" A few minutes later, someone started a chant: "Who! Who! Who! Who!" It was harmless enough, but for some reason it was a little scary for Jeff. He could feel a spontaneous energy rising from the crowd, and began to read an intense restlessness in the eyes of the people surrounding him. In less than a few minutes, he noticed that he and Marilyn were slowly beginning to be clamped in by other arrivals on the plaza. Jeff began to feel a squeeze around him that hadn't been there before. He was still fighting back the feeling of panic he had inherited from his previous bout with the crowd, but continued to try to hide it from Marilyn.

A few moments later, a young man in front of him pushed a friend, knocking him sharply back into Marilyn. He apologized cheerfully enough, but Marilyn's anger rose. Jeff knew that she could see the nervousness in his eyes, much as he tried to hide it.

PART IV

By 6:30, Jeff could barely see the end of the crowd at the back. The noise of the crowd had risen until it was hard to hear himself talk. "This is going to get crazy," he called to Marilyn. "We've got to want to see a band awful bad to go through this."

Marilyn was beginning to agree. Already their feet were being stepped on, and Jeff was glad he had insisted on them both wearing heavy boots. As the squeeze grew greater, Jeff finally took Marilyn's arm and said: "We've got to get out while we've still got the chance."

When they started to inch back out, he heard a voice yell, "Wow— we've got more room." Jeff was glad to give it up.

In spite of their position near the back of the crowd, it took almost five minutes to elbow their way out of the jam. When they finally burst out, the temperature seemed to change from boiling hot to biting cold. They hadn't realized how much they were sweating, and their wet clothing accentuated the chill.

They stepped up on some concrete benches, where they could get a broad perspective of the crowd. More spectators were spilling across the foot bridge from the stadium, a tapestry of faces illuminated by the full moon and the plaza lights. From this perspective, Jeff had an eerie, unreal feeling.

From the vantage point of the concrete benches, Jeff began to notice the waves of the crowd, as the digital clock showed 7:00. He could only visualize them as actual ocean waves that seemed to be controlled by a multidirectional spring. The scene now reflected a literal sea of people, roaring as well as swelling like ocean waves. As the crowd tilted toward the river, a roar would come up. "Whoooaaaa!" Then the side of the crowd by the river would push back and the recoil would spill the waves in the other direction, and the "Whoooaaa!" would rise again. Individual shouts and cries continued to be swallowed up. But Jeff noticed a strange thing. When he stepped down from the bench to the plaza level, there seemed to be no disturbance and the dull roar sounded friendly and jocular. He felt relieved. The scene was far gentler than that of the Zeppelin concert, and for that he was grateful. He resolved, however, that he would not take one step forward until the scene was looser and the crowd had thinned out. From where he stood, he had no idea that people like Debbie, Mike, Carolyn, Jim Krumrei or the Rosses were literally fighting for their lives in an embroilment they could not escape, and praying that the doors would open soon to get them out of their intense misery.

At the same time that Jeff Waddle was studying the waves of the crowd out on the plaza, Sgt. Jack Basham was inside the Coliseum, trying to locate promoter Cal Levy in the cavernous auditorium. It was some minutes after 7:00 and the musicians had just finished their sound check and were leaving the stage. Basham found Levy down near the stage area. Levy asked if he could have a few more moments to check a camera. But after his brief talk with Menkhaus, Basham was concerned about the mood of the crowd, even though up to this point, it had appeared to be placid. Basham suggested to Levy that he complete his camera check as the crowd was coming in. Then he headed toward the lobby of the main entrance to supervise the opening of the doors. On the way, he reached Captain Galbraith, of the private security force, on his radio. There was a problem with Basham's radio and his signal was being partially broken up.

Galbraith in turn passed the word along to the lobby, where ten security guards from the private force were waiting his instructions under the supervision of Lt. Floyd Bridges, also of the private Coliseum police. Back inside the lobby from the main banks of doors some twenty feet, were nine turnstiles manned by ticket takers who waited with the security guards for the inevitable rush that would follow. The view from inside, out toward the crowd, was much the same as any other hard-rock concert: a tightly pressed crowd, inevitable elbowing and intense pressure from behind. The faces on the spectators reflected anger and restlessness.

What had to be guarded against was the sudden overflowing of the lobby section. There would be an endless crush following on the heels of the first of the crowd that entered. The turnstiles could only handle a limited number at the time and if people were smashed against them, there would be a hopeless tangle as the lobby overflowed.

Ed Linedecker, the supervisor of the ticket takers, was well aware of this. Consulting with Floyd Bridges, they decided that they would open three of the doors on the northwest side, and two on the southwest, nearest the river. As the lobby filled up, the crowd would somehow have to be held back. When both Sergeant Basham and Captain Galbraith arrived, Bridges lined his ten private security guards up, and assigned

158

them to various doors and positions in the lobby. The time was somewhere between 7:05 and 7:15—no one is quite sure. What is sure was
that the press outside was so great that when the guards attempted to
push open the doors out into the crowd they could barely do so.

To force the doors open required enormous counter pressure. Not an
inch could be gained without sacrificing what little space remained in
the crowd. This meant further compression, while the doors were being
squeezed open. The scene was all too familiar, from the previous
concerts. This created the illusion of the commonplace, and a sense of
false complacency on the part of both the crowd and security. It had
always looked worse than it was in the past. This time was bound to be
the same.

Guard Mike Spoess put his enormous frame into the job as soon as he
got the signal to open the doors. At every concert, he looked on the
crowd as if it were his own kids. He did not like the looks of the situation
just outside his door, although he had actually seen worse in the past.

Meanwhile, several other guards were able to get doors open, at the
cost of further squeezing. The crowd burst in like a flash flood, swamping the lobby. Some of the turnstiles became clogged and inoperable.
Those who could, leaped or slid over them. There was only one thing
the security guards could do: try to hold back the flow and close some of
the doors again until the lobby could get untangled, and the nine
turnstiles could function. Ticket takers, half protected by metal stanch-
ions, took what tickets they could. Many spectators went through still
holding onto their tickets.

There was the pushing and shoving that everyone had now come to
expect as a matter of course. The pressure from the crowd of some eight
or ten thousand was relentless. People squirted through the door like
pumpkin seeds, many of them carried by the momentum of the crowd
without their feet even touching the ground. As they spilled in, they
were propelled against the backs of those who already filled the lobby. Others were tangled in the metal turnstiles so that they could not
turn.

Mike Spoess and the other security guards found that it was almost
impossible to stem the flow until the spectators could clear through the
turnstiles. It was like trying to hold back an avalanche, squeezed into a
tight chasm. Those who were carried into the lobby with their feet off the

ground had no control whatever. Some were carried like driftwood in through the doors where they stumbled or fell face forward.

Meanwhile, Richard Morgan continued to broadcast over the PA. He urged the crowd to split up and enter through the north doors. But there was trouble there. Sergeant Basham, still having problems with his walkie-talkie, learned that some of the crowd was trying to break through some of the closed doors on the north side, where there was a minimum of security guards and police, and less of a crowd. Basham was able to make radio contact with Post 7, manned by Officers Steve Kramer and Charles Klug. They were out on the plaza near the main doors, unable to get anywhere near the doors themselves because of the tight compaction of the crowd. Over the heads of the people, they noticed a struggle to open the doors outward against the tightly packed mass. When the doors finally were opened, they watched the crowd surge forward but were unable to do anything to check it. Not even a battalion of police could have done anything.

At 7:13, Officer Kramer caught Basham's weak signal on his own walkie-talkie, and offered to help. Basham asked him to relay the information to Lieutenant Menkhaus about the problem at the north doors, and possibly send some more officers to the trouble spot. Almost before he had time to snap his walkie-talkie back in his belt, Officer Kramer heard a crash of glass on an isolated set of doors toward the river on the south side of the arena. Part of the crowd saw this as an open door, broke away from the mass and rushed toward it. They began pouring through the hole left by the broken glass. Kramer and Klug ran toward it to try to hold back the crowd. For the first time in the evening, it looked as if someone might get seriously hurt.

Frank Wood, now general manager of FM station WEBN, was admitted into the Coliseum private entrance, away from the crowd, shortly after seven o'clock. He was on his way up to the Beehive Club to have dinner with Larry Magid, the Philadelphia rock promoter.

Before he went up to the Beehive, at the top of the Coliseum, Wood sauntered out on the lower ramp to take a look at the auditorium. The Who had just finished their sound check, and were moving off the stage. The crowd was beginning to file into the arena seats and the open-floor area around the bandstand.

Wood was a perceptive analyst of audiences beginning with Wood-stock and continuing on through his radio career. His FM station was singularly successful in Cincinnati, catering to the album-oriented rock listeners, rather than those who went for the Top Forty singles. As such, his station was preferred by many advertisers because the profile of WEBN's listeners consisted of a higher income and slightly older age-bracket, with more sophisticated tastes in the rock spectrum. Wood could pass easily as a partner in a Wall Street law firm in his dark, conservative suit and precisely-tied necktie.

Frank Wood had not often been in an auditorium when a festival-seating crowd had filed in. He was a little surprised to see that they were so orderly and well-dressed, matching in effect the image of his FM radio station listeners. Only about 3,500 of the seats were reserved; the remaining seats of nearly 15,000 were up for grabs, but the crowd seemed still relaxed and in a jovial mood.

From the dining table at the Beehive Club, Magid and Wood could see the audience through a large glass window, continuing to file in. Both agreed that it looked as if the concert was off to a good start. They would have the better part of an hour for a leisurely dinner, before the lights dimmed and the sound of music came up. To them, as well as to the police, there was still nothing to indicate that the biggest disaster in rock history was about to take place.

As Wood and Magid began their dinner shortly after seven, Sergeant McAlpin was down on the street level, underneath the crowd on the plaza, with the four officers assigned to him. They were having a relatively easy time. There were very few, if any, potential gate-crashers in evidence, and the main activity was in the shouts of the street vendors hawking T-shirts emblazoned with the logo of The Who. As at nearly every rock concert, these were popular items. They sold at three or four times the value of an ordinary T-shirt, and were worn with pride in high school corridors as a status symbol. Along with the uniformed, street-level patrol were two plainclothesmen, Terry Meiners and Dan Henson of the Cincinnati police. They were assigned for the sole purpose of checking the vendors' licenses, for it was a common practice for bootleg T-shirt vendors from out of town to flood the approaches to the Co-liseum without a city license. Along Second Street and Broadway, the late comers still continued to parade toward the arena. But as they filed by the street policemen on the way to the plaza ramps, they appeared to be relaxed and complacent.

Content with the situation below, Meiners and Henson decided to check the upper level, over the stadium, to see if there might be any bootleg vendors in that area.

Meanwhile, Officers Kramer and Klug were having a problem keeping the crowd away from the broken door, off to the side of the main entrance. Several spectators were breaking out of the main crowd, drenched with sweat, tattered and worn, and trying to get in out of the cold. They were ready to brave any broken glass to get inside the building. At 7:20, Kramer got a radio message through to Sergeant Lamping, still by his squad car behind the crowd, and outside of it. Lamping responded immediately. "One-sixty-one here. Copy. There is little we can do. We don't have enough policemen here—they haven't let this crowd in yet, and there must be eight thousand people standing on the outside trying to get in. It's the Coliseum's problem to take care of the door."

Although some of the doors of the main entrance had opened, it was impossible to see this from the back of the crowd. Further, the doors were opening and closing like flood gates. Some of them were pressed closed again by the squeeze of the crowd and remained that way. Other doors continued to be opened and closed by the security guards to try to hold up the flow until the lobby log jam could be cleared.

Coliseum Manager Morgan's voice, distorted and muffled, continued over the loudspeakers to implore the crowd to back up, to be patient, to move to the north doors. But the crowd was now so deep and wide that it reached across the plaza, all the way to the stadium footbridge, packed into a solid mass of humanity. The pressure against those in front was cumulative. There was no rush. There was only a relentless squeeze. The shape of the crowd was like the upper part of a giant hour glass, with only a few grains at a time able to slip through at the narrow waist that led into the lobby.

Kramer and Klug watched a few of those who were able to extricate themselves. They squeezed out and stumbled toward the wall by the river, out of breath and sweating profusely. But in a few moments, they caught their breath and were ready to try again. Few audible yells or screams were heard above the noise of the crowd.

Sergeant Basham, in an effort to assess the situation from outside, slipped out the police door, and moved behind the crowd to check the mood. There were the shouts, the dull murmuring, the normal crowd noises, but there was nothing markedly unruly evident. In fact, there was a complete lack of hostility between the crowd and the police. The broken door, in a section away from the main doors and crowds, was being taken care of and was well guarded. Although the movement through the main doors was painfully slow, it still appeared to be normal enough for the usual rock concert.

After a quick survey outside in the plaza, Basham moved back inside, and made his way to the lobby to check the flow from that point of view. At least one thing comforted him; none of the ugly action of the Led Zeppelin concert was anywhere to be seen.

If it weren't for Mike, Deborah Shumate was thinking, *I'd be dead by now.* From early afternoon now, until after seven, she had been gulping spasmodically for breath while Mike would rhythmically push his elbow out, then relax and start again, almost as if his arms were breathing. She tried to stop herself from crying because it was using up precious air. But she could not stop. Her sister Carolyn was still nowhere to be seen. *God,* she thought, *Carolyn doesn't have Mike to protect her. What is happening to her? Why couldn't she have held on to us?*

By now the swirling motion of the crowd had brought Deborah and Mike down to within five or ten feet of the doors. They had heard the band's sound-check, that seemed to continue for half an hour, but now it had stopped. Surely, they would open the doors by now.

But then another terror gripped her. What would happen when they actually opened the doors? The crush, the pressure would be bound to increase. She was filled with a new dread, worse than before. But was that possible? How could anything be more frightening than what she was experiencing now? In front of her, a girl suddenly slipped out of sight. Mike saw the girl, and grabbed her shoulders in a vise-grip, pulling her up to the surface again. Yet there seemed to be no space for him to do it in. All through the hour, this had been happening. Not just Mike, but others around her were trying to help each other, in spite of the desperation, in spite of the compression. People were actually helping each other, when there seemed to be no way in the world they could do so. Everyone near her was trying to back up, to keep the people in front of the doors from being crushed against them. But it was impossible. How could anyone back up with the pressure of what must be 10,000 people behind him?

It was as if it were a giant room filled with accordions. All the accordions were being squeezed from the rear of the room, toward the front. The bellows were pressed together by a tremendous force from behind them. This enabled more accordions to enter, as the compression allowed more room. But if an accordion up front tried to expand back again—as a human trying to inhale—it would face insurmountable pressure. The air would be expelled from it, but there was no way to take in air until the back-pressure was relieved.

The situation faced by Deborah, Mike and others up forward in the crush was not unlike this. With the crowd from behind leaning in with ten or twenty pounds of pressure, it could create a cumulative force of up to 600 pounds if the crowd were thirty deep—which it was in some places. The human lungs—like accordions—could expel air easily under these conditions. But to expand again to take air in against this force was a gargantuan job.

Deborah tried to reason why the ones far behind them didn't realize the situation. But then she thought there was no way for them to tell what was going on in front of them. Before the swirl had brought her so far forward near the doors, she herself had had no idea what it could be like up front. She had not even tried to get close. She and Mike, she realized, had not moved themselves at all to this position. They had floated there, sometimes with feet off the ground. It was a helpless, undirected drifting.

More minutes went by—or was it hours? In between her gulps of air, Deborah became convinced that they were never going to open the doors. If they haven't opened them by now, she thought, they have no idea of ever opening them.

Another girl by Mike started sliding downward. Another time he grabbed her, pulled her up, and used his shoulder to hold her slightly above the crowd. For a moment, he couldn't get his arms back to frame a small air hole for Deborah. She thought she was going to pass out, almost wished that she would. But somehow, he did it, and she began getting more spasms of breath.

Now Deborah, almost in a nightmarish dream, began analyzing why they were holding up opening the doors. A thought struck her: The security guards in the lobby had been through this so many times before at rock concerts. They thought that the crying girls around her was an exaggeration, a ploy to get in to the concert early. Then she suddenly thought of Mike's brother, Norman. They were supposed to meet him at the entrance. What an irony! He was just the opposite stature of Mike. Strong, but thin and wiry, under five foot five. If he was there in the crowd, how could he survive? Then there was Mike's sister, Mary, and her husband. The whole congenial family was supposed to meet and enjoy the concert. What would happen to them?

She began sobbing again, as the press of the packed crowd moved her even closer to the door. She could see a tall, beefy, security guard there through the glass of the door. But why wasn't he opening the doors? Didn't he see the girls around her crying and trying to yell for help?

Just inside the door, guard Mike Spoess did see the girls crying. He was worried when the order to open the doors did not seem to come at seven. He was to man two doors up near the wall of the northwest bank, and he was already figuring the strategy to get the kids in as fast as possible and safely on their way into the auditorium. He had beside him a large, heavy metal bar that he could hook in at the top of the door, so that the crowd wouldn't accidentally push it back closed again. This had happened before, and he was ready for it. He also was planning what he could do to open the doors—which had to swing outward—so that they would not increase the pressure on those just in front of him. He was figuring that he would hold the men back until some of the girls got in, for they were obviously less able to put up with the crush. Then there would be the problem of holding back the crowd after the lobby filled to capacity. With his six-foot frame, he was ready for that, but he did not like it. He knew that the front-line crowds would not be in control of their movements.

The first and most important job was to get the kids just back far enough so he could open the door. He would treat them just like his own, no matter what happened. He set himself, ready for the crush, and waited for the command to open the door.

ARE THE KIDS ALL RIGHT?

From his vantage point on the stone bench on the edge of the crowd, Jeff Waddle stood with Marilyn watching the waves of the crowd. The clock on the tower read a few minutes after seven. The images from his experience at the Led Zeppelin concert still stayed heavily with him. He could not get the terrified faces from that concert out of his mind. And now he was seeing them again, this time from a distance. He saw a few of the concert-goers come out of the crowd, panting for breath, sweat pouring off them in spite of the arctic wind. Finally, he saw the door open, half obscured by the heads of the crowd. It seemed to open half-way, then falter. He could hear moans and sighs over the dull, constant roar of the people that massed in front of his perch. There must have been nearly 10,000 of them, he figured. That would have to be a cumulative total of over a million pounds of humanity. He was frankly glad he was not among them, whether he got into the concert or not.

Jeff watched an enormous surge forward, as if a tidal wave were hitting the front of the building. Then he could partially see other doors opening, falteringly, as the doors pushed into the crowd. Then, after the forward-moving tidal wave, came a sweeping backlash, reaching all the way to the perimeter of the mass.

Jeff turned to Marilyn and said, "I'm not going to get us in that crush tonight for a million dollars."

Almost at the moment Jeff Waddle said this, Brant Ross was lying on the ground, trapped by the pressure of other bodies on top of him. He heard a series of shrill screams and muffled yells near him. Someone above him was yelling but barely audible: "We've got people down over here. Back up and give us room! We've got people down and hurt!"

There were more muffled yells, as he struggled to get up. He was soaked with a clammy sweat, his clothes sticking to his body. The more he struggled to get out from under those above him, the tighter the vise seemed to be. His long underwear and corduroys had burst through at the knees, which were being ground into the cement beneath him. Breathing was getting harder, and each time he strained to pull his locked feet out, he felt able to breathe less.

But he had to get out, to free himself and find Becky. He comforted himself that she had surely made her way out of the crowd. People had been helpful in starting her on the way out. People were being helpful now. They were trying to back away, to give him a hand. There was no malice from those behind in exerting the pressure. They simply didn't know what was going on in front of them. He felt no resentment toward the crowd. But he wondered why the police weren't clearing the mess. He wondered more about how he could continue to live under the crush above him.

Almost miraculously, he felt the pressure lift off his legs. He was able to get up on his hands and knees. A circle of people around him were helping to extricate the pile he was under. They worked desperately, lifting others, and helping him to his feet. They finally helped him regain his balance, and he stood up. He gulped for air, and couldn't believe the intense heat created by the tight pocket of others around him.

Then, straining to look ahead of him, he noticed that he was considerably further away from the door than when he first arrived. Standing up, he forced his feet apart, trying to figure a way to get himself out of the crowd. He turned sideways, squirmed, and was able to move back a few feet. Then he picked up momentum, and gradually found himself being expelled outward, as if by osmosis. The water had parted—but immediately closed in tightly after him.

The minute he got to the edge of the crowd, he understood why the police weren't cued into the trouble brewing up forward. From the back of the crowd, everyone appeared passive and quiet, with a calmness that belied the struggle he had just gone through. If people had told him then that there was trouble up ahead in the crowd, he would have thought they were crazy.

Brant made two quick swings around the crowd to look for Becky. He could not find her anywhere. He had mentioned an alternate meeting place, beside the flagpole over by the river, but she was not there. Against the wall there were the others who had fought their way out of the mass. They were leaning back against it, ragged, exhausted and battle-weary.

But all he wanted to see was Becky. He saw a lamp post beside him, and immediately took off his parka and gloves, and laid them on the ground. He had climbed the ropes in gym class, and still kept in shape from his days as a track man in school by workouts three and four times a week. He rubbed his hands, squatted down a little, and leapt.

The bronze pole was cold and slippery. But he made it to the top, then

167

hooked an arm over the cross brace that supported one of the five lamps on the pole.

From the top of the pole, he could see that several doors were open, but the crowd was moving through them at a snail's pace. Below him, he could see the slow, swirling motion of the mass, and the domino effect that had sent him sprawling. With their feet inevitably pressed together, there was no support that anyone in the crowd could count on, except for the backs of the people immediately in front. Near the doors, the motion of the crowd seemed to be like that of a stopped-up sink.

There was still no sign of Becky. He was hoping that at least she might see him. He couldn't stop a thought of horror that kept gripping him: What if Becky, with her small, delicate size, had not made it out of the crowd? Then he comforted himself. Since she was nowhere to be seen, she *must* have been fed up with the scene, and must have made her way back to the car in the parking lot to wait for him.

He slid rapidly down the pole, grabbed his jacket and gloves and headed toward the stadium parking lot.

Just about the moment that Peter Bowes disappeared into the crowd from his sight, Jim Krumrei noticed that two doors at the main entrance were opening. Jim's relief was tempered by the fact that the crowd had to move backward to let the doors open, so that the squeeze was intensified. He could feel his chest pressed inward, so that breathing was becoming impossible. Then he could see that one of the doors was closing again because of pressure from the people in front of it. This in turn slowed the flow that had already started into the entrance, and again the pressure increased from all sides. The one door now open did little or nothing to ease the crowding.

Jim fought desperately for air, head and nose pointed to the sky. The more he tried, the less air he could get into his lungs. Slowly, very slowly, he began to lose consciousness. He felt himself slipping to the ground. Then suddenly, he blacked out.

About thirty feet away from him, another group from Wyoming High School was going through the same terrifying experience. Rick Rauh, a classmate of Jim and Peter, watched the two doors open, and saw one of them forced closed, to his dismay. His glasses had steamed up, and when he took them off, he couldn't get his hands back to put them in his pocket. His position in the crowd was shifted so often, he couldn't keep track of where he was. Somehow, he was gravitating slowly toward the door without any motion on his part.

He saw Peter Bowes appear near him, and was surprised because he knew that Peter had entered the crowd far over on the other side. Both of them suddenly noticed to their shock and surprise that there was a pile of people in front of them, near the open door. Seconds before this, Rick had been totally unaware of it. The pile had been completely screened from view on all sides, obscured by the crowd, and unsuspected. Since the melee was so near the open door, it slowed the forward motion of those behind it, who were trying to detour around it to reach the door. It was a pile-up like a giant football scrimmage line.

Moving without volition, at the tidal mercy of the crush behind him, Rick saw that he was being inexorably propelled straight toward the pileup. Peter was just in front of him. Both watched as they floated toward the pile, helpless to do anything about it. In moments, they were right next to it, on the edge. Behind them, the pressure continued without pause. In only a matter of seconds, Rick knew he was going to fall.

Although the crowd still continued to appear placid enough at 7:30, Lieutenant Menkhaus was not pleased with the obviously slow flow into the sporadically opened and closed doors. The reasons for the erratic movement of the doors was obvious. When the lobby was packed to capacity, the flow had to be stopped or the choke-up inside the lobby, between the doors and the turnstiles, would be unmanageable. There was also the problem of the crowd itself inadvertently closing the doors, which then had to be forced open against the pressure. Although he had no authority inside the Coliseum, he knew that more doors had to be opened, and quickly.

From his position out on the plaza behind the crowd, Lieutenant Menkhaus called on his radio to ask Sergeant Basham to see that more doors were opened and manned.

But radio contact was impossible. Menkhaus went immediately to a private side door, and entered the Coliseum to find manager Richard Morgan, to request that additional doors be opened. According to

169

Menkhaus Morgan explained again that the doors had been a little late in opening because of the sound check, and that he had been obligated to keep the doors closed until it was completed. Menkhaus also explained that local promoter Cal Levy joined them, and explained the delay in opening doors in the same way. When Menkhaus pressed for the opening of additional doors, Morgan pointed out that there were no additional ticket takers available. According to Menkhaus, he then suggested that perhaps ushers could be used, but Morgan reportedly said he was unable to do this because of union contracts. Opening the doors without ticket takers would invite gate-crashers, who in turn would overflow the auditorium and create another safety problem.

Frustrated, Lieutenant Menkhaus went back out on the plaza to try to figure out how to handle a backed-up crowd of 18,000 with the twenty-five officers under his command.

Some time between 7:15 and 7:30, a door opened several feet in front of Deborah Shumate. Her prediction came true. She could feel an enormous crush swelling behind her back that jammed both Mike and her up against the people in front of them. Mike Shumate was holding onto her, steering her toward the door, bracing himself against the edge of it, turning to help several other girls to sweep through the opening and into the lobby. In spite of his husky frame, his back was crunched against the door's edge, and he cried out in pain. Deborah, just inside the door was helpless to get him in farther. Then suddenly she saw Mike's brother Norman, just outside the entrance.

With his small and slight build, he was being pinned back against another door, wedged between the side of the girl whose chest was being crushed by the door. Mike wrenched himself free of the pressure, and held the door back far enough for the girl to free herself, then turned to try to hold Norman.

Norman's face was now squashed tightly against the glass, pinched between it and the building. His arm was caught between the edge of the door and the building wall, and he was screaming for help to get out. The jam of spectators in the doorway was so tight that even Mike's strength could not budge it. Norman's arm felt as if it were being ripped out of its socket. He could feel and hear the glass of the door, as if it were ready to crack. *If it goes*, he was thinking, *I'll never live through it.*

PART IV

He tried to fight the pressure of the door with his free arm, but it was helpless. Then Mike braced himself, and was able to bend the door back just enough for Norman to escape and plunge through it into the lobby.

Deborah was being pulled with the tide through the lobby, toward the turnstiles. Mike waved her to go on through, while he began yelling for Carolyn. He held his position against the flow in the lobby. Deborah, also crying out for Carolyn, found herself propelled through the turnstiles. All she could think of was Carolyn. Mike was able to yell above the crowd to tell her to go inside the arena, to get out of the crowd. He would find her inside after he found Carolyn. Dazed, she followed his instructions. Mike stood his ground, squeezing through the lobby, still calling for Carolyn, but all he could see was an endless mass of people streaming by him.

Brant Ross, after his futile search from the top of the lamp pole, approached the parking space, reminding himself that it was often inevitable that people got separated during nearly every rock concert melee. It would be logical that Becky had retreated to the car in order to recuperate from the intensity of the crush. He was pushing down any thoughts of anxiety, and even preparing himself against it if he did not find her in the car.

In the semidarkness, he approached the parking space, went up to the car, and looked in. Becky was not there. He looked inside to see if her purse or gloves were around; perhaps she had just stepped away from the car a moment. They were not there; the car was just as he had left it.

But he still would not give in to his anxiety. He trotted back across the bridge to find the crowd still moving slowly in to the entrances, still tight and compact, but no sign of any great disorder.

He continued to swing in a pendulum motion, back and forth behind the crowd, reassuring himself that he would still find Becky.

Jim Krumrei slowly came back to consciousness. He had no idea what time it was. He found himself sprawled on the ground, pinned there by several people above him. But somewhere in the darkness he found he could breathe. He struggled to move, to extricate himself, but it was impossible. Then suddenly, he felt a weight move from his legs. He groped to his feet, and stood up. Then his feet left the ground again, but he was held up by the people around him. An open door was just in

171

front of him. He was swept toward it, like a canoe shooting down rapids. In seconds, he squirted through the door.

Not far from where Jim Krumrei had lain on the ground, Rick Rauh and Peter Bowes were still slowly being carried toward the pile near the other open door. They were being pressed on all sides by the avalanche of people surrounding them. Rick saw with horror the edge of the pile loom directly in front of him. Those already down were reaching up to others who tried to lift them. Instead, more people were pulled into the mass.

Just in front of him, he saw Peter's feet touch the edge of the pile. Then Peter fell on it. Rick reached down and yanked hard on Peter's arm. Rick pulled up with all his strength, and suddenly, Peter was on his feet. Then the avalanche behind them squeezed tighter. Both Peter and Rick fell into the pile again.

From then on, everything became blurred for Rick Rauh. He lost sight of Peter. At first Rick wasn't pinned down. He was on top of the pile. There were screams of "Help me! Help me!" that seemed to come from all around him. He was beginning to grope toward getting on his feet again, backing off from the people underneath him. There seemed to be a little room to maneuver for a moment. A girl was pushed toward him by the endless pressure from the rear, and he fell backwards over her. He landed on the cement, legs up. But as quickly they were pinned. Another girl fell on his chest. He was gripped in panic. He screamed for help, and lifted his hand upward. Other hands tried to help him, but it was useless. With the girl on his chest pressing harder, he could hardly breathe at all now. He regained some of his composure, turned his head to the side, and found little airways in between people's legs that way.

In five minutes of gasping, Rick finally got enough strength to push the girl carefully to one side. He lifted her as much as he could, and sat her next to him. Their feet were still pinned, but they were able to sit upright. The girl begged him not to get up, since she felt she would slip down again if he did. Behind them, the avalanche still moved toward the doors. The irony remained that few, if any, could tell that such a fire storm was raging except those in the immediate area, and they could do nothing about it. The second irony was that scenes like this were so commonplace that they had come to be expected at almost any hard-rock concert.

172

PART IV

It was not long after the doors on the southwest side had opened that Lt. Floyd Bridges of the private security force saw trouble brewing in front of two of the doors in his area. It had happened at many concerts before, and each time the security guards at the doors had been able to untangle a pile in the entrance ways. The problem was back-pressure. The kids were moving toward him, toward the entrance like ships floating toward the narrow entrance of a lock. The first pile up near the door began building and Bridges, along with his assistant supervisor, Albert St. John, rushed to the doorway to begin pulling in the victims.

Karen Essel, a female security guard at the door next to them, was experiencing the same trouble. She dove into the doorway to help untangle a mass of arms and legs, working furiously and with some success. Helping the guards were several kids, who tugged and pulled valiantly bringing the spectators in, and turning back to help.

Outside the doors, the cries for help were barely audible. But the inexorable pressure of the crowd made those in the forefront impotent to save either the others or themselves. Dozens of them were moving toward the entrance with their feet off the ground, with no control whatever of their movements. The guards themselves were going through a spectrum of terror, fear, concern, hostility, anxiety and panic in varying and shifting degrees.

Soon Lieutenant Bridges reached an impasse. He tried to extricate a girl from the jam in the doorway, and the more he pulled, the more he found himself hurting the girl. Meanwhile, the crowd flow was squeezing around the pile, toward his open door, making it impossible to continue to pull the downed victims inside. Bridges tried to get outside, to get the sides of the pile up, but found himself swept backward by the people coming in.

The only apparent solution was to close one of the eight doors by the biggest tangle, open some other doors of the bank toward the river, and hope that the oncoming crowd would steer in that direction, away from the helpless people who were stacked up. Otherwise, immediate assistance was impossible. He finally got the door closed, and it worked. The incoming flood veered toward the new door that was open, giving small but precious space to the people on the ground.

Officer Kramer, on duty guarding the broken door away from the main entrance, could only guess what was going on in the greatest concentration of spectators. He had seen so many similar scenes at other concerts that he assured himself that this was the same. It would end with scratches and bruises, and that was it. Inside the broken door, some Coliseum employees were putting up a sheet of plywood to close it off, which Kramer hoped would relieve some of the crowd pressure that he had been trying to hold back.

The events throughout the entire confused picture moved slowly and, above all, in pieces and fragments. Pockets of the crowd would open mysteriously, and then close just as mysteriously. Spectators, like Brant Ross, could escape at times. But most of the crowd was trapped hopelessly in position. In the worst pockets, none could escape to tell others what was going on in detail, or when they did, it was almost impossible to convey the genuine intensity of the scene. Security men, hardened by the succession of other chaotic concerts, could not admit that this concert was different. The fact that several in the crowd felt convinced that the crush of the Led Zeppelin concert was worse than this also obfuscated what was happening. No one could see the big picture.

A spectator rushed up to Officer Kramer and said that people were passing out in the crowd. Kramer could not leave his post, but he looked over to the rear of the crowd where Lieutenant Menkhaus was consulting with Sergeant McAlpin in his squad car. He referred the distraught youth over to the car.

Menkhaus was having a series of problems. Several others had come up to him to report that the jam up by the doors was getting worse and worse and that someone was likely to get hurt, that there already seemed to be injuries. At the moment, Menkhaus was discussing with his two sergeants, McAlpin and Lamping, what could be done about the situation.

There was no easy solution. The crowd was packed so tightly that not the slimmest gap showed anywhere. A battalion of police could not get through to the entrance ways without causing further compression. Menkhaus thought over the idea of trying to bring his entire detail of over twenty officers into the crowd, but it was obviously hopeless, and could make matters worse. It was then agreed that Sergeant McAlpin would carefully drive his squad car toward the rear of the crowd, using his bull horn to plead with the people to step back, to ease up, to let some officers in to help any injured up forward.

174

PART IV

McAlpin repeated his request several times, moving his vehicle as close to the crowd as he dared. Although some in the rear stepped back, others in the middle and up front either could not or would not comply. When the man referred by Officer Kramer reached Menkhaus, the lieutenant knew he had to take another course.

Gathering Kramer and Officers Bley and Watson, Menkhaus followed their guide into the pack, squeezing and elbowing as best they could from the side. Moving in, the cluster of rescuers kept yelling, "Where's the victim? Where's the victim?"

No one seemed to know. But the officers struggled to get farther into the crowd. They finally came on a small clearing. On the ground was a young man of around twenty. Several persons were trying to give him both heart massage and cardio-pulmonary resuscitation. In the crush, it was almost impossible to give first aid. The officers lifted the man and forced a path to carry him back through the crowd, toward the broken door that provided the only quick entrance to the first-aid room. They had to fight this way desperately because there was no space for anyone to step to clear the way.

When they reached the broken door outside the main crowd, they found that a piece of plywood was now in place, locked by a bar behind it. Officer Watson pounded on the door for the inside security to open it. But there had been so many demands made by the spectators that the door was not opened. Watson finally smashed his fist through the plywood, reaching in to push down the panic bar on the door next to it.

Thinking it was a gate-crasher, a security guard inside held the door closed. Watson yelled that he was a police officer with an injury case. Finally the door was opened, and the three officers rushed the victim to the first-aid room, while Lieutenant Menkhaus went back on the plaza to coordinate his forces.

Inside the lobby, Sergeant Basham was checking the flow of the crowd through the doors on the Northeast side of the main entrance. Here the concert-goers were moving with the usual pushing and shoving. But it was not a riotous mob and there was no stampeding. Then he heard Sergeant McAlpin's voice squawk loudly on his walkie-talkie.

"Emergency! One-twenty-eight with an emergency."

The dispatcher broke in immediately. "Go—unit with emergency."

Apparently, McAlpin did not hear the dispatcher's response. Basham

175

repeated the message over his radio. The dispatcher came in quickly. "Go ahead with the emergency."

"We need a life squad," McAlpin responded. "Coliseum, on the concourse level. We have a man down, a possible heart attack." The time was 7:54.

"Copy. Please stand by."

The dispatcher cued in to the central fire tower, equipped for the entire city-wide network of fire, police, medical, Red Cross and other emergency services. In moments, he was calling back to McAlpin.

"One-twenty-eight—are you near the first-aid room? Fire tower wants to know."

"We are near the first-aid room," McAlpin replied at 7:55. "We have two-ah-that we are having difficulty with. One is in the first-aid room. By the first-aid room on the plaza level, across the plaza level. I'll guide them in."

Sergeant Basham, in the meantime, hurried to Stairwell D. He saw a man on the table with two guards administering CPR and heart massage. Basham ordered them to carry the victim to the first-aid room and quickly returned to the lobby to check for further possible trouble.

Meanwhile, the radio channels continued to chatter. Seconds after McAlpin reported the two victims came the message: "Rescue thirty-eight responding." Shortly after that, the dispatcher, attempting to clarify the stream of messages, tried to reach Post 1, a key post on the plaza by the Stadium foot bridge. Squad car 163 on the street volunteered to help by relaying the message, as the dispatcher explained his problem: "One-sixty-three—I am unable to raise Post One at the Coliseum. Was it that unit that requested a car to meet him? It sounded almost like an assistance run."

This was the problem. There seemed to be so much going on in scattered areas, that no one officer or post could possibly be on top of the situation. The distant dispatcher was the closest thing to a focal point, but he was miles away at the fire tower, and he had to operate blindly. With an apparent crisis brewing, and with the uncertainty of where all the problems lay, the dispatcher began a fast roll call:

"Coliseum Post roll call. Coliseum Post Two—forty-four."

"Coliseum Post Two. Okay."

"Okay. Coliseum Post Three."

176

PART IV

"Coliseum Post Three. Okay."

But the roll call was interrupted. McAlpin came on with a frantic call. One-twenty-eight—with an emergency."

"Go ahead, One-twenty-eight."

"How many rescue units you got responding to the Coliseum?"

"Rescue thirty-eight is responding."

"How many rescue units can we get? We got seven or eight people up here so far—that aren't breathing."

Lt. Roger Moore, of Rescue Company 14, had had a rough day. As the medical officer-of-the-day, Moore headed up a company that averaged over twelve runs a day, nearly 5,000 a year. This day was no exception. He and paramedic Gary Pumplin had just attempted to rescue a worker whose head was crushed by a steel beam. It was a futile job. As they had so many times before, they drove the victim to the Cincinnati General Hospital for pronouncement by a medical doctor, then continued to the Hamilton County Morgue just behind the hospital.

Both Moore and Pumplin were proud of their jobs, proud of the service they performed, in spite of its frequent terror. Moore's philosophy was, "You see what you have to see. You do what you have to do. And you really put the rest out of your mind."

On the way back to the downtown fire station, the calls about the Coliseum suddenly came through from the fire tower. There was something going on there, and it was obviously serious. One engine company, a ladder company, and the four other rescue units—24, 46, 38 and 15— were already responding. Lieutenant Moore put on his siren, turned onto the direct route to the Coliseum and screeched through the city streets toward it.

The mission was unclear. There were people down and they were not breathing. There did not seem to be a fire. The obvious thing crossed the minds of Moore and Pumplin at about the same time: Bad drugs must be in circulation. Not just overdoses—although the bad drugs might be contributing to the intensity of the ODs. A mass poisoning would tax every rescue unit and hospital in the city. Racing toward the Coliseum, Moore and Pumplin were still confused about what was happening on the plaza.

177

As Lieutenant Moore's rescue truck rushed toward the scene, both the fire tower and dispatcher messages continued unbroken.

"One-sixty—" the dispatcher called to Menkhaus at 7:59, "One-sixty—we are trying to get all the rescue units we can. They are sending three rescue units. That's three rescue units responding."

Menkhaus called from his radio, "You got directions for them?"

"That's affirmative, one-sixty. That's affirmative."

McAlpin broke in again to the dispatcher. "Have one-sixty and a couple uniform men meet me at the two gates by the odd-even sections so we can keep the crowd away from the ten people that are down."

Moore and Pumplin, in the rescue truck, looked at each other. The count of people down had risen to ten? Whatever the situation was, they were going to have their hands full.

On the heels of the previous message came another, "These people are down and we don't know why."

From their long experience in the rescue squad, both Moore and Pumplin sensed the problem: People were down and not breathing, with no apparent injuries and little clue as to why. There was most probably a drug situation, as there had been so many times in the past. But worse than that—what if it were a new drug, with no known antidote available?

Moore thought of his seventeen-year-old daughter at home. "God," he said aloud. "Thank God she's not here tonight."

In the crowd outside the southwest doors of the main entrance, a spectator watched himself move toward one of the open doors. It was the only way he could describe it. His feet were not moving. They were tight together, off the ground. He couldn't even steer himself. It was as if he were on a moving platform. He noticed a girl in front of him, sliding along the tide of the crowd with him. Her eyes were closed. She had obviously fainted, or had passed out, yet she remained perfectly upright. He was able to get his hands up far enough to shake her by the shoulder. Then he slapped her cheeks. She did not respond. Suddenly both squirted through the door. The girl simply toppled over, straight down to the floor. He picked her up, carried her out of the path of the oncoming stream of people.

Karen Essel, the security guard, helped him, bending to her knees to begin giving CPR. Others were toppling too, as they pressed through the doorway, standing straight up, expressionless, eyes closed. They fell, one by one, until the lobby area was scattered with those who had fallen. The lobby guards and two paramedics on the Coliseum staff squeezed through the lobby crowd to administer CPR. Other guards pulled in several others who seemed to be unconscious. In a matter of minutes, there were five or six down on the lobby floor, as several officers and guards rushed in with stretchers to take them to the first-aid room.

Outside on the plaza, near the doors, it was impossible to tell how many people were down. Several of the police and Menkhaus's detail were squeezing stretchers into the crowd and fighting to carry the unconscious victims out beyond the crowd on the plaza so that the rescue units could immediately get to them with their medical equipment when they arrived. The dispatcher continued to coordinate the operation, trying to clarify a tangled situation without much success.

From Lieutenant Menkhaus came instructions for the fire department paramedics. "One-sixty here—can you get one of those rescue units and tell them they have to come up on the plaza level?"

"That's affirmative," the dispatcher replied. "We're calling them again."

Post Nine came in. "Are the people that are down on the inside?"

The dispatcher relayed the query to McAlpin. "One-twenty-eight—Where are—are the people? On the inside? We got the fire tower on the line now."

Menkhaus caught the message and came in. "We got them down on the inside and the outside. We're going to need the rescue units on the plaza level. We'll direct them as they get here."

"Okay," the dispatcher replied. "There are now four rescue units responding."

Menkhaus's reply was brief. "We're gonna need them."

Concentrating on their high-speed run through traffic, and still in the dark about the actual conditions at the Coliseum, Lieutenant Moore and paramedic Pumplin kept a close ear to the police communications dispatcher as they raced toward the scene. Behind them, in the ambulance section of the rescue truck, the equipment was stacked and ready for the first moment they arrived.

179

There was the M/D-2J, the Monitor Fibrillator Datascope that would immediately reflect signs of life through spikes on its EEG-type graph. There were the IV lines and needles, to administer dextrose intravenously. There were ampules of calcium chloride, diluted adrenalin and sodium bicarbonate, the latter to offset the acid that built up from lack of oxygen. There were intercardiac needles to go straight to the heart to stimulate it. There were Laerdal Suction Units, to remove vomit from a victim, along with a Foley Catheter to monitor urine output to the bladder—a vital life sign. There were several inflatable splints to instantly immobilize broken bones. The van was a superbly equipped micro-hospital emergency room.

On the fire truck radio, Lieutenant Moore heard Lieutenant Menkhaus instruct Post 1 to clear the area by the stadium bridge so that the fire equipment could get through. Lieutenant Moore then cut in to the dispatcher on his radio to get more information. He was still puzzled by the suddenness of the emergency, by the spotty information coming over the radio on his channel. All Moore knew from the radio was that some people were "down" for no apparent reason. The whole thing sounded crazy.

"What are those people who are down?" Moore asked on his fire truck radio. "Do they have a gas leak down there—or *what?*"

"That's unknown at this location," the dispatcher replied to Lieutenant Moore. Then he called to Menkhaus for further information. "Could there be a gas leak over there? Or it might be ODs?"

Menkhaus's reply was cryptic. He seemed to be trapped in the crowd and could not get out a full answer. "As the crowd pushes—uh— we—we really got a problem here."

Other garbled and fragmented messages criss-crossing on the air channels still failed to clarify the problem for Lieutenant Moore. He wanted to be prepared as much as possible for when his truck arrived on the scene. In a moment, he reached Menkhaus directly on Channel 4.

"What's the nature of the problem at the Coliseum?" he asked.

Menkhaus replied, still breathless, and apparently caught in the crowd. "The crowd down here became so large that people began to pass out. We've got—uh—some people down here who are in need of medical assistance to them now. We have the fire department sending rescue units down here, and we also have additional fire equipment responding."

As the rescue truck continued through the streets, Lieutenant Moore asked for further clarification. "What kind of an affair do you have down there tonight?" he asked Menkhaus.

Menkhaus came back on his radio. "There's a concert with a sell-out crowd. Sold out in advance. Approximately eighteen thousand people. Trying to get into the doors that opened at approximately 7:00 P.M. The crowd began building around 3:00 P.M. this afternoon."

A squad car broke in from I-75 Interstate and asked the dispatcher if any more help was needed at the Coliseum.

Menkhaus affirmed, as the dispatcher asked: "We have more emergencies?"

"That's affirmative," Menkhaus replied. "Tell them all to come to the plaza level. We'll direct them from there."

Promptly, the dispatcher called the squad cars citywide to respond. There were nine of them altogether, beginning to converge from all points in the city—cars 114, 115,116, 216, 316, 415, 515, 516. As each car was roll-called, the dispatcher instructed: "Make your run an emergency."

The strange part of the picture was that even the spectators who were catapulted past the prostrate forms in the lobby failed to grasp what was going on. To them, and even to the police who were carrying them to the first-aid room or out of the crowd to the edge of the plaza, it had to be the common enemy of the rock concert scene—the overdose.

Roaring up the curved driveway between the Stadium and the Coliseum, Lieutenant Moore reached the plaza level, and slowed down. Ahead, he could see the lights of the Coliseum, across the footbridge. There was not much of a crowd visible; nearly all were gone inside by now. But he could see that a ladder company and engine company had arrived, and they were just across the bridge, toward the flag poles. He carefully edged his van forward, waved on by the police Post One at the bridge entrance. They had done a good job of clearing the bridge of spectators, and Moore had no problem driving across.

The conventional fire truck had oxygen tanks, but was not equipped with the sophisticated equipment that the rescue units carried. As he reached the scene near the Coliseum, Moore saw four or five prostrate forms lying on the plaza. Around them was a strange sight—shoes, gloves, jackets, and clothing were scattered about on the plaza surface. The early-arrival firemen were administering CPR and heart massage. The spectators had cleared, except for a few stragglers. Lieutenant Moore was relieved to see three other rescue companies already at work on some of the victims. As medical officer-of-the-day, he would coordinate their work. Their equipment was out of the truck in seconds. With Pumplin, he turned to a victim, and both dropped to his side.

By instinct, experience and constant training, both Lieutenant Moore and Pumplin made a quick assessment. There were no physical marks or injuries visible, no bleeding. Moore's hand went straight to the pulse. There was none evident. Quickly he inserted an indo-tracheal tube into the trachea, an airway to prevent regurgitation. He squeezed the rubber bulb to shut the stomach passage off. Then he clamped the aspirator over the mouth, and set the automatic respirator into action. Almost at the same time, Pumplin examined the pupils. They were dilated. Not a good sign, but with ODs that symptom did not mean too much.

With the pupils dilated and not responding, Lieutenant Moore inserted the IV needle and drained the sodium bicarbonate into the veins to offset the acidosis that was setting in from the lack of oxygen. Then came the adrenalin, then the calcium chloride.

All this was done in a matter of seconds. Both Moore and Pumplin knew that the body will shut down its systems in reverse order of priority. The last thing to shut down would be the brain. The priority: Get oxygen there.

The Monitor Fibrillator Datascope showed some spikes on its computerized track. A good sign, but inconclusive. It was becoming more possible that a mass drug poisoning was extant, and that somehow it had to be determined just what the drug was.

Lieutenant Moore heard the shouts of a few kids standing by on the plaza. They were distraught and upset. One girl was kneeling down beside a friend, sobbing violently. Two boys approached Moore and said: "There's a whole flood of Quaaludes going around. Sopors—714s, you know. Are they bad? Can you tell if it's the 714s?"

The street name for Quaaludes, or "sopors," was 714—a number printed on each of these tablets. They were once a prescription drug in the U.S. —since banned. They were prescribed as downers. But in extra doses they became a strong hypnotic that would send the taker into a floating, exotic state. The kids reported there was plenty of LSD around, too. Maybe it was bad acid? Or both? The only way to tell was by an analysis of the blood.

Rescue 38 was already pulling bloods to be rushed to the General Hospital for analysis. This could not be done on the spot. Meanwhile, Lieutenant Moore instructed every fire and rescue unit on the scene to continue CPR and cardiac needles directly into the heart.

The wide cement plaza was in confusion, as if in the aftermath of a battle. Three engine pumpers were parked at random, their rotating lights splashing over the rescue workers who kneeled in silhouette over a half-dozen prostrate victims sprawled motionless in a random pattern among the vehicles. Two rescue trucks were parked elsewhere, doors open to reveal their stocks of medical supplies and instruments. Four squad cars stood by, their own rotating lights whirling to cross patterns with those of the fire trucks in an eerie pattern, a semi-illuminated scene from a disaster film. Nearly all the crowd was in the Coliseum, except for the other silhouettes of a dozen or so stragglers who stood in stunned silence, seemingly unable to grasp what was going on. Recorded music was blaring from the loudspeakers inside the hall, but the concert had not yet started.

As Pumplin and the other fire units continued their work on the outside plaza, Lieutenant Moore learned that there were more victims inside in the first-aid room. They had been carried there by the police who had formed a cordon to screen off the view from the last spectators who were straggling into the auditorium. The victims inside had been removed to the first-aid room so quickly that hardly any of the 18,000 spectators had been aware of what was happening. By the time the fire equipment had arrived, only a scattered few saw it, and as far as they were concerned, it simply had to be just part of the drug scene.

With paramedic Pumplin taking over to continue the CPR, Lieutenant Moore jumped into the rescue van, and called the fire tower. There seemed to be eleven people down now, five out on the plaza, and six inside the first-aid room. Oddly, there seemed to be few injuries at the moment, as the rescue attempts were concentrated on those who were unconscious.

As soon as he got through to the tower, he asked them to call the General Hospital and send out a city-wide call to the Hamilton County Disaster Team—an organized team of doctors and nurses that could respond in minutes to an emergency.

Inside the lobby, before the fire equipment had arrived, and before the people had fallen inside, Mike Shumate continued to yell for his sister-in-law, Carolyn. His wife Deborah had since gone into the auditorium on his instructions. Drenched in sweat, as if he had fallen into a swimming pool, Mike was calling so loud that his throat was sore. He had shooed his sister and her husband on through the turnstiles, asking them to find Deborah and his brother Norman and take care of them while he continued looking for Carolyn.

They were as soaked as he was, and there was fear and shock in their eyes. Mike moved away from the northeast doors as the crowd started to thin and crossed toward the southwest bank doors. He noticed one person on the floor, with several people trying to help him to his feet. He was either hurt, or an OD, Mike was thinking. As a matter of fact, he was wondering why there weren't several people hurt in the crush outside the doors. On the other hand, Mike figured that if he and Deborah had gotten through the crush safely, everyone else could.

Inside the auditorium, the seats were filling up rapidly. The relief of the crowd to get out of the cold and away from the incredible pressure in the doors was evident everywhere. To the thousands who were packing the Coliseum, the ordeal had been worth it. Except those who had passed by a case or two of apparent overdose, there had been no sign of any real injury. There were the tired, the exhausted, the breathless and the sweaty. But they appeared more as if they had had a strenuous workout on the football field. Most prevalent, though, was enormous relief—thank God the wait and the battle was over with.

Backstage, the members of The Who were waiting, tuning up, relaxing. Their greenroom was far at the other end of the arena, completely away from the crowd and the main entrance. The group was totally oblivious that there even had been a crush. Bill Curblishly, their manager, was watching the huge indoor stadium fill up, waiting to cue

PART IV

The Who onto the stage. But first there would be a 15-minute movie trailer of The Who's motion picture, *Quadrophenia*. The tour, in fact, was partially planned as a promotion trip for the film. The preview on a widescreen before the concert would show many of the choice but bloody scenes on the beaches, and the crowd was bound to love it.

While the projectionist waited for the cue to roll the film, Deborah Shumate found Brian and Mary Downey, along with Norman, inside the seating area. Norman seemed to be well-recovered from his terrifying experience behind the glass door, although he hurt all over. But Deborah was totally shaken and distraught. She learned that Mike was still calling for Carolyn in the lobby, and had not found her. The others begged her to stay with them, that they were sure there was nothing wrong and that the only problem they had seen was an anonymous OD case they could do nothing about. Deborah pleaded with them not to tell her about it—she hated that kind of scene. Brian, Deborah's brother-in-law, was able to find a row of seats, and persuaded Deborah to sit with them as they tried to comfort her. They would save two seats for Mike and Carolyn when they got there.

Deborah tried to get her mind off Carolyn. She had a pair of binoculars, and held them up to check them out. But her hands were shaking so hard she couldn't even begin to focus them. Then she comforted herself further by thinking Carolyn must have had an easier experience than she and Mike had. It calmed her down somewhat, as she waited for Mike and Carolyn to appear.

Out in the lobby, Mike could still not find Carolyn. He moved back toward the less crowded section, where the scene was more tranquil. Then he saw her. She was against the wall, bent over and sobbing hysterically. He tried to help her up, but she slid down again, still incoherent, still sobbing. Mike sat down beside her and tried to calm her down.

In between sobs, she told him her story. She had been swept away from Deborah and him by one of the swirling waves of the crowd. She found herself only eight or nine feet from the opposite set of doors from them, totally out of sight. Then she suddenly felt as if a giant vacuum cleaner was sucking her down. Like so many others, she slowly slipped down until she was on her knees. She knew she was going down, and

185

kept saying "No-no-no!" She was screaming until the press got so great she could barely breathe. She realized that no one could hear her over the noise and stopped. She was able to breathe slightly better. But it was almost intolerable.

Someone tumbled on the back of her legs, and she was trapped. She put a hand up in the air for help but it, too, was sucked down. Now she could neither scream nor breathe. She was convinced she was going to die. Then a miracle happened. A man in the crowd next to her suddenly grabbed her arm. He slowly began pulling her up. He got her half-way up, and then she slipped down again. The man shouted, barely audible, but hysterical: "Girl on the ground! Please help!" She could hear him faintly, but suddenly, three other men squeezed in by her. All four raised her to her feet. They lifted her above the crowd, as she tilted her head back and gulped for air. She fought to retain consciousness, knowing that if she blacked out again, she would surely die. In fact, she was sure she was near death and she screamed out again she was dying. She believed that she was held up that way for three-quarters of an hour, passing in and out of consciousness. She vaguely remembered being squirted through the door with her four helpers. She remembered a rush of cool air—and of falling face forward on the floor.

Mike sat with Carolyn on the floor while she began to calm down. The lobby was now almost empty. He helped her to her feet, and together they went through the turnstiles and into the auditorium. They found the rest of the family group in a matter of minutes. Debbie looked up, screamed with joy and wrapped her arms around Carolyn, who was still weak and trembling. Mike went out to get some Cokes. Perhaps, Debbie was thinking, the concert would take their minds off their horrible experience. If there was any group who could do it, it would be The Who.

As Jim Krumrei recovered from his battle in the crowd, he found his friends Greg MacDonald and John Roosa not far away from Stairwell D. They were battered, too, by the experience. But all three were so relieved to get away from it that their morale recovered fairly quickly. They looked around for Peter Bowes, who had arranged to meet them just inside the turnstiles. He was nowhere to be seen, but the arrangement had been made that whoever got in first would save some seats. It would be a simple matter, then, to wave in the others. Jim, Greg and John moved into the auditorium, and were lucky enough to find seats together. They saved one for Peter, and John went to try and find him.

He circled the ramp, down along the piazza past the soft drink stands, all around the Coliseum. He still didn't spot Peter, and came back to report this to Jim and Greg. But of course it was hard to spot any single person in a crowd of 18,000, especially in the confused rush through the doors. In spite of this, Greg decided to go out and look for Peter, while the others held the seats.

He searched the faces on the crowded floor section, where there were no seats, simply standing room. It was so packed that it was hard to pick out anyone. Obviously, Peter must have found a seat somewhere, and would join them after the concert at the parking garage. It was a common thing to split up in separate seats during a sold-out concert, and judging by the crowd in the auditorium, this concert looked packed.

Jim Krumrei was also watching the aisles to see if he could spot Peter in one of them, but without luck. Then somebody remembered that Peter had said he was going to look for his brother at the concert. Jim felt relieved. It would again be a simple matter to meet Peter at the garage, where they couldn't miss him. In spite of the sweat, which made him feel as if he had stepped out of a shower, and in spite of the bruised ankles and shredded shoes, Jim was determined to enjoy the concert he had waited so long to see.

Rick Rauh, of the other group from Wyoming High, was grateful that a third door had opened and that he had been propelled through it and into the lobby. He could not find his other friends in the crowd, and contented himself to find a single seat where he could recover and catch his breath. He had not seen Peter since their harrowing experience in the melee. But he knew that if he himself could get through it, Peter, who was stronger and bigger, could do so without trouble.

Before the distress calls had gone out, and before the fire and rescue units arrived, Jeff Waddle and Marilyn had held back resolutely from the crowd as it entered the doors. When it had thinned down, they finally fell in at the back of the crowd, and moved forward cautiously. There was still some shoving and pushing at the doors, and even a backlash at one point that made them reel. What surprised Jeff was the sight of coats and hats and shoes scattered aound the plaza, and inside the lobby when they finally went in. The scenes in the crowd must have been even rougher than he thought. If so, he had not actually observed any. This was true of so many spectators, impossible as it seemed. Again it was a question of being screened off by the crowd at the critical moments, and of the expected turmoil of a large percentage of the hard-rock concerts that cause many chaotic incidents to be shrugged off by all who experienced them before. If a spectator fell down, that was to be expected. If a person stayed down, it was probably an overdose. The bottom line was that the general scene from most points of view still looked no worse than a Led Zeppelin or Kiss concert—or many others like them.

There was only a steady flow through the turnstiles when he and Marilyn went in. They found two seats far up and away from the stage. They were not good seats, but they were the price they had to pay for hanging back. Jeff figured it was a price worth paying.

From their perch high in the bowl, the packed arena of thousands of featureless faces looked much the same as any other concert Jeff had been to. The floor area was jammed with several thousand, pressed close against the barrier that separated the stage from the crowd. The steep tiers of seats held an audience that showed little outward sign of the struggle and turmoil at the gates. As observant as he was, Jeff Waddle had no clue whatever of the tragedy that was taking place so close to him.

After he had come back from his futile trip to the parking space to find Becky, Brant Ross continued his patrolling of the plaza for some time. He completed a full circle of the building two times. He still would not let himself get panicky, because he was confident that Becky must have worked her way out of the crowd early. Suddenly, he saw the police making their way out of the crowd with a stretcher. They placed it on the ground over by the flagpole. From a distance, he could tell it was not Becky, and like so many others, he ascribed it to an OD.

For the first time, though, he was beginning to get genuinely alarmed. Since Becky was not outside, then she had to be in the building, Brant told himself. He made his way to the turnstiles, now cleared of the main rush. Brant was inside in less than two minutes, and he moved quickly along the corridor toward the Beehive elevator, where Becky had agreed to meet him.

188

PART IV

In moments, he was approaching the elevators. Someone who looked like Becky was standing there. He couldn't be sure, but he broke into a run. As he got nearer he was sure it was she. Then part of the crowd obscured the view and he ran faster. The girl was still there, looking toward him, but she made no move to come toward him. In between the people who screened the view, it was hard to tell.

It was only when he was within twenty feet of her that he knew it was Becky. He rushed to her, took her in his arms. They stayed that way for over a minute, not saying a word to each other.

For Becky, the wait had been agonizing. She herself could not recall how she escaped through the crowd. Everybody was incredibly nice in letting her squeeze out. She crossed over to the building, out of the main crowd, and leaned against the wall of the building to get out of the wind. From its outer edge, the crowd had looked absolutely calm and peaceful. Next to her was a bank of doors on the river side, not in use. Suddenly, she heard a crash of glass and looked up to see several people going through the broken door. Freezing in the cold and wind, she jumped toward it, entering it just before the police arrived to stop the rush to the door.

Then began the long wait inside. She had gone to the Beehive elevator, and stood there, for over half an hour. As she waited, her anxiety grew. She was determined to stick by where they planned to meet, and determined not to panic as she had outside.

But the wait was long, and the anxiety grew. Twice she saw people coming toward her who looked exactly like Brant in the distance. The second time, she was absolutely sure it was Brant. When it wasn't, she felt a terrible sense of loss. When a third figure approached that seemed to be Brant, she refused to let her hopes rise. She was convinced that her desire to see him had created another figment of her imagination.

But it wasn't imagination. In spite of that, she waited for Brant to come all the way up to her, just to be sure. She saw him approach, soaked with sweat, his corduroys ripped out at the knees, and it was the happiest moment of her life. They went in together to find a seat, determined to put the experience behind them.

As they did, the police teletype was clattering with a brief message: FIRE COMPANY AND THREE RESCUE UNITS SENT TO THE PLAZA LEVEL OF

ARE THE KIDS ALL RIGHT?

THE COLISEUM. SEVERAL PEOPLE NOT BREATHING. REASON NOT KNOWN AT THIS TIME.

Downtown in Cincinnati, at the Netherland Hilton, Dr. Thomas Gates was ready to take his first spoonful of creamed vegetable soup when his electronic beeper sounded. He was attending a testimonial dinner for a local congressman, to be followed by a speech by Tip O'Neill, Speaker of the House of Representatives and visiting Cincinnati for that occasion. There were many local notables there, including young Mayor J. Kenneth Blackwell who had just assumed office three days before.

The beeper sounded Dr. Gates' call number, 3-Lincoln-99. The doctor quietly put his soup spoon down and went immediately to a pay phone in the lobby. The message was brief: Proceed immediately to the Coliseum. There are at least ten down with probable massive overdose. Total casualties unknown.

Within minutes, Dr. Gates was at the parking lot and getting into his car. He carried in it a compact load of medical equipment for every possible type of emergency. Gates headed up Cincinnati's Medical Assistance Team, also known as MATS, or the Academy of Medicine Flying Squad. The team formed a carefully synchronized operation that involved the hospitals, the Red Cross, and a large group of doctors and nurses, all serving on a volunteer basis. At any disaster the team would set up a medical command post in conjunction with the fire department and police, known as a Triage Center. Here, the medical officers would decide on the priorities—which victims would receive first attention. The process was of critical importance. If the vital signs of life were totally gone, the priority had to be given to those who had a fighting chance to survive.

Driving at top speed toward the Coliseum, Dr. Gates was frankly puzzled by the emergency call. A massive drug overdose scene would set into motion all the conditions for a mass panic, not just for the victims, but for those who might have taken bad drugs, perhaps still circulating through the crowd. As he pulled into the lower level of the Coliseum, he dodged several squad cars both coming into and leaving the scene with sirens wailing. At the lower level entrance, he opened the trunk of his

190

car, grabbed his medical equipment and his green helmet that identified him as a member of the team and rushed into the building.

The policeman on duty waved him through the door and to the elevator that took him to the main concourse. From the policeman, he learned that Lieutenant Moore, as medical officer-of-the-day, had already set up a command post in the first-aid room. The room was chaotic. There were five unconscious victims jammed in the room, with the Coliseum nurses and rescue company paramedics working on them on tables, cots and the floor. Dr. Gates went quickly to the victim nearest him to see what possible could be done to augment the efforts of those who were on the scene before him. One thing seemed certain. There were no signs evident that indicated that traumatic injuries were the cause.

At almost the same time that Dr. Gates left the Netherland Hilton, Dr. Dan Storrer, also of the medical flying squad, was shopping at a downtown department store. When his electronic pager called him, he was in his car and on his way in minutes. The report on his beeper was sketchy, but the drug overdose was a common story of past concerts. But why so many, and so concentrated?

Outside the Coliseum a rescue truck was already working on a victim inside the truck. As they administered the CPR, they were drawing a blood sample, the best step to determine what kind of drug might be the cause. There were no physical marks on the unconscious form, no sign of trauma. As Dr. Storrer was directed to the command post at the first-aid room, he tried to anticipate what other cause might be at the root of the trouble. The thought of carbon monoxide crossed his mind, but it didn't seem likely without other evidence. There were so many drugs going around, it was easy for a bad lot to circulate among a large crowd. If this were true, the doctors would have to grope in the dark before the blood analyses could give them a cue. And that would take time.

Over the past year the medical squad had had to contend with a bewildering spectrum of things. Most recently there had been a lot of PCP—Angel Dust—extant, and before that, loco weed, jimson weed, LSD, Quaaludes and heroin. Alone or mixed with alcohol, almost anything could cause a dangerous overdose syndrome. Reaching the first-aid room, Storrer joined in with Dr. Gates and Lieutenant

Moore to lend whatever assistance he could. From a quick first appraisal, the outlook did not appear promising.

Gary Miller, director of the Red Cross disaster service of Cincinnati,
was at a church meeting when his pager sounded the emergency signal.
His information, like that of the others, was scanty: Multiple casualties
at the Coliseum. The Red Cross was an important cog in the Hamilton
County Disaster Program because it provided important backup to the
fire, police and doctors. Along with additional equipment for intuba-
tion, IVs, resuscitation equipment and medicines, the Red Cross could
supply in short order a corps of nurses trained for emergency service,
disaster vans and everything else from body bags to four-wheel-drive
vehicles.

In the absence of more detail, Gary's thoughts flashed to a previous
incident at the Indianapolis Coliseum where the explosion of a gas tank
had caused so many casualties that the emergency units of that city were
taxed to the limit. After putting out his own call on the Red Cross
network for emergency nurses, he drove to headquarters, picked up
emergency equipment and joined the others at the first-aid command
post. The entire disaster facilities of Hamilton County were now in
action, but the medical question still remained a critical mystery.

When the lights dimmed inside the giant auditorium, the crowd
jumped to its feet and roared with a decibel count that could have gone
off the meters. The thousands standing on the floor of the arena
squeezed forward near the barrier that stood between them and the
stage. Hands were raised high above heads, and fists pumped like
pistons. Near the bandstand, the spectators pogoed up and down,
bobbing in delight. As if some cosmic signal had been given, as many as
10,000 butane lighters flared in the darkness, adjusted to produce
spouting flames as tall as a foot in height. Others lit pieces of paper and
waved them in exhilaration above their head. A few cherry bombs
exploded loudly. A beer bottle, smuggled past the police inspection
posts, soared from a high seat and crashed in splinters on the lower
aisleway. The Who had come to Cincinnati all the way from
England—this was the rousing tribute to them, a spontaneous ovation.

Recollection of the whole ugly mess of the crush outside had suddenly
dissolved. Only a fraction of the spectators had experienced anything

192

worse than a terrifying squeeze or the sight of a few ODs. The point was that the concert was about to start, and the jammed auditorium was fused in passionate anticipation waiting for the band to begin.

Most did not know that the preview of the film *Quadrophenia* was to be a prelude for the band. As a result, the frenetic welcome was ahead of schedule. Instead, a large wide screen was dropped from above—"flown in " as they say in the theater—and the music from the sound track of *Quadrophenia* thundered from the speakers. Described by one critic as "a spectacle of exploding energy, and the euphoria of violence," the scenes from the picture began unrolling. A forlorn figure, moving along a desolate beach, approached the camera from a distance, dressed in the conservative clothing of a Mod. Then, in a series of shock cuts, gangs of Mods on their elaborately-decorated motor scooters, rolled along the road, culminating in a gang confrontation with the Rockers on a British seaside beach. Suddenly the scene exploded in a pitched battle on the sands. Tangles of bodies slugged and piled up on top of each other, until the bobbies arrived with their nightsticks, to break up the stacks of bloodied bodies on the beach. For some fifteen minutes, the scenes unrolled, as the title QUADROPHENIA zoomed in and out of action.

As the violence on the scene and the volume of the sound track grew in intensity, Mary Downey had to turn her eyes away. The scenes were almost a duplicate of the crush she had just gone through outside on the plaza. Deborah Shumate, sitting beside her, was still shaking from her own experience and Carolyn was numb, stunned and barely aware of her surroundings.

In another part of the arena, Brant and Becky Ross were sitting close together, trying to get back in the mood of the concert they had waited six weeks to see. But a friend they had met inside got up from his seat and said he was going home. The combination of the battle outside and the violence on the screen was too much for him.

Jim Krumrei loved the album from the *Quadrophenia* sound track, but he kept one eye on the screen and the other on the auditorium's darkened aisles to look for his friend, Peter Bowes. It was hard to identify anyone, and the aisles were now becoming packed with spectators who crowded them for a better view of the stage area.

Jeff Waddle sat with Marilyn in a seat high and to the rear of the auditorium. He was trying to get himself in a mood of enjoyment, but he

193

was not having much luck. He couldn't suppress the feeling that something was wrong. By the time the movie faded to black, and the wide screen was flown again to the ceiling, the crowd was now ready for The Who to appear. And when they did, the butane lighters flared again in every corner of the arena.

For nearly everyone, the agony of the long, cold wait dissolved when The Who began their first power chords. John Entwistle pummeled his electric bass as Peter Townshend crashed into a storm of chords. Roger Daltrey bent over half-backward to let go all his vocal energy. If there was anyone in the audience who was not now swept into the rising riptide, it was not evident. The sensory overload was taking over more than 18,000 different sets of ganglions with percussions that battered the body as well as the eardrums. For two hours, The Who would be holding the crowd as willing prisoners, with little cognition of either time or space. No hypnotist could have accomplished the job so swiftly. The hands in the air, the fists pumping, the pogoing in the aisles continued and grew more intense. The roar of the crowd rose to hurricane force, and blended with the music to become the sound of a cyclone.

Frank Wood had finished his leisurely dinner with promoter Larry Magid shortly after 8:00 o'clock. From the window in the restaurant, he had watched the tiers of seats fill rapidly. He was interested that the crowd still maintained its decorum, and there seemed to be no mad rush for seats. The floor area was packing up fast, however, and the usual crunch down by the bandstand area was evident. The floor seemed to be jammed as solidly as the crowds outside had been.

When the film preview started, Wood joined Magid to go to the Beehive elevator, to make a closer survey of the crowd from the floor. They waited for several minutes after pushing the button, but nothing happened. Then a passerby who had come up the stairs told them that it wasn't running. He said they were using the elevator for some kind of problem but he didn't know what it was.

When Wood went down the stairs to the main concourse level, he noticed that there was a crackle from the walkie-talkies of a few security guards there. There was an urgency in the electronic voices that was very unusual. From the scattered phrases, Wood could tell that there was some kind of emergency going on. Someone on the concourse spoke out to say that he had heard someone had died, although he had no details. Wood and Magid reached the same conclusion as nearly everyone else—there must have been an OD. Then the word passed quickly down the hall that there might be two or three OD deaths. Wood was shocked by the news.

On the way to the concert office, which was next to the first-aid room, Wood asked a couple of the rescue paramedics about what was up, but they gave out no information as they rushed by. Someone else said that the emergency was on the plaza. If all this turned out to be true, instead of rumor, he would have to confirm it and bring his newspeople into action. He went out through a side door and onto the plaza.

Lieutenant Menkhaus, coordinating the widely scattered events, was moving from position to position, both in and out of the Coliseum. There was a lot of ground to cover. At the same time, he was attempting to filter all the scattered information through the communications center, and organize the squad cars and fire department details as they arrived. It was obvious that a major disaster was in the making, and at 8:11 he reached the dispatcher: "I think you better start notification of the key people of the city. We've probably got at least eight critical emergencies here—and some of them may be fatal. Just let 'em know what's going on." Although the CPR was still continuing, there was no report of any success yet. There was still hope, but it was dwindling fast.

The primary thought on his mind was what to do about the concert. Should it continue in the face of the developing disaster? The music was blaring in the arena, which in a sense was a blessing. Hardly anyone in there suspected what was happening on the plaza or in the first-aid command post. The victims had been removed from the crowd swiftly, and the police cordon had served as an effective curtain to screen the lifesaving attempts from the sight of practically all. With two widely-separated areas for treatment, one in and one out of the building, even Menkhaus was finding it hard to stay on top of what was exactly happening. The paramedics and the nurses, expert as they were with the life support systems, could not make any official pronouncements on the grim probability that a life had ended. This was officially the realm of the doctors, who were just now getting into action from their disaster alarm.

The piecemeal radio reports that Menkhaus was receiving from all quarters were not good. The estimates kept changing. Now consensus of unconfirmed messages seemed to indicate that there were anywhere from two to eight dead, and the speculation was that the ODs alone might not be to blame. The clarification would have to come from the hospitals and the morgue. With the rescue work still in process there could be no clear-cut picture until either the resuscitation process worked—or the worst was confirmed. The news was bound to come soon—technically a limit of eight or ten minutes at most would reveal that the life signals could not be revived, and the "D.O.A." would be written on the police reports: Dead on arrival.

That time had well passed when Police Captain Espelage called for Lieutenant Menkhaus on his radio. "What's the situation there, lieutenant? Is it under control now? Do you have any known fatalities?"

There was a pause, then Menkhaus answered. "Uh—we have probably two, maybe three—may be as many as eight."

"Fatals!"

"That's affirmative," Menkhaus replied.

While the paramedics, the nurses and the firemen worked frantically with the resuscitators and IV solutions, Dr. Gates examined the vital life signs of one of the victims inside the first-aid room. As chief of the disaster services, Gates had seen the worst over many years. In spite of this, as a sensitive man, he could never remain totally detached in the face of major tragedies. He could repress his deep concerns, but the anguish was always there.

It was obvious from Dr. Gates' first glance that the life support systems were not effective. None of the five lying in the first-aid room was responding to the treatment. They were blue and lifeless, no pulse, no blood pressure, no spikes on the fibrillator read-outs. When Dr. Storrer joined him, they both went through the grim task of preliminary pronouncements: Death from unknown causes. But the question was still begging. Young, healthy people just didn't die like that.

As they moved from victim to victim, the music and the cheers reverberating through the building formed an eerie contrast to the scene inside the first-aid room. The festival was on, yet almost no one in the overflowing auditorium knew what was going on just outside the arena seats. Some few knew that there might be injuries. Some few might suspect there could even be a death from an overdose. But at the moment, there was no confirmation to back that up.

Both Dr. Storrer and Dr. Gates agreed about the most obvious danger to be faced: What might be happening inside the jammed auditorium right now? What was *about* to happen in there? Were others about to fall from a possible poison drug still circulating among the crowd? And if they fell, couldn't this trigger a mass panic? Even the news of several dead from causes unknown could signal a massive exodus up the crowded aisles and out through the exits—a terrifying possibility. And what if there were already fallen victims underneath the mass that filled the floor section, or even under the seats?

As the paramedics and police prepared to take the bodies to the General Hospital for final pronouncement prior to taking them to the morgue, the two doctors crossed to an open doorway that looked out on the throng that stuffed every available space. The music was roaring; the din was earsplitting. The tiers formed a solid, seamless blanket of humanity. The same thought was in both their minds: What if they had to get in there to help somebody who was down? It looked impossible.

As they watched, someone lit a Roman candle in the middle of the crowd, just as The Who were finishing a song. It sprayed a burst of fire and colors out and over the tops of the heads. Peter Townshend stepped forward on the stage, and yelled out to the audience: "If any bloody punk does that again, we're going to shove it up his ass! You can leave the fireworks to us."

Townshend meant the last part of his statement quite literally. On the next song, a loud, planned explosion on-stage punctuated the music, as the batteries of spots and floods burst into a blazing light show. The blast was part of the act. Dr. Gates fought back an involuntary shudder. The chemistry of the crowd was overpowering.

It was not just a concert, it was an exchange of energy between the spectators and the band who were fused together by an electrically-charged force. Was it an emotional catharsis, a magnificent, therapeutic release—or was it destructive abandon? Right now, it was a tough, hard problem because there was no way of telling what could be hidden in the middle of such a compacted throng of people swept into the fire and fervor of the moment.

There was one other element he had not even had time to consider. His own sixteen-and-a-half-year-old son had been thinking of going to the concert that night. Dr. Gates had left it to his son's good judgment, reminding him to assess his responsibilites to himself, and to think it through. Was he there somewhere in the crush? But that problem would have to wait. There were critical decisions and plans to be made against the contingency of a possible panic and further fatalities.

By now, five other doctors had arrived, along with the Red Cross nurses. But there was little more that could be done with those who had fallen—only the contingency plan for what might happen next. One of the doctors responding, a woman, arrived in distress and tears. Two of her children were somewhere in the crowd, but she knew her duty as a member of the disaster team came first.

There were eight or ten staggering on the concourse who had apparently overdosed. They reinforced the poison drug theory. They staggered along the concourse, some falling down, some slumping against the wall. The problem for the doctors and paramedics was to prevent them from hurting themselves further. Some hit their heads on the floor. Others fell near broken bottles. All the less serious cases had to be treated outside the first-aid room. One OD case was convulsive and throwing up, but able to talk in broken phrases. He indicated he had taken Quaaludes and bourbon—that there were a lot of Quaaludes going around, as others outside had said. Perhaps a bad batch had been loosed on the crowd?

Until some kind of report was available from the Hamilton County Forensic Medicine Center at the morgue, the medical teams were still working blind. If the pupils were contracted to a pinpoint, this could indicate barbiturates. If they were wide, it could mean any number of drugs—including new and unknown ones. For those who had fallen, a discovery of what new drug might be involved was of no use. But for those who might fall inside—now the major fear of the disaster workers—this was critical.

By now the fire marshal, the police chief and captain, and the city's safety director were converging on the scene from scattered parts of the city. As they did, Lieutenant Menkhaus, along with Lieutenant Moore and the medical team, set up a contingency plan. All the nurses and doctors from the Red Cross and Flying Squad would be stationed around the perimeter of the inside of the Coliseum, remaining as inconspicuous as possible. The police detail would remain on duty, also inconspicuously, in order to avoid any alarm on the part of the crowd. The teams would watch the crowd and wait—and hope that no more would drop or be uncovered when the Coliseum cleared.

The possible circulation of a bad drug was terrifying. The possibility of a panic resulting from it was worse. As far as any definite information was concerned, eleven had died in entering the building. The toll of a mass movement in trying to get out under panic conditions would be inestimable. As Dr. Gates took his post in an open doorway that looked out on the packed aisles and jammed-in spectators standing on the floor, he wondered what might be hidden there out of view, and prayed that no one else would fall that night. The long, tense watch had begun.

When the chiefs and some members of the city council arrived, it took only a matter of seconds for the decision to be made to let the concert continue until the end. No member of The Who had any inkling of what had happened outside. In consultation with Bill Curbishly, the British manager of The Who, it was immediately agreed that they would not be told until after the concert. Any attempt to cancel or shorten the concert could lead to a possible disaster that might dwarf what already had happened. Right now an audience of 18,000 was in control and stabilized, unaware of the tragedy. What might happen if an announcement were made from the stage, no one could picture. So as the radios crackled and the dead and injured were being lifted into the squad cars, the band played on. Shortly after, when Mayor Blackwell was summoned from the dinner at the Netherland Hilton, he quickly concurred. It was his first major decision after only three days in office.

Most baffling was that few injuries were apparent. Only five had been officially noted. Those who were dead had very few marks of external injury. All would have to wait for the coroner's final analysis. This strengthened the drug overdose theory and intensified the mystery.

Meanwhile, the police radios and communications center continued to chatter with staccato messages pouring out from the Coliseum, the hospitals, the squad cars, the command posts, police headquarters and

199

the county morgue. Though disjointed and disconnected, they formed an impressionistic picture of what was happening throughout the city:

> Have all the Coliseum posts meet me on the plaza level on the walkway from the Stadium. We—uh—have to move some people out of the way here . . .

> Can you get hold of General Hospital, tell them we have five D.O.A.'s that are going to be transported. Ask them if they can still do the pronouncements. . . .

At 8:34, a brief, laconic call to the District One Headquarters came through from Menkhaus:

> District One—will you notify the Clergy Team and ask three or four of them to respond and stand by to assist—uh—with the relatives of the deceased?

About half an hour before the doleful call for the Police Clergy Team went out, Frank Wood had reached the scene on the plaza, just outside the Coliseum doors. He found what he saw hard to believe. There were the fire equipment and squad cars scattered everywhere about. There were the clusters of silhouettes of people in separate groups. Several of them were bending down over prostrate forms on the paving. There were the others being placed into the police cars or vans, and sirens wailed as they took off down the Stadium ramp. Only police and fire officers seemed to be around, along with a few officials. "My God, what's happened?" was all Wood could say to himself.

Yes, there were people dead, he was told. Most probably they were ODs. Two, maybe three—maybe as many as five. The number seemed to keep going up. The next report he got was eleven! He rushed back to the concert office, where the scene had now become as confused as that outside. On the phone, he reached Craig Kopp, the WEBN news director, at home. Wood quickly sketched in the fragmented details of what had happened. It sounded so incredible that Craig thought it was some kind of a black humor joke—not uncommon around the radio station. He soon realized it wasn't.

"The problem is," Wood told his news director, "everybody is extremely concerned that there might be more victims inside—under the crowd. Or more to come."

PART IV

"Is it bad drugs?" Craig asked.

"Nobody is sure what has happened, " Wood replied. "Can you reach Rick Bird and get him down here to cover the story right away?" Bird was a newsstaffer at the station. "I'll start checking the scene right now."

"I'll call Rick immediately," Craig told him. "Then I'll head for the newsroom. Be there in minutes." He hung up.

The implications of the disaster flooded Wood's mind. There were multiple mysterious deaths. Kids, all of them, most probably. There were 18,000 or more kids inside the arena, screaming their heads off and enjoying the concert. There might be twice that many parents, spread across the city and in Ohio, Kentucky and Indiana who would get the news on radio and television. None of the victims had been identified, at least as far as Wood could learn. What would happen if between thirty and forty thousand parents rushed in their cars to the Coliseum, the police station or the hospitals to find out if their children were among the casualties? It would be total chaos and terror.

Wood's first job was to get more information for his newsman Rick Bird when he arrived, grim as the job was. Whatever news went out on the air would have to be very carefully handled. He would instruct Craig to do whatever was intelligent, whatever was proper. He had faith in Craig's sense of perspective. WEBN-FM was a rock station, and a good one. It stuck for the most part to the best, established groups, and avoided the Top Forty mania. But tonight there would have to be one purpose in mind: Cautious, articulate information, information that would clarify, sort out and help the desperate parents who had no way of knowing whether their own kids were part of the tragedy—and to help the police and hospitals in dealing with what was bound to be chaos.

Although Wood tried to fight it, alarm went off in his head as he looked at the scene inside the auditorium. The floor area was so jammed that people could hardly move. An army of ushers could not prevent the aisles from being packed with people. In the excitement and hysteria, fire and safety laws had gone by the board. The whole roaring, cheering crowd was unaware that anything had gone wrong.

To check further, he squeezed down on the floor, into the crowd. To his relief, it was not as tight as it looked. It would be hard for anyone to be down on the floor without someone knowing about it. Yet he could not see everywhere, and the tension still remained. The thought of those thousands of fans suddenly breaking for the exits was unspeakable.

When he squirmed back out of the crowd on the floor, he learned from a security guard of the decision to keep the concert going. He was grateful. If it had been canceled, he could picture a riot breaking out in addition to the panic. Over the guard's walkie-talkie, he could hear more of the police communications going on. "Sixteen—" the dispatcher was calling. "Are they still going ahead with the concert? We're being plagued by phone calls up here."

An officer's voice, weary from hundreds of inquiries, came on the radio to say: "Our phones are ringing off the wall."

It had started already, and Wood could believe it. If he had had children who were there, he would call every place in town to find out if they were safe. The radio calls punctuated the need for Wood to get out as much documented information as possible, and he set his mind to that job.

Even on the concourse and in the lobby, the concert music and cheers blasted every corner. Wood found Rick Bird in the lobby, already interviewing officers, but the information was still scanty. Lieutenant Menkhaus had scheduled a news conference back at District One Headquarters, but that would be an hour or so away. Meantime, Rick Bird had to go with the sketchy information he and Frank Wood could scratch together.

It wasn't much. There were apparently eleven dead, and the reason would not be known until the coroner reported. Several had not been carrying ID cards or billfolds for fear of losing them. Or where there were IDs available, the names were being withheld until the next of kin could be notified. This looked a long way off. The bodies would have to go through the formal pronouncement at the General Hospital, then shipped next door to the morgue at the Hamilton County Forensic Medicine Center. There would still have to be the slow careful process of the autopsies, which could go on through the night, or more probably, the next day. Most important, parents were urged *not* to call the Coliseum, police or hospitals because the lines had to be kept open for further possible emergencies.

Rick Bird gathered together what information he could. He was lucky to find the pay phone in the lobby free. He reached Craig Kopp at the station, both of them having made record-breaking trips from home to get on the job. Outside the glass doors, Rick could see the remote broadcast trucks from the local TV stations already in action.

Inside at the phone, the music was echoing and reverberating off the concrete wall. He could hardly hear Craig on the other end of the line, but was able to gather from him that the phone report would be piped out over the air, live from the Coliseum. Rick shouted the news over the phone as loudly as possible, competing not only with the volume of the music, but the noise of the crowd.

As he filed his phone report, Rick suddenly became aware that he was standing on an enormous pile of shoes, coats, gloves, wool hats and even glasses. He realized with a shock what chaos there must have been when the crowd had rushed into the building. On the air, he described what he was standing on — mute testimony to the intensity of the push to get in.

Back in the concourse, Dr. Bill Gates was still tense as he checked the scene from an open doorway, both inside the seating area and along the hallway. Gratefully, no new casualties—dead, injured or ill—had developed, but the strain of waiting to see if they would was great. The concert was thudding at fever pitch and he was thankful that the decision to continue was made. The thousands inside the hall seemed to have left their individual identities behind to join in a massive group experience. It was almost unreal, a Fellini scene, unintelligible to an outside observer.

The scene of the giant butane lighters, the burning paper that had been waved, the Roman candle going off, all hung in his mind. Even the smallest fire, a jacket, a shirt, someone's long, flowing hair—and panic and turmoil could follow.

A kid staggered along the concourse beside him, his face pale and deathlike, carrying a bottle of Jack Daniels. Suddenly he stopped, poured it on the concrete floor, laughed hysterically and then smashed the bottle down beside him. Another stumbled along the concourse with a tray, weaving and trying to balance it. He slipped and cracked his head hard on the concrete. It seemed almost a miracle that he got up again. Others were wandering through the concourse, crying and sobbing. It was impossible to tell whether they were ODs or not. Was all this an

203

outlet to demonstrate a sense of freedom and participation? Dr. Gates had no answer.

An usher struggled across a row of seats to him, reporting a minor injury in the crowd. When Gates tried to get to the location, the ranks had closed in. There was literally no place for either him or the usher to step. The injury — apparently a twisted ankle — would have to wait until the crowd cleared. The long watch by the medical team, all around the arena, continued.

Lieutenant Moore was also keeping his rescue team on standby, watching the crowd, patrolling a wide beat. At one point, he moved out into the lobby, saw the piles of clothing lying there. It looked like a disaster area, which in fact it was. But he suddenly became aware that there were people outside the long bank of doors. They were pleading to get in to find if their children were there and safe.

It was a heartbreaking sight, and Lieutenant Moore's sympathy went out to them. Many looked as if they were in shock, standing there as the music punctuated their sorrow. Others pointed to the piles of clothing and wailed. One man was screaming through the glass that he would pay a thousand dollars to get in. Moore wished he could let them in, but it was impossible. There was no way they could find where their children were, even if he could allow them in. The hall was overflowing, and the entrance of frantic parents into the arena could trigger the panic they were all trying to avoid. But could the parents out there understand why the festival was allowed to continue in the face of the disaster? The scene outside the doors was as painful as the tragedy itself.

There was an unbridled energy in Daltrey's vocal command, Townshend's combination of acrobatics and music and Entwistle's overpowering riffs on the electric bass. Beyond that, Kenny Jones was proving himself a percussion giant on the drums with his cyclonic bursts that served for many as a fit memorial for the late Keith Moon.

At her seat, Deborah Shumate was thinking that whatever the terrors of the long and painful wait outside, it was certainly no fault of The Who. She was also glad that no one had apparently been hurt. With Carolyn, Mike and the others safe, she could give herself up to the surging crescendo of the music. With the action, the blazing light show, the hypnotic beat and the lyrics that she could recite before they were sung, she submitted to the sensory overload and was swept away by it.

Brant and Becky Ross, in another part of the house, were also getting into the mood of the concert, still euphoric about finding each other and lost in the growling resonance of the music. Part way into the concert Brant made his way out through the aisles, stepping around the people blocking them, and went to the refreshment stand. While waiting he glimpsed a partially obstructed view of the plaza. There were one or two TV crews out there, and he speculated that The Who was such a big draw, they were probably going to be interviewed after the show. Then he noticed the police cordon blocking the way to the first-aid room.

As he was leaving the stand, a kid next to him asked, "Did you hear that they say that seven or eight people died tonight? There must be some bad stuff around."

Brant simply did not believe him. He struggled back through the aisles to Becky. She did not see how such a thing could be possible, and they turned their attention back to the show.

It was painfully ironic when they played a number from *Quadrophenia* called "The Punk Meets the Godfather." Townshend himself had described the film as a study of divine desperation that is "at the roots of every punk's scream for blood and vengeance." Jimmy, the central character in the film, is a reflection of Townshend and Daltrey's own search for identity in the Mod scene. In the picture, pills are poured down open throats as if they were on a coal chute. And in the Godfather song, Jimmy's lyrical railings against the adult establishment state in no uncertain terms that the nation is dying, and the establishment exists only by temporary permission of the young. Pumped out of Jimmy's drugged ruminations, the song is sonorous and paced with operatic cadences.

As the song reached its melancholy refrain, the starkness of the irony was lost on the Coliseum audience who remained unaware of the grim scenes going on at the morgue.

Daltrey was singing the painfully ironic lyrics about broken glass on the dance floor, about bloody faces passing by, about empty rows of numbered seats, himself unaware of what had gone on outside.

Jim Krumrei divided his attention between the stage and the aisles to see if he could catch a glimpse of Peter. At one point, Jim was sure he saw him for a fleeting moment. It turned out to be someone else. He turned back to try to concentrate on the concert. He felt the performance was lukewarm. With still no sign of Peter, he concluded that Peter had found his brother somewhere in the crowd and joined him.

Back at the radio station WEBN-FM, news director Craig Kopp was feeding what information he could to the listeners, trying hard not to be an alarmist, but faced with accumulating news that indicated that a major disaster had struck. At length, the enormity of it was confirmed with certainty. The cause was still unknown, pending the completion of tests and autopsies. Positive identification was not possible in some cases, and no names would be released until the victims' immediate families had been notified.

It was painful news to report. Not only would the terrible uncertainty for thousands of families be agonizing, but there was no way of safely informing the 18,000 people inside the Coliseum to call home. The basic news, sketchy as it was, went out over the wires, across the country and overseas. Within minutes, the WEBN phones began ringing, with calls from Los Angeles, Philadelphia, Miami, San Francisco—and as far away as Perth, Australia. Over fifty calls came in from other radio stations. There were already misconceptions. Many thought the disaster was some sort of massive riot. Craig painstakingly pointed out that it was not. Other calls rushed in from frantic parents, begging for news of whether their sons or daughters were among those who had died. There was no way Craig could tell them. He was as much in the dark as they were.

In the meantime, local television programs were being interrupted for the fragmented news: Captions streamed across the bottom of screens: "11 DEAD AT RIVERFRONT COLISEUM CONCERT . . . . NONE YET IDEN- TIFIED . . ." Most important, was a police telex to all the media: "WILL YOU ADVISE LISTENERS THAT IT IS OF NO USE TO RESPOND TO THE COLISEUM OR TO CALL THE POLICE OR THE HOSPITALS. IF THERE IS ANY INFORMATION THEY WILL BE NOTIFIED."

This was of critical importance. With the police phones already "ringing off the wall," the newspaper and broadcasting offices jammed with callers and the hospital phones clogged with callers, the city communications were already paralyzed. It was not a question of the fatalities alone. It was a question of 18,000 and at least twice that many

206

relatives and friends who were desperate to learn if these concert-goers were alive.

At shortly after nine that night, Deborah and Carolyn's mother, Betty Naumann, was sitting quietly reading at her home in Covington, Kentucky, just across the river from Cincinnati. Deborah and Carolyn had called that afternoon, just before they left for the Coliseum. They were full of anticipation for The Who concert, and glad to be on the way early to get good seats. Betty Naumann marveled at their enthusiasm and wished them well.

Now, as she read her book, the phone rang. She crossed to answer it, wondering who it might be. It was her sister-in-law, and her voice was frantic.

"Have you heard?" she said. "Have you heard the newscasts?" Betty Naumann had not. She asked the news.

"Hundreds have been killed, and hundreds have been stomped to death at the Coliseum. We have no other information."

Betty froze. It sounded so unbelievable that she couldn't take it. Almost in shock, she dialed the Cincinnati police as soon as her brief conversation was over. All the lines were busy, including the emergency numbers. She tried again, several times. It was useless. She reached the Covington police, but they could tell her nothing. Then she called a friend, who reminded her of the messages being relayed over the air to all relatives of the concert-goers: Stay home and keep off the phone lines. All involved would be notified as soon as possible.

Betty Naumann wanted to follow instructions, to keep off the phone, but she couldn't. The strain was too great. She was divorced and living alone, and she could not bear the tension of waiting without someone to share her anxiety. Nearly hysterical, she ran to her car, and started out toward the Blue Ash section of Cincinnati, where Mike's family lived.

On the way over, she learned to her partial relief that there were not hundreds dead—but eleven was still a horrifying number, and there was no way of knowing about Carolyn and Debbie's safety. As she drove, Betty kept praying that her children were safe, feeling a surge of guilt for thinking only of that. She thought of Mike and Debbie's tiny children, suddenly stripped of their parents. It so overwhelmed her that she could hardly drive the car straight.

ARE THE KIDS ALL RIGHT?

At the home of Mike's mother, Jeannette, and stepfather, Jim McFalls, both were spending a quiet evening watching television. At nine that evening, Jim got up from his chair to switch from Channel 12 to Channel 9 to find a new program. Instead of the program, the screen flashed to the plaza of the Riverfront Coliseum. In the foreground, the fire rescue team was giving CPR to a teen-age girl, as she lay on the concrete—several other casualties were receiving the same attention. The lights of fire engines and police cars were flashing and rotating, illuminating a scene of chaos. Then the news came: eleven dead; cause unknown; no identification.

Shannon, Mike's eleven-year-old sister, watched in horror. Then she screamed and became hysterical. Jeannette tried to comfort and reassure her, but inside she was just as terrified. Not only were her sons, Mike and Norman there, but her daughter Mary and son-in-law, Brian Downey, themselves parents of small children. When Deborah's mother arrived from Covington, she was praying that Mike's family would have news. But there was none. It was now approaching 10 P.M. The concert was still in progress. Ironically, the only ones who knew of the catastrophe were those outside the Coliseum, listening to the broadcasts. Practically all inside the Coliseum were insulated from the news. The family sat in anguish, waiting and silent except for Shannon's sobs.

Brian Downey's mother and father were facing the same anguish. The interlocked families were all close friends. Mrs. Downey had both a bad heart and a bad back, and the news on TV left her almost traumatized. For a moment, Mr. Downey was thinking that he'd have to rush her to the hospital. In the meantime, he called every major hospital in Cincinnati: the General, the Good Samaritan, the Jewish, Bethesda and others. Either they had no news, or the lines were choked.

Throughout the city, the same scene was being repeated in thousands of homes, where the only answer lay in waiting.

Back at the Coliseum, the concert was approaching its end. The audience remained at a high pitch, as high as during the initial ovation. The lyrics continued to accent the group's astringent attitude toward the established order—although The Who, most in their mid-thirties, were fast on the way to becoming the older generation. Still, The Who's old musical leaning post, "My Generation," brought a surge of approval, as

208

PART IV

Roger Daltrey sang the classic lines: He hoped his generation would die before it got old, and suggested that those who disagreed with his outlook should fade away.

As the band went into its finale, manager Bill Curbishly waited anxiously in the tuning room backstage. He had been sitting on the appalling news for nearly two hours now, with The Who onstage still unaware of what had happened. He would have to let them know when they came offstage prior to the traditional encore. Curbishly was upset because no one had told him about a problem until 8:45, and then only the false information that there were two fatalities from ODs and two from other causes.

When the last chords of the finale decayed into the auditorium shell, the group bowed and smiled as the volume of applause and cheers rose. The veteran members hoisted drummer Kenny Jones to their shoulders, and marched off triumphantly. Again, thousands of butane lighters, pushed to the highest flame possible, lit up the auditorium. The salute was joined by flame-thrower jets from hairspray cans, butane cannisters and even whipped-cream cans. Combined with blazing paper cups, the effect was dazzling and pyrophoric. But the scorching tribute brought chills to the fire rescue and medical teams as they stood around the periphery at various exits. Even a minor fire could start a panic.

None of them knew for sure if the tragedy was already over. They could not be actually sure until the last spectator had filed out of the arena. Dr. Gates and Dr. Storrer stood at their posts, tense and concerned until the floor would be cleared.

Down in the tuning room, Bill Curbishly spoke briefly to the members of the band as they entered from the stage. He did not tell them the whole story. The encore was yet to be played. No hint of the scope of the disaster should be leaked, even inadvertently, by The Who to the audience. Curbishly simply told them that something serious had happened, and they were to wait until the crowd had cleared. The chances of a rushing, mad exodus were as great as before.

When The Who came back onstage for the encore to the continuing ovation, they followed instructions, cutting the brief medley to the minimum. Then they hurried offstage as the cheers came to a climax and faded off. The time was about 10:30.

ARE THE KIDS ALL RIGHT?

An hour before the finale of the concert, Jack Leach was relaxing at his home, watching the Oakland Raiders play the New Orleans Saints on television. As special investigator for the Hamilton County Forensic Medicine Center, he worked as a liaison between the police and public prosecutor, sorting out cases where crime might be involved, searching for evidence, coordinating the work of the toxicologists and criminalists at the center. It was a taxing job, and he was exposed to tragedy daily. But he never got used to it. Asked how he was able to put up with such constant exposure, he told a friend: "That's why we have rose gardens and fishing rods." Leach was an expert on both.

When the news flashed on the screen, Leach went straight to the phone and called the coroner's office. The lines were all busy. In moments, he was in his car on his way to the forensic center, which housed not only an extensive crime and medical analysis laboratory, but the morgue as well.

Approaching the neighboring General Hospital, Leach found the streets choked with automobiles, hopelessly seeking parking spaces near the morgue and hospital. In the cars were parents, family and friends of the concert-goers who still remained in the Coliseum. The faces in the cars were drawn and anxious. The cars crawled toward the medical complex on a desolate pilgrimage. The announcements on the car radios could only repeat the same shred of information: eleven had died at Riverfront Coliseum; cause unknown; identification not made.

Leach was able to grope to his parking space, down by the morgue entrance. Several police cruisers and vans were there, carefully moving the fatalities from the vehicles to the morgue bay. In his office, the four telephone lines were being manned by the center's staff, quietly attempting to forestall the anxiety of the callers. All the staff could tell them was to please call back later. The moment a phone was hung up, it would ring again.

In the morgue next to Leach's office, the police and attendants were filling out Form 316, the impersonal slips that recorded the tragic fact: Dead on Arrival. Several were listed as DOE, JOHN. SEX-MALE. AGE-UNKNOWN. OCCUPATION-UNKNOWN. And beneath that: DOA FROM WHO CONCERT, PLAZA LEVEL, COLISEUM.

Leach joined in to search for clues of identity, including description of clothing, physical description and markings, coins, currency,

210

jewelry—any clue that would enable the morgue to notify the closest of kin. The moment the clues came together, the families would be notified and summoned to the morgue to complete the identification.

At the General Hospital, less than a block away, the staff doctors were making the official pronouncements. It was purely a confirmation process, legally necessary before the fatalities were transferred to the morgue for the coroner's staff to make tests and to perform the autopsies.

Under the supervision of the Hamilton County coroner, Dr. Frank Cleveland, the tests prior to the autopsies were being completed as fast as possible. But the process had to be slow and meticulous. Most important was the determination of whether there was a mass of tainted Quaaludes flooding the streets, the discovery of which was critical to prevent other fatalities. Bootleg pills were not uncommon. It was known that sometimes methaqualone, the active ingredient in the pills, was at times replaced by the bootleggers with the potent horse tranquilizer, PCP. Results could be disastrous, including wild and uncontrollable psychosis.

With the puzzling lack of major injury, both the cause of death and the question of drug poisoning had to be settled quickly. The facilities of the forensic laboratory, as modern and well-equipped as they were, were pushed to their capacity. The full autopsies could not be completed and signed until the following day, after the lab tests gave some kind of clue to the drug question.

The gas chromatograph was down for repairs at the time, but the scanning electron microscope and mass spectrometer were available, both representing the most sophisticated scientific instruments available for analyses.

Using the mass spectrometer was not simple. The half-million-dollar instrument is painstakingly slow. Tiny samples of vital organs have to be dissolved in a phosphate buffer solution, and spun to 9,000 G's in a centrifuge. What remained floating on top of the solution—called a supernatant fraction—would then be pushed up to 100,000 G's to produce a solid pellet in the bottom of a tube. Diluted in alcohol and squirted into the injection port of the spectrometer, the specimen would be bombarded with high-speed electrons to measure the type and quantity of specific drugs, down to infinitesimal quantities. Blood and urine analysis, less complicated, were done first.

211

From the bloods, evidence was carefully searched for the presence of alcohol, methaqualone (the Quaalude active ingredient), cocaine, phecyclidine, morphine, marijuana, salicylates and other drugs. The urine samples were tested for alcohol and amphetamines. As the tests went on, the identification process continued, prior to the painful job of notifying the bereaved families.

At 10:26, Sergeant Lamping, at his post on the plaza, picked up his radio and called the dispatcher.

"General information," he said. "Would you advise all District One cars—the concert is now over. The crowd is coming out."

Practically no one in the crowd who moved out of the exit doors yet had an inkling of the enormity of the disaster as they walked toward the parking spaces. Some were casual and quiet; others still carried the euphoria and exhilaration of the music. Most were hardly aware of the parents who stood by the doors with drawn faces, looking for their children. There was none of the crush of the frantic scenes in entering the building.

Inside, the medical and paramedical teams watched the aisles and seats slowly empty. They were still tense. The eleven casualties had taken place, unobserved by all except those who had been entangled in the crush. The same situation could theoretically develop inside as the crowd went out. Or it might even have already happened.

Mike and Deborah Shumate, along with Carolyn, saw nothing unusual as they walked out of the Coliseum. They hurried toward their car to get out of the cold. The throngs that walked with them were calm and relaxed. Mike was able to clear the parking space in very little time, and drove casually along I-75 toward the suburb of Fairfield, twenty miles north of Cincinnati on the way to Dayton, where Deborah's brother-in-law Bobby and his wife Roseanne were taking care of the children. They had no car radio, and contented themselves with talking about the musical prowess of The Who, as well as the terrible crush in getting into the building.

They were just beginning to feel the pain and stiffness from the experience. Mike's back was hurting badly from his crunch against the edge of the door, and he was starting to feel the bruises on his arms and legs now that the distraction of the music had stopped. Carolyn, numb and shaken by her experience, wondered why more people didn't get seriously injured. Both she and Deborah realized they were aching all over, and in retrospect, found themselves wondering how they ever got out alive.

When they walked into Bobby and Roseanne's living room, Deborah noticed that both looked numb and rather strange. Roseanne's eyes opened enormously wide, as she ran to Deborah and threw her arms around her.

"Thank God," Roseanne said. "Thank God!"

Deborah was stunned by the greeting. Her first thought was that something had happened to her children, and that Roseanne was too confused at the moment to tell her. And then she was told the news.

Both Deborah and Carolyn broke into tears. Mike stared blankly, unable to believe what he heard.

"You'd better call your mother," Roseanne said quietly. "She is worried to death. She's over with Mike's parents. Couldn't stand to be alone in Kentucky."

Deborah called her mother at once. She had been frantically waiting for Deborah's call from the time the concert had ended, not realizing that Deborah could have been in the dark about the tragedy. Deborah comforted her, and asked her to pass the word along to other family members. Then she called her father, who, with his weak heart, was breathing so hard he could barely talk. "I'm all right," he said, "now that you've called. I'll be fine. But thank God."

The others in the family group at the concert had left in their cars separately. Brian and Mary Downey were a little surprised at the TV camera truck on the plaza when they left, but thought only that it was a post-concert interview. They left the Coliseum quickly, taking I-71 out to the Norwood section.

As they turned off the highway near their home, Brian decided to stop at a King Kwik convenience store for a couple of Cokes to take home. The woman behind the counter was an acquaintance of theirs, and knew they had been to the Coliseum. But she was not her usual cheery self.

"How was the concert?" she asked grimly.

"Fine," Brian told her. "Once we got in, it was worth it."

The woman answered shortly. "It wasn't worth eleven dead, was it?"

213

Brian gasped. "I can't believe it," he said.

"You will when you turn your TV set on," she said.

Brian rushed to the pay phone to call his parents. The line was busy. He tried several times, then he ran out to the car to tell Mary. She began to shake and cry, as Brian sped in the car to get to their home phone.

Jeff Waddle, who had remained almost aloof from the crowd as a detached observer, saw nothing unusual as he and Marilyn left the Coliseum. They went to Marilyn's blue Honda sedan, parked on Eastern Avenue. With Marilyn driving, Jeff turned the radio to WSAI-FM, one of his favorite rock stations, then leaned back to listen. There was a female disc jockey on the air, but her voice did not sound as lively as usual. In seconds, it became apparent why. There was no music—only the news of the Coliseum disaster. Jeff listened, then dropped his head on the dashboard. "Terrible," he found himself muttering. "Just *terrible.*"

His thoughts went instantly back, back over two years, to the article he had written for the University of Cincinnati magazine *Clifton* in 1977. On crowd control at the Coliseum, of all things. "Through Trial and Error," it was ironically titled. Phrases he had used in the article two years earlier rushed to his mind.

"The event more closely resembled a violent riot, rather than the concert it was supposed to be. . . .

"All the trouble experienced at the Coliseum has occurred almost exclusively at rock concerts. . . .

"Why are so few doors opened so late? . . .

"At general admission concerts, everybody wants to get good seats, so they get there early and they get in front of the doors . . . I think it would help to have reserved seating. . . . "

There had been much more in the article, written so many months before. Much of it pointed to a potential catastrophe. The strange part was a catastrophe had happened this night—and he had been totally unaware that it had happened.

Brant and Becky Ross had had as uneventful an exodus from the Coliseum as the others. Nothing they saw indicated that there had been trouble—except for the possible OD cases. In the car on the way home, Brant turned on WEBN-FM, where Craig Kopp was in the middle of his many news broadcasts that night. Becky almost went into shock. Brant, in retrospect, and with the memory of his fall and entrapment, could see the picture now, in hideous detail. Quickly, they pulled off the road to phone each of their parents. For the parents, the worst two hours they ever spent were in waiting for the calls.

Jim Krumrei, along with Greg McDonald and John Roosa, sauntered out of the Coliseum, keeping an eye out for Peter as they did so. They scoured the plaza and the exits for nearly ten minutes, but saw no sign of him. The scene seemed peaceful and normal, without even a heavy crowd. They finally decided that Peter had probably gone back to the P&G garage to wait for them. Either that, or he had decided to go home with his brother Ben. They walked up to the garage, several blocks away on Sixth Street, still keeping an eye out for him.

At the garage, they sat in the car for some twenty minutes, with no sign of Peter yet. They checked the attendant, who told them that he had seen no one waiting around. The consensus of the three was that Peter was probably still waiting at the Coliseum for them, if he had not already gone home with his brother. Either reason was a logical explanation for the delay.

They drove back slowly to the Coliseum, scanning the sidewalks as they did so. Except for some stragglers scurrying to get out of the cold there were few people now. They pulled into the lower level entrance, and again canvassed the area, without luck. Deciding to give the parking garage one more try, they kept another sharp lookout until they reached it. There, the attendant told them that no one had gone in or out of the garage since he had last spoken to them.

Confident that Peter had gone home with his brother, Jim Krumrei went to the pay phone and called Ben Bowes at home. No, Ben told Jim, he had not found Peter at the concert, and had assumed that Peter had sat with the rest of his group from Wyoming High School. Strangely, neither Ben nor Peter's friends had yet turned on a radio, and none was aware of what had happened. Ben suggested that they take another look around the Coliseum, where Peter was probably still waiting for them.

Bringing the news back to the car, Jim jumped in as Greg headed the station wagon back to the Coliseum again. They retraced their route slowly, searching for Peter as they did so.

Backstage in the "cheering up room," the four members of The Who

215

sat in bleak, atrabilious silence as Bill Curbishly filled in the story of what had happened. Although he had few details, Peter Townshend knew with certainty that the group would be accused of inspiring drugs, and drunkenness, even though The Who had come out openly against drug use in recent years. There would be the inevitable comparison between the violent scenes in the film *Quadrophenia* and their tempestuous history, with the smashed instruments, amplifiers and hotel rooms.

In many of his reflections over the years, Townshend had revealed his concern and sympathy for the young generation. He often stated The Who was trying to explore the energies of the kids and guide them through their inner turbulence. He also felt that the group's macho, aggressive image was tempered with idealism and fecund vision, that his lyrics and music expressed for the young what they couldn't express for themselves. Townshend claimed he cared more about them than some of their parents did. Now, he was filled with horror at what happened.

Roger Daltrey felt sick and totally helpless. He had long thought that the group's bittersweet attacks on the falsity and pretension of the world were helping young people through their frustrations and deep-seated emotions. Along with the others in the group, he agreed that the decision to continue the show was wise. If he had known during the concert, he was sure he would have broken up on the stage, and the crowd would have been triggered perhaps into desperate behavior.

Because of the enormity of the disaster, the decision would have to be made whether to continue on with the fourteen-city tour at all. That would have to be decided quickly. Meanwhile, there was nothing to do except go back to their hotel rooms in sadness and anguish.

In the almost empty auditorium, the fire and medical teams still waited. The question still remained: Were there bodies lying hidden, screened from view, that no one knew about? Lieutenant Moore and Gary Pumplin, seasoned as they were to daily crises, were tense. Psychologically, they prepared themselves for anything. They were still befuddled by what had happened earlier. People just don't die like that, Moore kept saying to himself. How could they benefit by this experience in the future? How could they prevent it? Where did the roots of the problem lie? If it was a new drug, what kind of antidote would be available? What was the suction power, the magnetic force that drew the crowd into such a compaction? Fatalities in trying to escape from buildings could be expected. But a crush trying to get into a building, on an open plaza? Who could expect or anticipate that?

With the building almost empty, the life squads left their quiet observation posts, and combed the auditorium. They made a close inspection, behind and under seats, the stage, the floor. Only after the last square foot was inspected did they relax their vigil. The relief of the teams was measurable. But the impact of the disaster still hung over the scene.

Dr. Gates and Dr. Storrer, still in the dark about the full nature and extent of the casualties, called their flying squad together, along with Gary Miller and the Red Cross volunteers. Lieutenant Moore stepped forward to thank them all for their efforts on behalf of the Cincinnati Fire Division. The grim facts were summarized: Four had expired on the plaza level concourse. Five had died in the first-aid room. One had died en route to the hospital, and another on the lower level. All the efforts to revive the victims had been carried on long after hope had faded; all were without success. Uncounted injuries had been treated, most of them minor cuts and bruises. Five who were found to be more seriously hurt, had been rushed to the hospital in police squad cars, none of them critical.

Less than an hour after the discovery of the first fatality, Lieutenant Menkhaus had summoned the Cincinnati Homicide Squad to begin the job of discovering how and why so many people had died so basically unobserved by so many thousands of people—including the police. There was no visible stampede, no riot, no fights, no enormously mad rush. Could it have been plain and simple compaction, the lethal squeezing to death of eleven healthy young people? The thought was staggering.

Specialist Dan Jones and Sgt. Paul Morgan of Homicide were on the scene quickly to begin the investigation of the confusing affair. Officer Kerry Rowland from Post 6 by the main doors, pointed up the terrible dilemmas he faced to Specialist Jones: "At one time there was a woman that came up and said her husband was injured inside the crowd. We asked her to tell us where, you know. And we had to tell her there was no way we could even possibly get inside the crowd to get to him. It was right around this time we saw Sergeant Lamping. He was in a police vehicle. He was on the microphone and trying to clear a hole for us to get in and assist people. We couldn't even get in the crowd, even with the vehicle."

Homicide Sergeant Morgan tried to get a picture of the scene as observed by Private Security Guard Gerald Beckman, on duty in the lobby area. "As the doors were opened," Morgan asked, "and the people began to pour through, how much time went by before you were able to actually clear the area somewhat?"

"Well," Beckman responded, "most of the time, if the lobby gets jammed up, we block off the entranceway, you know. One or two of the doors to let all the people inside to mill on in through the turnstiles, so we can let the rest of the people in. We do that off and on until they all get in."

"Was there anyone who was actually injured to the point where they had to be taken to the hospital from your location?"

There was, as Beckman described: "Yes sir. There was the ones we got from underneath the pile. We dragged them in, you know, we pulled them in or they stumbled in. It was about five or six of them inside the lobby area on the ground."

"Were they still conscious when you got them inside the lobby area?"

"Not all of them, no sir," Beckman replied. "One of them I worked on and tried to revive, but to no avail. There was a nurse there that I knew, name I don't know—I know her to see her. She tried to help me, but at that time, I think the Life Squad was called."

The fragments began to gradually come together, as the Homicide men continued their inquiry. Private Security Supervisor Floyd Bridges could not fully understand what had happened himself when he talked with Sergeant Morgan.

"We have handled a lot of shows, a lot of rock concerts, and I thought that some of them was worse than this one was. But undoubtedly it wasn't. Because we never had any casualties in the other shows. That's what makes the difference."

Bridges went on to tell the sergeant how he had tried to work his way out of the door to help. "I wanted to get these people untangled," he said. "We tried but really we couldn't make it through there because they was all jammed in the door." Then he added, "It was kind of an upset thing with me. Because I felt like being in charge, I would have to do everything in my power to free those people."

The investigation by the homicide officers was long and desolating. Karen Essel, the woman security guard in the lobby near the southwest bank of doors, told Sergeant Morgan: "First of all, it was hard getting the doors open. People all pressed up against the doors. Once we got the doors open, there were people on the bottom of the pile we couldn't get out. We just couldn't get to them."

She had administered CPR to several of the victims. What puzzled her was that they didn't appear to be the same as the OD cases she had seen at other concerts. "A lot of times they come in, and they pass out from drinking or drugs or whatever. But this was different. This was totally different. They were completely knocked out. Six of them came in and they were out. Because we turned around, and they were all inside. So I don't know if it was the kids who completely brought them in, or what it was."

In the hospitals, the General and the Good Samaritan, the latter known by the police as "Good Sam," Homicide continued its probe, taking statements from the injured in the hope of more clarification. "I was with my friends," said one, "and I got separated from them. And the next thing I know, a bunch of people in front of me were just falling down, and I went down with them. I was fighting to stay up, and I couldn't stay up. And there were people trying to get up. There was just such a massive crowd, everybody was just trying to get in that door."

An injured girl told Homicide: "They opened one door, and everybody started pushing forward. Then people started pushing backwards. And it was getting hot, and people started passing out. And they were falling to the ground, and we were trying to pick them up. And I got pushed to the ground, and a guy told me to hold on to his neck. Then he said, 'I'm sorry I can't hold you any more, there's nothing I can do.' And I just started praying to God as loud as I could. People around me kept saying 'Pray louder, pray louder.' And I did. And all of a sudden a couple of people cleared a way."

Yet all of this happened in a small pocket among the spectators, out of the sight and knowledge of most, a pocket of quicksand in a forest of thousands of trees. Even most of the security guards were screened by the crowd from the actual casualties. Mike Spoess had concentrated so hard on getting the crowd through on the northeast bank of doors, away from the critical area on the other side of the lobby, that he didn't learn what had happened until ten o'clock that night. At that time, another guard came up to him and told him about it. Spoess was literally sick when he heard the news. He felt that it was his own personal loss. When his detail was dismissed, he got in his car, his 298-pound frame shaking with sobs. He cried all the way home.

The press conference was held at the District One Headquarters at 10:30 P.M., just as the crowds were beginning to file out of the Coliseum. There was still no news to release on the identification of the fatalities. Some were not yet identified. Other identification was withheld pending the notification of next to kin.

Mayor J. Kenneth Blackwell, the youngest mayor to be elected in Cincinnati's history, sat at a table next to Lieutenant Menkhaus. Blackwell pointed out that the general admission ticket system had apparently resulted in a disorderly rush for seats. He told about the critical decision to permit the concert to continue. Both he and Safety Director Richard Castellini, whose son was at the concert, agreed that attempting to stop the concert would have resulted in absolute chaos.

Lieutenant Menkhaus agreed also. He went on to summarize the scattered events of the evening in its basic details. The full detail of the city police had arrived on the plaza at an early hour, knowing that the concert was a sell-out. At about 7:54 P.M., some of the crowd kicked in a glass door. It was obvious that there was trouble brewing, although the crowd was not basically disorderly. Shortly after that, some of the entrance doors were opened, and the crowd surged forward. At 7:54 P.M., the police were directed to the first fatalities, about fifteen feet from the southwest bank of doors on the plaza. The concert began several minutes later. The city police had no control over the time the doors should be opened, but Menkhaus added: "The doors should have been opened much earlier."

Mayor Blackwell announced that he had asked Safety Director Castellini for a full report, and the brief conference was over. Meanwhile, the mass anxiety across the city and the area was still not relieved as the phone lines were jammed and many still remained in the dark as to the fate of their children.

PART IV

At the morgue, both the cause of death and the question of drug poisoning had to be settled quickly. As each fatality was examined, the grim truth slowly emerged. In none of the cases whatever did drugs or alcohol contribute to the cause of death. Whatever small traces were found were in miniscule, non-intoxicating quantities. The tentative cause in every case appeared to be: Asphyxia by compression of the chest. The victims had been squeezed to death. Official confirmation would not come until several days later.

The most feared cause—ODs or bad drugs—ironically played no part in the catastrophe. No one would know how many there were—nor were they important considering those who had died, except for one reason: They were expected and commonplace. They thus provided a camouflage for the real cause. In doing so, both spectators and security forces had been lulled into that false sense of complacency that over-looked the possibility of people being squeezed to death—some of them literally standing up and moving as corpses, feet off the ground, until they fell face forward, swept into the lobby by the force of the crowd.

Fire Lieutenant Moore watched at the morgue as the tests were completed. Jack Leach, living with the phone to his ear for hours, continued to try to comfort and inform the myriad of callers, still in the dark. Outside, a young husband stood by a police cruiser, completely broken and sobbing. His wife had been pronounced dead, and he had two small children at home. He called out curses to the sky, in spite of the friends who tried to comfort him. "Why did she have to die?" he kept asking.

Families were being called in as the identification process continued, faced with the appalling task of confirming the fatalities. An extra room was opened at the morgue for the Police Clergy Team and psychiatrists from the Central Psychiatric Team to try to comfort the bereaved, and to administer sedatives for those who were breaking down with remorse. Reactions varied from obscenities to blank, stolid silence hiding abysmal grief. Both the clergy and the psychiatrists were helping not only the families but also police and firemen who had worked in the rescue attempt and shared the shock and sorrow.

Lieutenant Moore watched one father escorted to the morgue to identify his son. As he came back along the hall, the lieutenant watched

221

the blood drain from the father's face. Then he leaned back against the wall and seemed to disintegrate. To Moore it was worse than the whole experience of the night, worse than most of his harrowing rescue missions all through the year. Here was a strong, healthy man melting before his eyes, and there was nothing Moore could do to help. "I would rather go through all the things we have to do with our rescue unit," Moore said later, "than to have to watch a thing like that."

As Greg McDonald pulled his car out of the garage and on the street, Jim Krumrei leaned over and switched on the radio. Within seconds, the tone of the newscaster reflected a major crisis. Then the full news emerged. *Eleven* fatalities—at the concert they had just attended? And they knew nothing about it at the time? It created a shock that neither Jim nor the others had ever experienced.

They drove toward the Coliseum, still looking for signs of Peter. They jumped out of the car at the lower level, and told a policeman there that their friend was missing—could they find out anywhere what had happened to him? The officer suggested they try the press box, inside the Coliseum.

At the building, the doors were locked. They pounded on them until another officer let them in. He let them go through to the press box, but it was jammed, and they were unable to get any information.

Frustrated in their attempt to learn anything from the press box, Jim suggested they go to the police headquarters. They drove toward Ezzard Charles Drive, where the District One Headquarters was. They waited as the officer checked with the coroner's office. "There is no confirmation yet," the officer said. "But they do have a fatality with Peter Bowes' ID card. That's about all I can tell you right now. Please wait here a minute."

The officer went back to the desk, and Jim could overhear him talking to the Bowes family. He could not make out exactly what he was saying. Jim and the others refused to believe that the worst had happened. There was some mistake, they were sure. Peter, with his smile, his zest for life, his cheerful sense of selflessness *simply could not be dead.* The idea was unacceptable.

But when two officers came out and asked the trio to guide them out to Peter's house in the Wyoming suburb, the strength of their convictions

222

faltered. The group divided up for the long ride to Wyoming. One officer drove Greg's car, with Greg and Jim in it. The other drove a police cruiser, with John Roosa riding with him. The trip was mainly silent in both cars.

On his way out of the concert, Rick Rauh, of the other group from Wyoming High, had sensed that there was more confusion on the plaza than usual. The TV remote unit was in action, not at all customary. He stopped and asked a policeman what had happened — were there serious injuries involved in the crush he had been through? The officer told him that he was not permitted to talk. Then Rick overheard someone talking about what had happened. He simply couldn't believe it. On the way home, he stopped at a White Castle restaurant to phone his family. His legs were severely brusied and he was forced to hobble. His parents were frantic, but their relief was immeasurable. He continued the drive home, listening to the news, thankful that he was alive.

Back at the Coliseum, the Homicide Squad was continuing its probe into the causes of the deaths. Security Guard Albert St. John tried to analyze why he had not been able to observe the actual conditions, even though he was stationed at one of the entrance doors. Asked by Specialist Ray Meyer when he first noticed anyone injured, St. John replied: "Well, that's when I looked outside and I saw all this equipment out there. And I thought, well, what in the world's going on? And all of a sudden I looked up, and my God, we got firemen all over — life squads all over."

Officer Richard Vogel, of Post 1, told Homicide how he tried to find out why the crisis had remained basically undetected: "I walked completely around the Coliseum, and spoke to approximately a hundred to a hundred and twenty-five people who were still outside walking around, in an effort to find anyone who might've been a witness to whatever happened. And no one had seen anything. I was unable to locate any witnesses. If I could find any, I was going to detain them for the Homicide Squad."

Said another patrolman: "We wanted to possibly prevent anybody from getting hurt or storming the door where there was glass, still jagged and broken out. And after we got there, I didn't observe any violence or rowdiness or anything else. It was just a steady flow of people, and they were all funneling into the turnstile gates."

A storm of controversy would obviously be gathering. The reasons would be probed in depth. The overriding purpose would be to prevent such a tragedy from ever happening again, in Cincinnati or anywhere else.

The police squad car and Greg's station wagon turned off Springfield Pike and onto Walnut Street, the quiet tree-lined land of pleasant, inviting homes, most of them dating back to the 1800's. An old barn or two sat back comfortably on the spacious lawns. The two cars pulled up quietly at the Bowes home, 15 Walnut Street, the gracious century-old home where Peter had lived all his life.

Jim Krumrei and his two classmates waited in silence, as the police went in to the Bowes' house. There must be hope, Jim was thinking. There could be a mistake. Peter's identification card might have dropped, and someone might have picked it up. There was no confirmation yet, and as long as there wasn't, there was still hope. As they waited, they saw Peter's sister, Nancy, come running to the house and in the doorway.

Images of Peter went through Jim's head. His crazy antics when he imitated Chuck Berry with his guitar; his easy swing with a golf club; his mastery of the recipe for eggs benedict; his effortless turns down a ski slope; his lively energy on the Fender guitar; his powerful strokes in a freestyle swimming race. Peter was singularly deathless. No one who expressed the joy of life as much as he did could possibly die young.

After several minutes, one of the police officers came out of the house. He thanked the group for guiding them to the address, and said they needn't wait any longer. The officer made no comment about Peter or his family, and no one asked. With Jim Krumrei and John Roosa in the car, Greg McDonald drove off to drop them at their homes. Instead of the four lively concert-goers who had driven to the Coliseum earlier that evening, there were now only three, and the car seemed almost empty.

Mary Bowes, Peter's mother, was an intelligent, sensitive woman of quiet courage and serenity. As the head of the local Montessori school,

224

and as a mother of four, her life was built around children. Along with Dick Bowes, her husband, she had nurtured a loving home that was reflected by the closeness and warmth of the family. The affection among Peter and his brothers, Andy and Ben, and his sister Nancy was marked. The closeness of Peter and his parents was rare in an age where a generation gap was supposed to exist.

At the Hamilton County Morgue, a friend and neighbor volunteered to help with the inescapable task of confirming the identity. She was strong, and not a member of the family. The grief that had struck the entire Bowes home was so stunning, so pervasive that total shock reigned.

For her part, Mary had to summon all her courage to enter the morgue, determined to face the facts, whatever they might be. She pondered the decision of whether she should identify Peter directly—or whether her neighbor should do it to spare her the anguish. Mary faltered in making the decision, but called on her deepest resources to give her the courage to do so. If it was Peter and she was sure that it was—she wanted one last glimpse of him, to touch his head, to give him one last kiss. She informed the attendant that she would go with him, and started down the hallway.

Part way down, she learned that she would have to identify Peter through a glass observation window. She would not be allowed in the same room. It was a strict regulation. Mary stopped. To see him like that would be worse than not seeing him at all.

Instead she sat and waited as her friend went to complete the positive identification. As she waited, she asked for the necessary papers that would fulfill Peter's wish to help others—to donate whatever organs could be used to someone who needed them. She thought of his lovely, soft brown eyes—and how they might be put to use to help another see. Part of him, at least, would live on. And his memory would remain so strong in so many minds—his family, his friends, his teachers, with all who had even brief contact with him that somehow he would seem to be alive.

With the identification of all the victims only partly made before 2:00 A.M., the police department planned to hold every name from the public until all were identified by families or friends. Through a misunderstanding, the coroner's office released a partial list, and the police sent a telex out over the wires to confirm the incomplete information at 0200 hours:

BULLETIN REFERENCE COLISEUM

REFERENCE MEETING DISTRICT ONE PERTAINING INFORMATION OF PERSONS DECEASED AT COLISEUM. THE FOLLOWING INFORMATION WAS ACCIDENTALLY RELEASED BY THE HAM CO CORONERS OFFICE AND SO IT IS BEING RELEASED TO NEWS MEDIA VIA THIS BULLETIN.

THE FOLLOWING LISTED PERSONS HAVE BEEN IDENTIFIED BY RELATIVES OR FRIENDS AND ARE DECEASED.
REMAINING INFORMATION AS WE RECEIVE IT WILL BE RELEASED IN THE AM ACCORDING TO AGREEMENT.
PETER D. BOWES, WHITE MALE DOB 10/5/61 RESIDENCE 15 WALNUT STREET, WYOMING, OHIO
TEVA LADD, WHITE FEMALE IN HER 20's, NO FURTHER INFORMATION
CONNIE BURNS, WHITE FEMALE, 18 YOA, NO FURTHER INFO
JAMES WARMOUTH, WHITE MALE 20 YOA, NO FURTHER INFO
BRYAN WAGNER, WHITE MALE, DOB 2/1/62, RESIDENCE 107 TREMENT IN FORT THOMAS, KY.

The names of the six others could not be released until identification had been completed. All the friends and families of the deceased shared the same anguish as Mary Bowes. Michael Ladd had desperately held on to his wife Teva, until she had been swept away by the tidal current of the crowd. They had two small children. Bryan Wagner had waited in front of the Coliseum entrance from three in the afternoon. His brother Eric watched him disappear into the crowd four hours later. James Warmouth was a star basketball player in the Dayton area, and failed to survive the crush. Connie Burns had arrived at the Coliseum on a chartered bus bearing an informal group from Dayton, two hours away. The bus sat late into the night outside the darkened Coliseum, waiting for three of its passengers who failed to show up. Slowly, the news became apparent. One of the missing passengers was injured, in the hospital. The other two would never return. Connie Burns was one of them.

PART IV

With only the partial list available, Cincinnati remained a restless, anxious city. Brian and Mary Downey's phone kept ringing for half the night, from worried friends who wanted to see if they were all right. Carolyn, Mike and Deborah could not sleep as the pain from their bruises increased, and as the terrifying scenes of the evening kept repeating themselves in their minds. Brant and Becky Ross were restless and tossing. Jim Krumrei listened to the news at home in disbelief, still not sure that Peter had been among the fatalities. He prayed for a mistake in the identification. Rick Rauh could not stop himself from listening to the news on the radio. Frank Wood worked with WEBN staff to assure that the programming remained at low key. Album selections for the next day were carefully screened. One song was quickly removed from the list. It was Led Zeppelin's "Trampled Under Foot." And back at Stouffer's Cincinnati Towers, Peter Townshend drank himself to sleep with a bottle of cognac.

Early the next morning, a tired-looking man entered the newsstand shop at Stouffer's Towers. He was wearing a T-shirt, blue jeans, and saddle shoes. He bought several copies of the *Cincinnati Enquirer* and left the shop quickly. It wasn't until after he left that Paula, on duty at the shop, realized that it was Roger Daltrey, lead singer of The Who.

The banner headline of the *Enquirer* streamed across the front page in enormous type: STAMPEDE KILLS 11 PERSONS AT COLISEUM ROCK CONCERT. Below on the front page were other headlines: DEATHS SHOCKED SOME, BUT OTHERS DIDN'T CARE — WHO IS THE WHO? — COLISEUM'S HISTORY OF CONCERT TROUBLES. The front page dealt exclusively with the story of the concert. "People couldn't care less," a girl concert-goer was quoted as saying. "There were broken bottles all over the place. People were kicking and shoving. They would rather see The Who than help someone who was dying."

But the news headlines and stories infuriated Deborah Shumate as she read the papers. To her, there was no stampede. She had seen acts of heroism everywhere, including Mike's, whose back was severely injured in doing so. She resolved that she would set the record straight, to make it known that 18,000 people couldn't possibly squeeze into a single entranceway and a subsidiary door in a single instant.

At about 9:30 A.M., several members of The Who contingent slipped

227

down the back way to L'Empril, where breakfast was being served. They looked tired and washed out. They carried with them a stack of newspapers, and read them in silence as coffee was served. As they read, the sadness in their faces was apparent. They stayed only a short time, then went up through the back way to the suite of manager Bill Curbishly, where a small press conference was arranged.

Roger Daltrey was fighting back tears as the interview began. He defended The Who's energetic antics on the stage, saying that the group in no way encouraged its avid followers to rush the entrance of the Coliseum. Now dressed neatly in a jacket and corduroy slacks, he said none of the group could sleep after the concert.

"I think three gates for 18,000 people is a bit of a joke," he said. "We have an energetic show, but it's not violent. We're not on drugs, and that's difficult for rock groups."

He added that if the deaths had happened inside the hall, The Who's career would have ended. "But our group was not responsible for crowd control," he concluded.

Curbishly backed Daltrey up on this point, and defended the group against the accusation that The Who had arrived late to cause the delay in the opening of the doors.

"The group was onstage checking equipment between 6:30 and 7:00," he said. "And the doors opened at 7:05 — a delay of only a minute or two."

Daltrey added that he had three children of his own, with his fifteen year old the same age as some of those who had died.

"I do know what it's like to be a parent," he said. "We came back here after the concert and choked. What can anybody do? It's not going to bring anybody back." Then, for the parents, he added: "Words are truly inadequate. Anything I say, I'm sure I'm not going to help. I feel totally helpless."

The press conference was brief. The Who contingent turned to packing their bags for their U.S. Air flight to Buffalo that morning. With considerable soul-searching, they had decided that the show must go on, and that the rest of their fourteen-city tour would be fulfilled.

When Rick Rauh woke the following morning, his legs were aching from his contusions and abrasions. He woke up slowly, his mind going

228

back over the struggle he had in the crowd and the overwhelming news of the tragedy. Suddenly, he heard a loud cry from the other room. It was his sister. She had just turned on the news. The name of Peter Bowes was among the victims.

Rick felt too numb to move. He sat there on the edge of his bed, frozen. Peter Bowes dead? He found it impossible to believe. He had been right with him in the crowd, right next to him. He had pulled Peter to his feet in the struggle, before he himself went down. Suddenly, Rick felt his entire world collapse. He prepared to go to school in a state of shock.

Jim Krumrei woke with the hope that the events at the Coliseum were only a nightmare. There still had to be a mistake about Peter, he told himself. He turned on the news and waited. It wasn't long before a preliminary list of victims was announced. Peter's name headed the list.

He forced himself to get dressed. He arrived at school about nine o'clock, and found the hallways full of students who were openly crying. Hardly anyone could believe it was Peter. He had no enemies. His buoyancy, humor and idealism touched everyone who knew him. His classmates and those closest to him were devastated.

Ken Hammel, the senior guidance counselor, was prepared for the reaction. He knew it would be severe and long-lasting. He had already talked with his colleagues at Finneytown High School, where two students and a recent graduate had been killed in the disaster. All agreed that the kids must talk it out, must get the agony out and must be encouraged to do so. The regular school routine was out of the question. Hammel himself was stunned. No one had thrown himself more into his volunteer work at the mental hospital than Peter. Five days a week. Sliced out of a time when he could have been enjoying himself. Actions like that made it all the harder to accept his death.

Jay Aronoff, another member of the Wyoming High group at the concert, walked to school that morning to talk with Hammel. His own experience in the crowd had been strange. The incredible wave motion swept him in every direction. He had no volition or control over his movement, and he was separated from his other friends from school.

As a door opened, he had been suddenly catapulted directly toward it. The movement kept going inside the lobby, where he felt he was going to be flipped over the turnstiles. Then he was grabbed by someone who stopped him. The wave he was riding carried him through the door many minutes ahead of people who had waited in front of him. Two of his friends who followed him found themselves swept through the door on their backs, holding on to people's legs.

When Jay sat down at Hammel's desk, Hammel asked him, "Have you heard the news?"

"It was terrible," Jay said. "Eleven people."

"I mean about Peter."

"What about Peter?" Jay asked.

"He was one of them," Hammel said.

Jay leaned back in his chair. He was wearing a sweater, and underneath it, a Who T-shirt he had bought the night before. He stood up, reached under his sweater, ripped the T-shirt off and threw it in the wastebasket.

Driving on his way to the Longview State Hospital that morning, Mark Carle, Peter's supervisor at the hospital school, snapped on the car radio to learn more about the disaster. Again the list of casualties came over the air, with Peter's name heading it. He gripped the wheel of his car tighter. Then he cried as he drove toward the hospital. He recalled Peter's face the previous afternoon, flushed with excitement about the concert.

Carle turned off Paddock Road, pulled up to the top of the hill where the sprawling brick building of the hospital lay. In the classroom, five of the students were waiting for him. Carle quietly explained that Peter had died the previous evening. Three of the students didn't seem to take it in. Perhaps death was beyond their comprehension. Tony, a big, deaf twenty-year-old struggling with first grade problems, had enough hearing for Carle to get it across to him that Peter would never return. Instead of stamping and cursing as he usually did, he sobbed. Byron, who had just learned to write his name the day before with Peter's help, looked out the window in silence. Then he turned back to the classroom and screamed.

Carle and the staff prepared a letter for the Bowes family that they read to the students in the class. "Our deepest sympathy goes out to you and your family," it read. "Peter's contributions to our staff and students were many. He was a good person and a hard worker. We will miss him very much."

230

PART IV

The teaching staff signed the letter on the right hand side; the students on the left. At the top of the list was Tony's name, boldly printed. Just beneath it, Byron signed his name. For the second time in his long efforts, he spelled it correctly.

The final confirmed list of the victims was compiled and issued by the coroner's office, stark and impersonal:

> Walter Adams, Jr., age 17
> Peter Bowes, age 18
> Connie Burns, age 21
> Jacqueline Eckerle, age 15
> David J. Heck, age 19
> Teva Ladd, age 27
> Karen Morrison, age 15
> Stephan Preston, age 19
> Philip K. Snyder, age 20
> Bryan Wagner, age 17
> James Warmouth, age 21

On each report, without exception, the identical notation was repeated: Asphyxia by compression of the chest. Some trace quantities of drugs or alcohol were found. None were instrumental in the deaths.

All over the city, people were asking *why?* Lieutenant Menkhaus, who had been in both the eye of the cyclone and around its perimeter, was determined to find the answer. He assembled every shred of information from his past experience to find answers. In the past he had consulted experts on crowd control, on the psychology of crowds, on the peculiar nature of anatomy of the rock audience. There was no question that the hard and heavy-metal rock attracted some violent types. Yet most of the spectators were clearly not of that category.

Lieutenant Menkhaus was also conversant with the history of rock concerts in other cities. He had investigated an Aerosmith concert in Cleveland two years before, where teams of medical doctors were required to treat ODs. He had consulted with Dr. Terry Pulse of Dallas, where 50 percent of the spectators at one concert were on drugs or alcohol. He had conferred with Tampa police when Led Zeppelin failed to show up for a concert, and the crowd had torn the stadium apart. But drugs and intoxication were not the major factors of The Who concert, although other crowd action characteristics were similar.

Ironically, the persistent pattern of these scenes in Cincinnati and other cities made the event on Riverfront Plaza look "normal" and expected. The appearance of the crowd served as a decoy. The action had occurred at so many times and in so many places before that no one could believe what was happening. If someone appeared to be losing consciousness, it was automatically attributed to the overdose. If someone yelled out over the noise of the crowd, the yell was attributed to "normal" crowd hysteria. The surface symptoms that appeared to the rescue squads and doctors at first glance suggested that bad drugs might be circulating. This was the assumption they had to go on. The previous scenes at the Led Zeppelin and other concerts actually appeared worse on the surface. All these elements diverted attention and reduced the ability to diagnose the situation promptly.

These conditions made it all the more difficult to answer the question: Where was the main villain? Even though the investigation of the Homicide Squad showed no criminal roots to the disaster, there had to be a cause that could be clearly defined. The search for the cause extended beyond the police and out through the city officials, the legislature, the people, the press and elsewhere. What complicated the situation was that the villain appeared to be a complex combination of factors. Which was the major cause was hard to discern.

There were the many suspects. The architecture of the building. Crowd control planning. Poorly defined responsibilities. Drugs and alcohol. The nature of the crowd. The nature and image of the rock group. The failure to open enough doors on time. And festival seating, a prime suspect.

The question was whether these added up to a composite villain, or whether any of them stood out most in the chaotic conditions that led to death. The detective story that was about to begin would extend far beyond Cincinnati and have an impact on every city in the country where rock concerts were scheduled.

PART V

THE AFTERMATH

MAYOR

J. Kenneth Blackwell reached his office in City Hall the next morning after a sleepless night. Few mayors had encountered such a trauma within a handful of days after taking office. He was confident that his approval of letting the concert continue would be understood as a safety measure to prevent an extension of the disaster. It was. What he sought now was action to prevent any such tragedy happening again.

He acted quickly. He instructed City Manager Sylvester Murray to take both short-range and long-range steps to deal with future problems, including legislation, public hearings and the setting up of a nine-person task force that included businessmen, lawyers, security men and both high school and university student leaders.

On Mayor Blackwell's mind was the necessity that all concerned cooperate with the task force in its probe. This would include the Coliseum management which had not been cooperative in the past. There was also the big question of festival seating, a term that suddenly became known nationwide. Blackwell considered a ban on this beyond debate. The city council was already exploring ordinances on this before the day was long underway.

There was another question that Blackwell pondered. The hard-rock concerts appeared to nurture the loosest conceivable standards of public behavior. He observed that the crowd at such concerts took it for granted

235

that normal rules did not apply. In a letter to the quickly-formed task force he wrote: "Attendance at a rock concert does *not* constitute a license for any unruly few to violate the rights and sensibilities of the many decent citizens, young and old, who attend these events. Public intoxication, public consumption of marijuana and other controlled substances, public urination, setting open fires — none of these acts are permissible whether they occur at a Coliseum rock concert or at a music hall symphony performance."

Newspapers across the country responded with stinging editorials. "A lot of Americans are moved to wonder again," wrote *The New York Times*, "whether the glamorization of violence by some rock groups may not itself explain the tragedy." The *Louisville Courier-Journal* stated: "It was not just promoters' greed, nor police insensitivity, nor the emotional flammability of alcohol and drugs alone that caused the murderous stampede, although all of them together may have been factors. What happened was a manifestation of mob hysteria. . . . "

Said the *Atlanta Constitution:* "This tragedy should not be dismissed as just another unfortunate incident by an unruly mob. It should serve as a warning to other cities about what can happen when not enough planning is involved."

The *Indianapolis News* added: "It's tragic that it took the lives of eleven young fans to say it, but the message should ring perfectly clear: Rock 'n roll — clean up your act!"

At the same time, the editorial added that the situation could possibly have been avoided with wise adult leadership on the part of the promoter, the hall management or the security force.

The promoter and the Coliseum management made no statements. Looming in the background would be millions of dollars' worth of lawsuits that probably no insurance policies would ever be able to cover. The Coliseum's Heekin was unavailable for comment. Larry Magid, the Philadelphia promoter who had booked the Cincinnati concert, told a *Rolling Stone* reporter: "I hear this idea that it happened because the promoter didn't have his shit together. You hear people saying 'It couldn't happen here in Providence,' or whatever. Bullshit! It's a symptom of a society. In fact, it has happened at soccer games in other countries. I just think it goes a lot deeper, where the responsibility lies and who to blame, no matter who didn't do what. After all, *we* didn't

236

trample anyone to death, and we didn't step on anyone, and we didn't push anyone."

But Monica Williams, a resident of Covington, Kentucky, had different ideas. She wrote about the concert to the editor of her local paper: "It makes me question our culture. That we allow ourselves to become so fanatical about something so inconsequential as a rock concert baffles me. That our sense of perspective and human lives are lost, all for the sake of entertainment, makes me sick. This may sound like it was written by someone's Great Aunt Mathilda, who is completely out of it, and is down on all teenagers and anyone under 35. It isn't. I'm just as into rock and roll and having a good time as any teenager, but I've stopped to think. When rock and roll becomes the be-all and end-all of our lives, it's time to take a good hard look at ourselves and our culture. How real is our perspective? Hopefully, though, these eleven people will not have died in vain. Perhaps this useless tragedy will touch our lives, causing us to take a harder look at our shallow culture."

The letter suggested another suspect: The prevailing culture itself. But it also brought up the question of whether rock was inconsequential or not. A force that could catapult so many into such a disastrous situation, a force that had become a passion of a whole generation, had to be considered a prime mover on the cultural scene. Were The Who, and other hard-rock superstars at the top of the pyramid, aware of their own power and the responsibilities laid on them because of that power? Was the image of these groups of such magnetic or gravitational force that they literally pulled the mass together and sucked it into the arena to its self-destruction?

The official probes that were being set in motion would deal with the hard evidence of the event. The evidence was important, but it reflected only surface conditions. Underneath them were underlying causes that superstars, rock managers, promoters and officials appeared to be largely unaware of. Even if they are academic, an understanding of them can define the problem for the future, for without this understanding, corrective measures can only remain ineffective.

While the theory of mass hypnosis by a charismatic superstar could explain many of the hard-rock disturbances inside the concert halls, the Cincinnati tragedy did not fall into this category. The music hadn't started, except for a few beats of the tune-up. What's more, there was no stampede, as many news stories reported. There were also many instances of selflessness, even heroism, in the crowd—the exact opposite of antisocial violence.

There was obviously brutally stupid crowd planning that city officials had no control over. Only a handful of doors were opened in the face of Lieutenant Menkhaus' pleas. No football stadium of any consequence opens only a single main entrance for a large crowd to funnel through; gates are opened all around the perimeter. From the days of the Roman Coliseum, this practice has been followed. In the face of the untenable position in which both the crowd and the police were placed on the plaza, there was what appeared to be a mindless, zombie-like forward movement, creating a squeeze of massive proportions. The deep causes of this phenomenon were obscure.

When the film *Love Story* was playing in theaters throughout the country, many young girls buying tickets at the box office burst into tears, anticipating the emotionalism of the film. Most had not even read the book. When *Jaws* was breaking box office records, it was observed that people standing in line exhibited extreme signs of jumpiness. Behind both instances was a single motivation: intense anticipation.

In comparison to a film, the anticipation created by a superstar rock band is magnitudes stronger. The empathy and identification with the superstar is far more intense for the devotees than for any comparable type of performance. The audience and the superstar are one, even in a poor performance. The image is there, and many rock fans have commented that the image is more powerful than the performer himself.

The spectators arriving on the Riverfront Plaza for The Who engagement arrived there for the most part in a preconditioned state that characterized most superstar concerts. The anticipation had been reinforced from constant listening to The Who's recordings, from the moment the tickets had gone on sale six weeks before. A Harris poll has revealed that 87 percent of teen-agers listen to rock music, many from early morning until night. The lyrics and beat are pounded into both ears and body at high decibels.

A survey by the Media Information Department of the McManus, John & Adams agency found that young adults listen to rock music on the radio an average of over five hours a day. They spend less than half of

238

that watching television. In addition to radio listening, there is the constant reinforcement of rock music on hi-fi tapes and records. The excitement created by the forthcoming concert adds to this intensity, creating a focus of anticipation that is unique in the field of the performing arts. One Who fan slept three nights in a sleeping bag outside the ticket office of the New Haven Coliseum at 40-degree temperatures, and claimed he wouldn't sell his $10 ticket for $500.

The incessant preconcert listening creates several conditions that are not obvious on the surface. Further clinical observations by Dr. John Diamond began to reveal other palpable facts. One was that the academic records of his young patients improved measurably when they stopped listening to rock while studying. In another case a precision engineering company switched from rock to soft music on its music broadcast system, and found that productivity increased as errors went down. The decision was not popular among the workers, but production still went up.

The constant rock music has become addictive, as it appears to be across the board with the young adult population. This addiction, in turn, leads to another subtle aspect of hypnosis and the trance state that is just as powerful as the direct induction of a trance and more insidious, since a subject is totally unaware of what is happening.

The condition is known as posthypnotic suggestion. In the case of addictive album listening, the beat and the rhythm create the trance state on the spot. It's not uncommon for an avid fan to walk down the sidewalk with a portable transistor and earphones, oblivious to the world. Others remain glued to a pair of stereo speakers at high volume. If the lyrics and heavy beat are strident and commanding, as they often are, it is possible for posthypnotic suggestions to be planted, suggestions that a subject feels compelled to carry out.

Lyrics of many superstars are frequently forceful and commanding. A singer like Jimi Hendrix had exceptional power. When he sang his own "Electric Lady Land" on a recording, he could, as he said, "put anything you want into that gap."

The lyrics of this song, for example, ask the listener if he or she has ever visited "Electric Lady Land," where a magic carpet is waiting, and where the listener can take a ride with sound and motions without hang-ups—all suggesting and recommending an hallucinogenic trip.

239

On a souped-up stereo, these become vocal commands, especially to a young and impressionable mind that might be in a waking trance from long hours of listening. Under these conditions, the lyrics can have the same effect as a strong posthypnotic suggestion. They suggest directly to the listener to go out and get both stoned and laid—a suggestion that is likely to be unconsciously followed. If the parents of a thirteen- or fourteen-year-old are not happy about this idea, a heavy conflict can follow. The young adolescent may have no idea why he has such compulsions. No parental or police restraint is likely to override a suggestion made through effective hypnosis if it is implanted firmly and often enough on a subject in a receptive, sensitized state. The same applies to the posthypnotic condition.

Clinical experiments on this state have shown dramatically how effective posthypnosis is. While in a trance, a subject can be instructed to do something at a later time that is markedly absurd, such as putting his jacket on backwards or patting a dog that isn't there. When out of the trance state, he will feel an irresistible compulsion at the instructed time, and will act out the instruction without knowing why.

The posthypnotic suggestion can last for a considerable time. Estabrooks reports one such incident that lasted over twenty years. Wolberg describes a suggestion planted this way as a "spontaneous self-limited posthypnotic trance" that the subject can't resist, even though he knows the act is ridiculous. A basic characteristic of the trance state is that the subject will take any suggestion literally, including posthypnotic suggestion.

Through six weeks of compulsive listening to the hard-rock albums prior to the concert, many of the crowd can arrive for a concert hypercharged emotionally, in a waking trance, and not even aware of it. By the time psychoactive drugs or alcohol or both get working the posthypnotic state can deepen, and the behavior can become more irrational.

Instead of the conventional labels "good kids" and "bad kids" arriving at a concert, there would be "susceptible subjects" and "resistant subjects." According to statistics on hypnotic induction, up to 30 percent of the crowd could arrive in a posthypnotic condition, with the absence of rational conscious thinking.

All through the long weeks leading up to the concert, the focus has been on the superstar in a highly-intensified and aroused way. He

240

emerges as all-powerful and omnipotent. Through the phenomenon of hypnosis, a transference has taken place, roughly similar to that of psychoanalytic therapy. This willing transference leads in turn to an exaggerated emulation of the superstar's lifestyle and behavior pattern.

What a star might do in reasonable moderation, the willing subject in a trancelike state might do in excess. An adolescent who wouldn't dream of shoving a needle in his arm, of driving a car so as to endanger others, throwing a beer bottle into a crowd, smashing through windows or doors or tossing an M-80 in a crowded auditorium, could literally do any of these things, and still not know why.

Dr. Michael Lieberwitz, of the Institute for Research in Hypnosis, notes: "This exaggerated attachment (of the hypnosis transference) may lead to an identification with and an emulation of the superstar's behavior patterns. This might range from emulating one small aspect of the admired star to attempting to copy his personality and interactive characteristics in a global sense." Applied to the apparent death wish of Joplin, Hendrix, Morrison, Brian Jones, Moon and others, this could have serious consequences.

Not only has the repetitive preconcert listening invariably been at high volume (many try to match the decibels of the concert), but the hard-rock lyrics are frankly based on aggression. In his clinical practice, Dr. Lieberwitz has further noted: "The dynamic and auditory aspects of the music are capable of increasing and amplifying the state of arousal of the person. With this scenario, you have an increased tendency towards suggestibility, and the possible evoking of latent, aggressive, angry, and hostile feelings that are present in all of us, some of which might not be that latent."

Thus on December 3, 1979, the crowd that arrived on Riverfront Plaza was in a highly preconditioned and sensitized mood, drawn there by the uncontestable charisma of The Who, and flowing toward the narrow funnel of the doorways as described in Peschel's analogy of granular particles flowing into bins, or Henderson's picture of molecular particles of water moving toward a dam. In either way, there would be a squeeze as the human molecules inexorably moved forward, a large percentage of them open to posthypnotic trance conditions, and the others subject to their resulting irrationality.

But all these aspects were not quite enough to explain why eleven people had to die. There were other factors that intensified this hypnotic state. Reason and logic were dulled. The crowd was jammed as tight as a pack of cigarettes over a three- to four-hour period. Lifting an arm or hand was almost impossible. Once the bodies were pressed together, the biting cold changed to suffocating heat. Food or drink or the chance to go to a restroom were denied, contributing to exhaustion. All this could break down the strongest of resistance.

More than this, though, is the reaction of an individual as he becomes part of the crowd itself. Here an overall umbrella covers the scattered contributory reasons and draws them together under its cover. It was Gustav Le Bon, the turn-of-the-century social commentator who had great influence on Freud's thinking, who said: "Behind the visible facts are hidden at times thousands of invisible causes."

As one of the most profound students of crowd behavior, Le Bon probed deeply for these invisible causes, and came up with unique and articulate answers. Among his major conclusions is that the crowd automatically creates a condition of superhypnosis on its own, far more potent than in ordinary individual hypnosis. In a crowd, the individual finds that his conscious personality has entirely vanished, that his will and discernment are lost.

"We see then," Le Bon writes, "that the disappearance of the conscious personality, the predominance of the unconscious personality, the turning by means of suggestion and contagion of feelings and ideas in an identical direction, the tendency to transform the suggested ideas into acts—these we see are the principal characteristics of the individual forming part of the crowd. He is no longer himself, but has become an automaton who has ceased to be guided by his will."

From this description, all the long series of scenes from the Mods and Rockers on the beaches of Brighton, through riots and disturbances of the mid-sixties in Britain, Germany, Sweden, Austria, Warsaw, Isle of Wight or Altamont, plus the continuous crowd problems with Morrison, Joplin, Hendrix, the Stones, Led Zeppelin and The Who, reveal the characteristics of the individual drawn into the rock concert crowds, although Le Bon's words were written more than a half century before.

But Le Bon examines carefully the other "invisible causes" that contribute to the large picture. A collective mind forms that becomes a single being in itself. It possesses properties that are different from those of the bodies in it. Contagion sweeps through the mass, which Le Bon says "must be classed among those phenomena of a hypnotic order." The contagion is such that the individual sacrifices his personal interest to the collective interest. Merely by forming part of a crowd, he descends several rungs in the ladder of civilization, as Le Bon puts it, and becomes a primitive being. In a state of expectant attention, he is an easy prey for suggestion. At that time, Le Bon says, everything depends on the nature of the suggestion to which the crowd is exposed. And it is suggestion that forms the base of hypnosis.

The continuous disturbances of the hard-rock scene made it clear what the nature of the disturbances were. With a crowd that is already hovering on the borderland of the unconscious mind, Le Bon notes that the brain tends to transform itself into action, with little if any individual sense of responsibility.

But at Cincinnati, there was no superstar directly on the scene at the time of the tragedy to create direct suggestion. How does that jibe with Le Bon's theories? First, Le Bon is dealing only with the hypnoid condition caused by the crowd itself, without any directed induction. He had no data on what would happen when a preconditioned crowd would assemble in an electronic age, already in a posthypnotic state. In this way, an unusual situation arises: a double layer of hypnotic influence, one from the crowd, the other from the preconcert conditioning. This double layer intensifies a vulnerable situation.

The electronic age concept still fits in with Le Bon's historical theories. "Thousands of *isolated* (italics added) individuals," he writes, "may acquire at certain moments, and under the influence of certain violent emotions . . . the characteristics of a psychological crowd . . . to at once assume the characteristics peculiar to the acts of a crowd." In other words, the preconcert masses exposed individually through incessant listening to albums and radio, idolizing the image of the superstar, and steeped in the anapestic beat and strident, and often violent, lyrics *have already become a crowd before they arrive at the concert hall.* In a sense, this creates a third layer of hypnosis when the crowd physically arrives to assemble.

What then comes into play Le Bon calls "the psychological law of the mental unity of crowds." The crowd is put into possession of a sort of collective mind that makes those in it feel, think and act in a manner quite different from that in which each individual would feel, think and act when isolated from the crowd.

This mental unity of the collective mind is particularly susceptible to magnetic and charismatic influences. The more powerful the magnetism and charisma of the superstar, the more impulsive and mobile the crowd becomes. As Le Bon states it: "The crowd is not prepared to admit that anything can come between its desire and the realization of its desire." In Cincinnati, the desire was to get in to see The Who, who represented an irresistibly magnetic image. In this regard, several of Le Bon's axioms come into play:

- A crowd thinks in images.
- A crowd is only impressed by excessive sentiments.
- Sometimes the sentiments suggested by the images are so strong that they tend to transform themselves into acts.
- To the individual in the crowd, the magnetic image or leader becomes the goal and guide of the individual's actions—the crowd demands a god before everything else.

Le Bon does not define just any assemblage of people as a crowd. They do not become so until they surrender their individuality. This inevitably follows under the sway of the charismatic leader and an atmosphere of contagious excitement and energy. The superstar, whose albums have supplied the electronic preconditioning over the weeks before the concert, fulfills just that situation. The waiting crowd outside and the crowd that later fills the auditorium are the same. The presence and image of the superstar are perceived before they go to the concert hall, and before they physically see him on stage.

The crowd, says Le Bon, is always in need of a leader, and it instinctively recognizes men of energy as masters. The master is able to wield almost absolute power. He feels the overwhelming playback, especially in the unequaled energy of a rock concert. His ego swells, and he demands more from the crowd, which willingly gives it to him. The two forces build on each other in a rising spiral. Both move to a trance state.

If Le Bon is right, the basic conscious character of the individual in a

244

crowd makes little difference. Le Bon is convinced that the most inof-
fensive personality in ordinary circumstances can turn into a savage
member of a crowd. "From the moment they form part of the crowd, the
learned man and the ignoramus are equally incapable of observation.
. . . The intellectual standard is immediately and considerably low-
ered."

On Riverfront Plaza in Cincinnati two opposing forces were at work.
One force was the mindless forward movement as the crowd sought its
superstar gods under the triple layer of hypnotic conditions: direct
hypnosis, posthypnosis, and hypnosis caused by the crowd itself. When
it was almost too late, another force began to show itself: one of courage
and selflessness, as people struggled to hep each other under impossible
mental and physical stress.

Again the studies of Le Bon come up with an answer. He discerns that
while a crowd may be capable of violence and destruction, it is simultaneously capable of acts of devotion and sacrifice, and to a much
loftier extent than the isolated individual is capable of. In the paradox,
selfless actions are taken unconsciously and without reasoning, as in the
negative actions. They do occur, however, in striking contrast to the
destructive impulses, but in much less frequency.

It is only through understanding this subtle combination of forces that
the persistent hard-rock violence can be explained—especially since a
sometimes similar demographic audience does not react this way at a
John Denver, Ravi Shankar or Bob Dylan concert. These audiences are
operating under Le Bon's crowd hypnosis, too. They have also under-
gone passionate preconcert listening over an extended time, and have
been exposed to post-hypnotic suggestions. But the suggestions are of a
different nature. Although some of this music embraces social protest, it
does not feature mindless aggression or aimless destruction. It does not
consistently pound out a tribal or anapestic beat. The decibels and
sensory overload are much lower. The musicians do not smash their
instruments and amplifiers onstage, or direct the audience to demolish
the seats and rush the stage. The charismatic image is there, but it is
different, and the crowd follows the image.

Awareness of all these "visible facts and invisible causes" is easier to
come by in retrospect than in foresight. Whether the superstar, hall
management or promoter were aware of the mechanics of the phenom-

PART V

enon of powerful triple-layer, triple-reinforced hypnosis or not, the
history of the predictable disturbances and their dangers made it clear
that something was going on that needed correction, and little if anything was being done about it.

The hard-rock superstar sits on the top of a pyramid formed by the
promoter and the concert hall manager. The star has inordinate power
by virtue of complex mass-psychology mechanics in an age of instant
mass communication. Because of the mass communication, the power
holds sway even before a concert begins. With rock music being one of
the most potent forces of the age, the need for a strong sense of
responsibility on the part of the superstar becomes urgent. The question
after Cincinnati was: Was this need taken seriously?

The action that followed in the wake of the disaster centered on two
hearings of the city council, and Mayor Blackwell's immediate request
for emergency ordinances. In addition, the new special task force began
its inquiry to consider the long-range problems dramatized by the events
of December 3.

From Blackwell's point of view, any further debate on the question of
festival seating and of the necessity of police decision-making authority
was out of the question. He noticed that there had been nothing but
study and discussion about the crowd problem for four long years. He
blamed much of the delay on the fact that the managers of the Coliseum
had been part of past public-safety study teams, and this brought about a
conflict of interest. Safety was simply nonnegotiable. The new task force
would not include any representatives of the Coliseum.

The emergency ordinances were passed quickly by the city council.
There would be no more festival seating at any gathering of 2,000 or
more spectators. Further, the authority and responsibility for crowd
control decisions would rest with the city police, whose hands had been
tied at the time of The Who concert.

The two hearings were held in the City Council Chambers at City
Hall on December 11 and December 18. They were not of interest only
to the legislators, officials or police. The concert-goers who had lived
through the experience were determined to testify, to express their
anguish, their anger and their feelings.

Most were furious at the press for labeling the tragedy as a stampede.
"Calling what happened at the Coliseum that night a stampede," said

246

Michael Kanser to the council members, "is a distortion of the facts. A stampede implies a sudden mad rush. This did not happen. Instead, there was a slow, inescapable and constantly more dangerous crush that built steadily for over an hour. After I attempted to exhort people to back up, I was told by several people around me that all big rock concerts were like this. . . . I found it personally appalling that such a dangerous situation had come to be considered normal. . . . The rock concert industry has been either incapable or unwilling to provide the assurance to its paying customers that they can expect that personal safety is included in the price of the ticket."

Another witness, Ron Duritsch, agreed with Kanser. "The tragedy was no stampede," he said. "It was a churning, suffocating crush of people who failed to communicate with each other and those in charge. These people did not willingly step on others. They had no way to move individually once they were upon those who were down. . . . They tried to turn and retreat, but this was useless for they could not even turn their bodies around. The pounding of the waves was endless. Many times your feet would not touch the ground. There was just no space. They began to fall unnoticed by all but those immediately surrounding them. People in the crowd ten feet back from them didn't know what was happening. The person in front of you went down, then you would follow for there was no one to lean against."

Forrest Buckley traced the long history of opposition to festival seating, and his efforts since 1976 to combat the constant fire violations inside the building. "I hope and pray," he said, "that if there's another disaster, it's not because of violations of the fire code. But we do feel strongly that if people are going to be suffocated or stomped to death, as happened December the third, the next time—unless we do something about it—it may happen *inside* the Coliseum. We cannot place the profits of a private enterprise above the safety of the people that go to those events that are held at the Coliseum."

The issues that emerged during the hearing boiled down to the question of public safety versus public enjoyment. Coming out of the Cincinnati tragedy was a parallel to the ancient axiom of not yelling "Fire" in a crowded theater. The freedom of expression did not include throwing beer bottles, setting off fireworks, lighting butane cans, or burning paper cups, or inciting the crowd, in or out of a packed theater.

247

ARE THE KIDS ALL RIGHT?

Deborah Shumate and her sister Carolyn, Brant and Becky Ross and Jim Krumrei were not able to speak until the second hearing on December 18. Deborah and Carolyn each wore "Who" T-shirts, reaffirming their loyalty to the group whom they held harmless for the event. Deborah was filled with scorn, as other speakers had been, at the reference by the media to a stampede. She spoke firmly: "I consider myself a responsible citizen. Not an animal. I was not drinking, smoking or using any drugs."

She went on to tell of her experience in detail, of how she felt she was going to die, of how she felt that the private security people were indifferent, of her disbelief that more doors weren't opened. Her main question she left unanswered: "How did they expect eighteen thousand people to get through two doors in forty minutes?"

Although there were more than two doors opened and the private security force was more than concerned, her question was relevant. When Carolyn spoke, she echoed her sister's thoughts as she went through her experience for the hearing. Both lauded the efforts of the people in the crowd who tried to help each other under the most frightening circumstances.

Brant Ross carefully broke down what happened to him, almost minute by minute, to chronicle the event for the city council. When Jim Krumrei followed him to the microphone, his grief at the loss of his friend, Peter Bowes, was apparent.

"It bothers me," he said, "that I was there and one of my best friends who went with me was killed. I counted only nine ticket takers for eighteen thousand people. But there was nothing the police outside could do." He told of seeing two doors closed because people inside the doors were being crushed. Like so many others, he spoke with sadness and frustration. The damage was done. Nothing could bring Peter back—or any of the other ten who died that night.

The Who continued its tour, with beefed-up security everywhere. The Buffalo concert the next night was dedicated to the kids who had died in Cincinnati. Daltrey was bitter about the report that not enough doors had been opened. He told a reporter that in the future the group would insist on having better control—"Anything we can do to stop it from ever happening again."

248

PART V

For the remainder of the tour concerts, there was only reserved seating. There was no trouble. Only Providence canceled the concert scheduled for that city.

Pete Townshend showed variable stresses in his interviews following the Cincinnati concert. Frequently brooding and dour, and alternately articulate and confused, he reflected the strain he was undergoing at those times he was persuaded to talk. He appeared to be hit with disconnected tides of thought as he was interviewed by Tom Bender on WRIF, the Detroit radio station. Several days after Cincinnati, he told Bender: "I went down for a while, but I feel happy now. But I don't care, I don't give a shit. I really want rock. I'm not worried about my neuroses or problems anymore. I just want to work and be happy. We didn't know anything about the accident. But everything in my life tells me to stop—my two little girls, my brain, body, everything tells me to stop. I'm not going to stop. I just don't *care*, really. I really don't *care* what happens anymore. I really have gone blind. I mean I've done the rock and roll thing, and I'm paying and I'm paying and I'm paying, and *I do not want to stop now*. And I don't even care anymore."

Townshend was hard to follow, but he sounded anguished and sincere. He continued: "I'm so upset for the kids that died in Cincinnati, and their folks and friends and families, and all that . . . but The Who isn't the only band that can cause a stampede. Led Zeppelin can do it. Yes can do it. Genesis can do it," he said, referring to other hard-rock Riverfront concerts. "In fact, in Cincinnati, all those bands did it before we even arrived there."

The facts were correct enough. But it was the persistence of this kind of uncontrolled situation that everyone in the city of Cincinnati was struggling to prevent in the future. Townshend's contradictory thoughts continued with his characteristic frankness: "It's rock. It's not The Who. It's rock and roll. Everybody—all of us—we're all bloody responsible. We make terrible mistakes, you know, by indulging our macho instincts."

In his obvious sadness there was both pathos and bathos, a sense of longing for the higher aspirations inspired by Meher Baba versus the strident aggressiveness of rock.

Although the rock scene that Townshend appeared to be blaming was the target of the task force and the legislators, their inquiry was not one of

249

condemnation. There was no great cry for an outright ban. If anything the task force was leaning over backwards to see if the concert scene could be carried on without violent excesses that had consistently accompanied the parade of hard-rock groups. There were practical reasons.

On December 3, the day of the concert, the Coliseum management had made a prompt and full payment of $1.4 million to the bondholders exactly on schedule. The question in the back of the investors' and city fathers' minds was: How could these payments be made so promptly without the support of the lucrative rock concert business? The ideal would be that the concerts could be conducted in such a way that public safety was assured. The answers lay in the new ordinances and their strict enforcement.

The two concerts scheduled to follow The Who in December had been promptly canceled, as the task force pulled its organization together. Shortly after its formation, the panel gave its go-ahead to the scheduling of future 1980 rock concerts. Scheduled for the new year were three concerts that included the soft-rock Linda Ronstadt, the hard-rocking Texas group, ZZ Top, and the heavy-metal idols of the macho-adolescents, Van Halen, with 45,000 watts of sound and three tiers of amplifiers. These three groups would be the acid test and could, in effect, demonstrate whether the safety rules and precautions could stand up in the face of reality.

What was forming was a confrontation that could not be avoided by promoters, fans, officials or the groups themselves. Safety was not negotiable, as nearly everybody agreed. At the bottom line, the superstars on the stage at the time could either increase safety by encouraging the crowd to do so — or threaten it by flaunting the efforts of the fire and police details to keep things in hand.

First on the list was ZZ Top, on March 22, nearly four months after the fatal Who incident. Only a few days before, Cincinnati Safety Director Richard Castellini called a meeting that included Richard Morgan of the Coliseum, and Cal Levy, Electric Factory's promoter for the concert. He asked to see specific, written operation procedures planned by the Coliseum for the renewal of the rock concert series. He was appalled by what they told him. There were no written procedures whatever for compliance with the fire and building codes and none for the handling of crowds inside or outside the facility. Further, Levy and Morgan indicated that they planned to open only ten or twelve doors.

After Castellini blasted Brian Heekin, a new set of ground rules were laid out. Reserved seating was already in force. But now there would have to be twenty-eight doors open and sixteen turnstiles manned. The doors were to open at 6:30 sharp, ninety minutes ahead of show time. Public address announcements were to be made, instructing the ticket holders to proceed either to the odd- or even-numbered entrances, depending on what tickets were held. There was to be strict enforcement of the No Smoking rule, not just grass, but cigarettes. The promoter was instructed to turn on the houselights if people lit the matches and butane lighters for the encore. There were to be thirty city police on hand, plus some twenty plainclothesmen. Supporting these were to be thirty private security guards, and twenty-five members of the youthful T-shirt peer security men—more respected by the crowd than any of the others.

Thanks to the new restrictions forcibly imposed on the Coliseum, the concert came and went, without serious incident. There was no jam on the plaza. When the doors opened at 6:30, only a scattering of spectators were on hand. Others filed in later, without a sign of a crush. By the time Linda Ronstadt arrived the following Tuesday, the scene was placid throughout.

The future began to look brighter. Mayor Blackwell cautiously awaited a full report on the success of the new regulations from his Safety Director. But he indicated that it was too soon to tell what the long-range aspects would be. Neither of the first two concert stars asked for trouble from the stage, and both cooperated with the new safety regulations.

The focus of attention turned to the next superstar group that would not appear until a month or so later, on April 24. This would be the band known as Van Halen, featuring two Van Halen brothers, and a lead singer named David Lee Roth. It was among the heaviest of the heavy-metal superstar groups, riding a high wave into the Top Ten, with record sales of some seven million copies. At a time when many thought that heavy-metal was giving way to New Wave and Punk Rock, Van Halen was soaring on the charts to disprove the theory. The group, especially Roth, deliberately bragged about being obnoxious, bragged about how many women they could lay at a single session, bragged about $10,000 worth of damage they inflicted on the University of Southern Colorado's dressing room area.

Roth looked and acted as if he had created the primeval sex drive. The group played as if they had invented the thunderclap. They had been called the American Led Zeppelin, but some of the Zeppelin's numbers were pale by comparison with the strident fusilades erupting from the Van Halen amplifiers. A favorite piece of theirs was called "Runnin' with the Devil," a breathless number that meant what it said, and could blast the fans half out of a hall.

Van Halen was fond of its strident vulgarity and proud of its ability to shock. It was natural that this event in the offing was a little unnerving to a city still freshly anguished and desolated by its recent disaster and desperately trying to forestall any sort of repetition. The attitudes of officials were sharply provisional in the light of the reputation of the Van Halen group.

To emphasize that the city of Cincinnati meant business, Mayor Blackwell and the chiefs of both the fire and police departments met with the manager of the Van Halen band just before the concert. The officials made it clear that there would be no compromise with safety, and that the cooperation of the band was critically important.

Thanks to reserved seating and the beefed-up security patrol, the crowd entrance for the Van Halen concert was uneventful. The electric announcement sign sharply warned against smoking and against the traditional butane salute—for the encore or any other time. Fire inspectors were posted at strategic positions, and the concert began. The music exploded through two numbers, and then led into "Runnin' With the Devil." The crowd exploded with it.

When the number was over, the acclaim resounded as loudly as the music. Then lead singer David Lee Roth stepped forward to speak to the crowd. Some wondered if he were going to give some kind of sermon about how the safety rules were important. Roth cleared his throat and spoke:

"I heard on TV some shit that you can't smoke in here. If you came here, you can smoke anything you want. You can tell them to stick that shit back up where it came from."

He turned and indicated the backstage area. "I swear to God when I came through those doors, I smelled dope. *Can you hear me?*"

PART V

The crowd did hear. It rose and gave Roth a roaring salute. Someone lit a butane lighter, and thousands followed. The packed hall blazed in flickering light. The concert continued.

When it ended, Roth went backstage. On his heels were several officials of the Cincinnati police and fire departments. They waited outside his dressing room for half an hour, until Roth finally consented to let them in. When they entered, Roth was the reverse of his macho image on stage. He was meek, subdued, quiet.

The officials lost no time in slapping him with a citation. They charged him with a misdemeanor for complicity in inciting others to violate the fire code. Later, it was discovered that the wrong section of the code had been cited. The charge had to be withdrawn, to the distress of the city officials and others who feared for the future safety of rock audiences at the Coliseum. Roth got off scot-free, and announced that he was thinking about suing the city for infringing on his rights of free speech.

James Chute, writing in the *Cincinnati Post* the next day, brought up the question of a rock band's responsibility for the actions of a crowd.

"Many elements in the Van Halen show," he wrote, "are calculated to arouse the audience to exactly the kind of behavior the city is trying to prevent. While security guards are trying to get people to sit down and clear the aisles, the band's lighting is set to shine on the audience, to make it part of the show."

He continued: "Fans and security officers are caught between rock-and-roll and a hard place. The fans are being urged to react by the group, but are warned and even ejected for responding in a manner other than specified by the Coliseum and the city. Security guards are asked to police what in many regards seems unpolice-able as long as the impetus to react comes from the stage."

This was the root. James Chute caught it in one short sentence: When the impetus to react come from the stage, the conditions remain unpoliceable, especially when the concept of the stage is expanded to include the long preconcert conditioning.

Mass hypnosis, including posthypnotic suggestions and the mechanics of crowd psychology, are facts of life. Intrinsically, they are neither good nor bad. Like a television set or computer, everything depends on what is fed into them. It is an unavoidable conclusion that the hard-rock scene consciously or unconsciously programs a situation that can, under certain conditions, lead to destruction, damage, injury and even death. As programmers of this ambiance, the hard-rock superstars are the only ones who can effectively deal with it. A few hundred feet away from where the disaster happened, the Van Halen group showed no signs of getting the message.

Nor did Peter Townshend when he was interviewed by *Rolling Stone* about the Cincinnati concert in June 1980, six months later. Townshend said that The Who was deeply moved by the horror and loss of life. He spoke of love and affection for the families of those who had died. But then he made a mercurial turn. He told interviewer Greil Marcus that when he heard the news of the deaths, the group dropped its guard, but just for a second—before it went back up again.

Speaking in his own italics, Townshend said: "It was, fuck it! We're not going to let a *little thing* like this stop us. This was the way we *had* to think. We had to reduce it. . . . We had a tour to do. We're a rock and roll band. You know we don't fuck around, worrying about eleven people dying. We *care* about it, but there is a particular attitude I call 'tour armor.' When you go on the road you throw up an armor around yourself, you almost go into a trance."

In his ambiguity, Townshend did not appear to be facing the issue. This failure was even more apparent when he got into the subject of festival seating: "I think the way festival seating was blamed, wholesale, for practically all the problems, was quite a nasty, negative overreaction—because I *like* festival seating. When I go to a concert I don't want to have to fucking sit in a numbered seat. . . . I like to be able to move about . . . or push my way to the front if I want to, or hide in the back if I want to. I also know, from the stage, that you get the best atmosphere with festival seating."

With every large coliseum in the States reviewing its policies on festival seating, Townshend's statement had a hollow ring. Nor was he showing recognition of the power turned over to him by the hypersuggestible crowd. The power was his, whether he wanted it or not, as well as the responsibility that went with it.

Then he spoke some lines that brought Peter Bowes' brother Ben up short when he read them: "We did all the things," Townshend told Marcus, "we thought were right at that time: sent flowers to the fucking

254

funerals. All . . . wasted. I think that when people are dead, they're dead."

Ben Bowes lost no time in throwing the rose he had been saving in his brother Peter's memory in the waste basket. One *Rolling Stone* reader wrote: "Couldn't he (Townshend) at least have deleted the word *fucking* out of respect?"

The generation that had grown up with the first fifteen years of the hard-rock age found that rock gave them a communication of their own, and a release and escape from the harsh or bitter or routine lives that many lived. They felt that rock was more of an experience than music. They felt it attacked the shame and hypocrisy of a world gone sour.

Deborah Shumate felt deeply that rock made her feel like a free spirit—free to move or tap or clap in creative self-expression. Her husband Mike felt that he had made many close friends, including Deborah, through a mutual interest in rock. Carolyn felt its frankness spoke of reality, a reality that made her feel alive.

Becky Ross felt that the music sang of many sensitive and personal things that helped her understand her own feelings and emotions, and she had met Brant through rock. Jeff Waddle felt that it encouraged a loving brotherhood among its listeners; that it made strong, intelligent social statements and criticisms. Jim Krumrei felt simply that it represented his generation more powerfully than anything else. Peter Bowes had found it a rich source of vitality and energy.

Any wide sample of spectators massing at a hard or heavy-metal rock concert would show fundamentally that "the kids are all right." Yet collected en masse for this specific kind of concert, something happens, something that even the concert-goers are not aware of. As for the promoters, the arena managers and the superstars, the phenomenon goes to the heart of their exploitation of a whole generation.

Only the deepest kind of analysis reveals the base problem. It lies in those "thousand of invisible causes" that Le Bon so painstakingly analyzed, that Dr. John Diamond revealed with palpable evidence, that Wolberg and Estabrooks pinpointed, that Lieberwitz defined, that Erikson, Freud and Rollo May anticipated—and that promoters, arena managers and hard-rock superstars ignored.

The eerie part is that there is no conscious awareness of these invisible causes on the part of those in the crowd—the ones who are most victimized by them. They are blindly unconscious of the preconditioned mood and state they arrive in. They are unaware that the "impetus to react comes from the stage"—before and during the concert, as almost any roadie will confirm. They are unaware for the most part of the unconscious death wish that is at the center of the world of hard rock, and that has revealed itself clearly over the past fifteen years. They have not seen or tested the results of the muscle weakness arising out of exposure to the constant hard-rock beat, exclusively. They have not discerned that the almost pain-level volume—on the stereo or at the concert — exacerbates this to produce physiological and emotional changes that seriously damage the will to live and to be creative.

There is a disturbing paradox here. The generation growing up from the mid-sixties on has been finding release and energy that literally appears to carry with it the seeds of despair and even a death wish. This conclusion is based on evidence, not opinion. It is ironic that the young, the bright, the intelligent are subject, in effect, to latter-day Pied Pipers who show little sign of changing the tune of the pipes. It is equally ironic that the exploiters, old and young, continue to profit, blind to almost everything but the almighty buck. Without wanting to be so, Cincinnati has become a symbol. If the tragedy there can create a widespread sense of awareness of the pitfalls involved, another such senseless tragedy might never have to take place.

BIBLIOGRAPHY

Books

Bancroft, Ann, *Twentieth Century Mystics and Sages*. Chicago, Henry Regnery Company, 1976.

Banta, R. E., *The Ohio*. New York, Rinehart & Co., 1949.

Becker, Ernest, *The Denial of Death*. New York, The Free Press, 1973.

Bejerot, N., *Addiction and Society*. Springfield, IL., Thomas, 1970.

Black, P., ed., *Drugs and the Brain*. Baltimore, Johns Hopkins Press, 1969.

Blythe, Peter, *Hypnotism: Its Power and Practice*. New York, Taplinger, 1971.

Boeckman, Charles, *And the Beat Goes on*. New York, Robert B. Luce, Inc., 1976.

Brenman, M., and Gill, M., *Hypnotherapy: A Survey of the Literature*. New York, International Universities Press, 1947.

Brill, L., and Harms, E., *Yearbook of Drug Abuse*. New York, Behavioral Publications, 1972.

Burke, Charles, *Aggression in Man*. Secaucus, NJ, Lyle Stuart, 1975.

Canetti, Elias, *Crowds and Power*. New York, Viking Press, 1962.

Carey, J. T., *The College Drug Scene*. Englewood Cliffs, NJ, Prentice-Hall, 1968.

Caserta, Peggy, *Going Down With Janis*. New York, Dell, 1973.

Chapple, Steve, *Rock 'n' Roll Is Here to Pay*. Chicago, Nelson Hall, 1977.

Chase, Gilbert, *America's Music*. New York, McGraw-Hill, 1955.

Christgau, Robert, *Any Old Way You Choose It*. Baltimore, Penguin, 1973.

Clarke, Steve, ed., *The Who in Their Own Words*. New York, Quick Fox, 1979.

Coles, Robert, *Erik H. Erikson: The Growth of His Work*. Boston, Atlantic-Little Brown, 1970.

Cressey, Donald, and Ward, David, *Delinquency, Crime and Social Process*. New York, Harper & Row, 1969.

Dalton, David, *Janis*. New York, Popular Library, 1971.

Dalton, David, ed., *The Rolling Stones*. New York, Quick Fox, 1979.

Dean, Stanley R., M.D., ed., *Psychiatry and Mysticism*. Chicago, Nelson-Hall, 1975.

Deren, Maya, *Divine Horsemen: The Voodoo Gods of Haiti*. New York, Dell, 1970.

Diamond, John, M.D., *Your Body Doesn't Lie*. New York, Warner, 1979.

Drug Abuse Council, *The Facts About Drug Abuse*. New York, The Free Press, 1980.

Duster, Troy, *The Legislation of Morality*. New York, The Free Press, 1970.

Dylan, Bob, *The Songs of Bob Dylan*. New York, Alfred A. Knopf, 1970.

———, *Writings and Drawings of Bob Dylan*. New York, Alfred A. Knopf, 1973.

Edmunds, Simeon, *The Psychic Power of Hypnosis*. London, Aquarian, 1968.

Eisen, Jonathan, ed., *The Age of Rock: Sounds of the American Cultural Revolution*. New York, Random House, 1969.

Eliade, Mircea, *Shamanism: Archaic Techniques of Ecstasy*. Bollingen Series. Princeton, NJ, Princeton University Press, 1970.

Emerson, Ralph Waldo, *Selected Essays, Lectures and Poems*, Spiller, R. E., ed. New York, Pocket Books, 1965.

Erikson, Charles W., ed., *Behavior and Awareness*. Durham, NC, Duke University Press, 1962.

257

BIBLIOGRAPHY

Erikson, Erik H., *Childhood and Society*. New York, W. W. Norton, 1950.

———, *Toys and Reasons*. New York, W. W. Norton, 1977.

Estabrooks, G. H., *Hypnotism*. New York, E. P. Dutton, 1957.

Ewen, David, *Complete Book of the American Musical Theater*. New York, Henry Holt, 1958.

———, *History of Popular Music*. New York, Barnes & Noble, 1961.

Fast, Julius, *The Pleasure Book*. New York, Stein & Day, 1975.

Ford Foundation, *Dealing With Drug Abuse*. New York, Praeger, 1972.

Freedman, Jonathan, *Crowding and Behavior*. New York, Viking, 1975.

Freud, Sigmund, *A General Introduction to Psychoanalysis*. New York, Garden City Publishing Co., 1943.

———, *Collected Papers*. New York, Basic Books, 1959.

———, *The Problem of Anxiety*. New York, Norton, 1926.

Friedenberg, Edgar Z., *The Vanishing Adolescent*. New York, Dell, 1962.

Friedman, Myra, *Buried Alive*. New York, William Morrow, 1973.

Fromm, Eric, *The Heart of Man: Its Genius for Good or Evil*. New York, Harper and Row, 1964.

———, *The Sane Society*. New York, Fawcett, 1955.

Gibson, H. E., *Hypnosis: Its Nature and Therapeutic Uses*. New York, Taplinger, 1978.

Gilbert, Douglas, *Lost Chords: The Diverting Story of American Popular Songs*. New York, Doubleday, 1942.

Goldberg, Isaac, *Tin Pan Alley*. New York, John Day, 1930.

Goodman, L., and Gillman, A., eds., *The Pharmacological Basis of Therapeutics*. New York, Macmillan, 1975.

Grayson, J., *Nerves, Brain, and Man*. New York, Taplinger, 1960.

Grinspoon, Lester, *Marijuana Reconsidered*. Cambridge, MA, Harvard University Press, 1971.

———, and Hedblom, Peter, *The Speed Culture: Amphetamine Use and Abuse in America*. Cambridge, MA, Harvard University Press, 1975.

Grossman, Lloyd, *A Social History of Rock Music*. New York, Doubleday, 1976.

Handy, William C., *Father of the Blues: An Autobiography*. New York, Macmillan, 1941.

Henderson, Dave, *Jimi Hendrix*. New York, W. W. Norton, 1975.

Herman, Gary, *The Who*. New York, Collier Books, 1971.

Hilgard, E. R., *Hypnotic Susceptibility*. New York, Harcourt, Brace and World, 1965.

Hopkins, Jerry, and Sugarman, Daniel, *No One Here Gets Out Alive*. New York, Warner Books, 1980.

Howard, John Tasker, *Stephen Foster America's Troubadour*. New York, Thos. Y. Crowell, 1934.

Inglis, Brian, *The Forbidden Game: A Social History of Drugs*. New York, New American Library, 1958.

Jones, Ernest, *The Life and Work of Sigmund Freud*. New York, Basic Books, 1951.

Jones, Hardin B., and Jones, Helen C., *Sensual Drugs: Deprivation and Rehabilitation of the Mind*. Cambridge, MA, Harvard University Press, 1975.

258

BIBLIOGRAPHY

Judson, H. R., *Heroin Addiction in Britain: What Americans Can Learn From The English Experience*. New York, Harcourt Brace Jovanovich, 1974.

Jung, C. G., *Archetypes and the Collective Unconscious*. New York, Pantheon, 1959.

Junod, Henri A., *The Life of a South African Tribe*. New Hyde Park, NY, University Books, Inc., 1962.

Kaplan, J., *Marijuana, The New Prohibition*. New York, World Publishing Co., 1970.

Karlins, M., and Andrews, L., *Bio-Feedback: Turning on the Power of Your Mind*. Philadelphia, Lippincott, 1962.

Kenville, K., ed., *Where to Get Help for a Drug Problem*. Hauppauge, NY, Award Books, 1971.

Kisker, Geroge W., *The Disorganized Personality*. Tape Series. New York, McGraw-Hill, 1963.

Kline, Milton V., *Freud and Hypnosis: The Interaction of Psychodynamics and Hypnosis*. La Jolla, CA, Agora Press, 1966.

Kolb, Lawrence, *Drug Addiction: A Medical Problem*. Springfield, IL, Charles C. Thomas, 1962.

Kooper, Al, with Edwards, Ben, *Backstage Passes*. New York, Stein & Day, 1977.

Larsen, Stephen, *The Shaman's Doorway*. New York, Harper & Row, 1976.

Larson, Bob, *The Day Music Died*. Denver, BLM Publishing, 1972.

Le Bon, Gustav, *The Crowd: The Study of the Popular Mind*. New York, Viking, 1960.

LeCron, Leslie M., *The Complete Guide to Hypnosis*. New York, Harper & Row, 1971.

Levy-Bruhl, Lucien, *The Soul of the Primitive*. London, Allen & Unwin, 1965.

Lommel, Andreas, *Shamanism: The Beginnings of Art*. New York, McGraw-Hill, · 1967.

London, Perry, *Behavior Control*. New York, Harper & Row, 1969.

May, Rollo, *Love and Will*. New York, W. W. Norton, 1971.

———, *Man's Search for Himself*. New York, W. W. Norton, 1953.

Miller, Jim, *The Rolling Stone Illustrated History of Rock & Roll*. New York, Rolling Stone Press/Random House, 1976.

Miras, C. J., *Cannabis and Its Derivatives: Studies on the Effects of Chronic Cannabis Administration to Man*. London, Oxford University Press, 1972.

Montagu, M. R. Ashley, *Man and Aggression*. New York, Oxford University Press, 1968.

Moore, Allen J., *The Young Adult Generation*. New York, Abingdon Press, 1969.

Nisbet, Robert A., *The Sociological Tradition*. New York, Basic Books, 1966.

Nite, Norm N., with Newman, Ralph, *Rock On: The Illustrated Encyclopedia of Rock 'n' Roll*. New York, Thomas Y. Crowell, 1978.

Nugent, Stephen, and Gillett, Charlie, *Rock Almanac*. New York, Anchor Books, 1978.

Perry, Dick, *Was You Ever in Zinzinnati?* Garden City, NY, Doubleday, 1966.

Pike, Jeff, *Rock World*. New York, Bookthrift, Inc., 1979.

Redfield, Robert, *The Primitive World and Its Transformations*. Ithaca, NY, Cornell University Press, 1953.

Rice, Julius, M.D., *Ups and Downs: Drugging and Duping*. New York, Macmillan, 1972.

BIBLIOGRAPHY

Richards, Stanley, ed., *Great Rock Musicals*. New York, Stein and Day, 1979.

Rochlin, Gregory, *Man's Aggression: The Defense of Self*. Boston, Gambit, 1973.

Rogers, Dorothy, *Adolescents: A Psychological Perspective*. Monterey, CA, Brook/Cole, 1978.

Rowes, Barbara, *Grace Slick*. New York, Doubleday, 1980.

Sanchez, Tony, *Up and Down With the Rolling Stones*. New York, William Morrow, 1979.

Schur, Edwin, *Crimes Without Victims*. Englewood Cliffs, NJ, Prentice-Hall, 1965.

Shaw, Arnold, *The Rock Revolution*. New York, Crowell-Collier Press, 1969.

Sheehy, Gail, *Passages*. New York, Dutton, 1976.

Solomon, D., *The Marijuana Papers*. Indianapolis, Bobbs-Merrill, 1966.

Sommer, Robert, *Personal Space: The Behavioral Basis of Design*. Englewood Cliffs, NJ, Prentice-Hall, 1969.

Spitz, Robert S., *Barefoot in Babylon*. New York, Viking, 1979.

Stearn, J., *The Seekers*. Garden City, NY, Doubleday, 1969.

Stein, Jeff, *The Who*. New York, Stein & Day, 1979.

Thompson, C., *Psychoanalysis: Evolution and Development*. New York, Hermitage House, 1950.

Ulanov, Barry, *A History of Jazz in America*. New York, Viking, 1952.

Various authors, *Twenty-Five Years of Rock and Roll*. New York, Harrison House, 1979.

Wertheimer, Paul L., *Crowd Management: Report of the Task Force on Crowd Control and Safety*. Cincinnati, OH, City of Cincinnati City Manager's Office, 1980.

Whitman, Walt, *The Portable Walt Whitman*. Mark Van Doren, ed. New York, Viking, 1945.

Witmark, Isidore, and Goldberg, Isaac, *From Ragtime to Swingtime*. New York, Lee Furman, 1939.

Wolff, Tom, *The Pump House Gang*. New York, Farrar Strauss, 1968.

Periodicals

Blumberg, H. H., "Surveys of Drug Abuse Among Young People," *International Journal of Drug Addiction*, 1975.

Campbell, A. M. G., et al, "Cerebral Atrophy in Young Cannabis Smokers," *Lancet*, 1971.

Essig, C. F., "Newer Sedative Drugs That Can Cause States of Intoxication and Dependence of Barbiturate Type," *Journal of the American Medical Association*, 1966.

Ewing, J. A., and Bakewell, W. E., "Diagnosis and Management of Depressant Drug Dependence," *American Journal of Psychiatry*, 1967.

Eysenck, H. J., "Suggestibility and Hysteria," *Journal of Neurology, Neurosurgery and Psychiatry*, 1943.

Frosch, W. A., et al, "Untoward Reactions to Lysergic Acid Diethylamide (LSD) Resulting in Hospitalization," *New England Journal of Medicine*, 1965.

260

BIBLIOGRAPHY

Goode, E., "Marijuana and Sex," *Evergreen Review*, 1969.

Goode, E., "Drug Use and Sexual Activity on a College Campus," *American Journal of Psychiatry*, 1972.

Heilpern, John, "The Who," *Observer Colour Magazine*, 1966.

Kline, M. V., "A Note on 'Primate-like' Behavior Induced Through Hypnosis: A Case Report," *Journal of General Psychiatry*, 1952.

Nahas, G. G., et al, "Inhibition of Cellular Meditated Immunity in Marijuana Smokers," *Science*, 1974.

Schenck, J. M., "The Unconscious Relationship Between Hypnosis and Death," *Psychoanalytic Review*, 1951.

Sperry, R. W., "Left Brain, Right Brain," *Saturday Review*, 1975.

True, R. M., "Experimental Control in Hypnotic Age Regression States," *Science*, 1949.

In addition to the specific articles listed above, information was drawn from various issues of the following periodicals.

Billboard magazine. Issues from 1965 to 1980, inclusive.

Cincinnati Enquirer. December 3, 1979 through August 31, 1980.

Cincinnati Post. December 3, 1979 through August 31, 1980.

Creem magazine. Issues from 1979 to 1980, inclusive.

Hit Parader magazine. Issues from 1967 to 1980, inclusive.

Rolling Stone magazine. Issues from 1968 to 1980, inclusive.

Information on the following topics was drawn from the issues of *The New York Times* listed below.

HENDRIX, JIMI.

May 5, 1969; Aug. 19, 1969; Sept. 6, 1969; Jan. 1, 1970; Sept. 1, 1970; Sept. 19, 1970; Sept. 26, 1970; Sept. 27, 1970; Sept 29, 1970; Oct. 1, 1970; Oct. 2, 1970; Oct. 18, 1970; Oct. 27, 1970; Nov. 3, 1970; Nov. 29, 1970; Sept. 14, 1971; Dec. 22, 1973; July 15, 1974; Aug. 16, 1974; Feb. 14, 1975; July 7, 1977.

ISLE OF WIGHT.

Aug. 26, 1970; Aug. 27, 1970; Aug. 31, 1970.

JONES, BRIAN.

Jan. 14, 1969; June 9, 1969; July 3, 1969.

JOPLIN, JANIS.

Feb. 12, 1969; Feb. 23, 1969; March 16, 1969; Aug. 17, 1969; Aug. 4, 1970; Oct. 5,

BIBLIOGRAPHY

1970; Oct. 6, 1970; Oct. 8, 1970; Oct. 11, 1970; Oct. 18, 1970; Oct. 27, 1970; Oct. 29, 1970; Nov. 29, 1970; Jan. 16, 1971; Jan. 31, 1971; Feb. 20, 1972; Aug. 12, 1973; Aug. 15, 1973; Nov. 11, 1973; Nov. 25, 1973; March 15, 1974; Feb. 13, 1975; Dec. 10, 1978.

MOON, KEITH.

Sept. 8, 1978; Sept. 9, 1978.

MORRISON, JIM.

March 24, 1969; April 5, 1969; April 9, 1969; April 13, 1969; Jan. 19, 1970; Sept. 21, 1970; July 9, 1971; April 27, 1974; Jan. 7, 1979; Jan. 9, 1979.

THE WHO.

May 19, 1969; Aug. 17, 1969; Nov. 30, 1969; May 16, 1970; June 8, 1970; Feb. 7, 1971; July 31, 1971; Sept. 19, 1971; Dec. 17, 1972; Dec. 4, 1973; Dec. 7, 1973; June 8, 1974; June 12, 1974; June 13, 1974; July 14, 1974; Oct. 11, 1974; Nov. 17, 1974; March 20, 1975; March 21, 1975; March 30, 1975; Sept. 19, 1975; Oct. 3, 1975; Oct. 31, 1975; Dec. 17, 1975; Jan. 29, 1976; Feb. 12, 1976; March 11, 1976; March 13, 1976; March 18, 1976; Jan. 20, 1978; Sept. 8, 1978; Sept. 9, 1978; June 29, 1979; Sept. 12, 1979; Sept. 16, 1979; Oct. 1, 1979; Nov. 13, 1979; Dec. 4, 1979; Dec. 5, 1979; Dec. 6, 1979; Dec. 7, 1979; Dec. 8, 1979; Dec. 10, 1979; Dec. 12, 1979; Dec. 16, 1979; Dec. 17, 1979; Dec. 18, 1979; Feb. 7, 1980; Feb. 29, 1980; March 2, 1980; March 22, 1980.

WOODSTOCK.

June 27, 1969; July 17, 1969; July 18, 1969; July 23, 1969; Aug. 13, 1969; Aug. 15, 1969; Aug. 16, 1969; Aug. 17, 1969; Aug. 18, 1969; Aug. 19, 1969; Aug. 20, 1969; Aug. 21, 1969; Aug. 22, 1969; Aug. 23, 1969; Aug. 24, 1969; Aug. 25, 1969; Aug. 26, 1969; Aug. 27, 1969; Aug. 28, 1969; Aug. 29, 1969; Sept. 1, 1969; Sept. 2, 1969; Sept. 3, 1969; Sept. 7, 1969; Sept. 9, 1969; Sept. 16, 1969; Oct. 5, 1969; Nov. 6, 1969; Nov. 21, 1969; Jan. 7, 1970; March 2, 1970; March 27, 1970; April 5, 1970; April 19, 1970; June 16, 1970; June 19, 1970; June 27, 1970; Nov. 22, 1970; July 5, 1971; Aug. 25, 1971; Nov. 2, 1971; April 16, 1972; June 6, 1972; Feb. 10, 1973; July 28, 1974; Oct. 19, 1976; April 6, 1979; July 22, 1979; Aug. 12, 1979; Aug. 13, 1979; Aug. 15, 1979; Aug. 26, 1979; Sept. 3, 1979; Sept. 9, 1979; Sept. 14, 1979.

Unpublished Dissertation

Ishiyama, Toaru. "Music as a Symbolic Representation of Human Sentiments, and Its Application in Therapy With a Regressed Mute Catatonic." Master's thesis, Western Reserve University, 1958.

JUl